WHEN THEY BLEW
THE LEVEE

WHEN THEY BLEW
THE LEVEE

Politics, Race, and Community in
Pinhook, Missouri

David Todd Lawrence and Elaine J. Lawless

University Press of Mississippi / Jackson

www.upress.state.ms.us

The University Press of Mississippi is a member
of the Association of University Presses.

First printing 2018
∞

Library of Congress Cataloging-in-Publication Data

Names: Lawrence, David Todd, 1972– author. | Lawless, Elaine J., author.
Title: When they blew the levee : politics, race, and community in Pinhook,
Missouri / David Todd Lawrence and Elaine J. Lawless.
Description: Jackson : University Press of Mississippi, [2018] |
Includes bibliographical references and index. |
Identifiers: LCCN 2017057200 (print) | LCCN 2018002938 (ebook) | ISBN
9781496817747 (epub single) | ISBN 9781496817754 (epub institutional) | ISBN
9781496817761 (pdf single) | ISBN 9781496817778 (pdf institutional) | ISBN
9781496817730 (cloth : alk. paper) | ISBN 9781496818157 (pbk. : alk. paper)
Subjects: LCSH: African Americans—Missouri—History. | African Americans—
Missouri—Social conditions. | African Americans—Land tenure—Missouri—His-
tory. | Disaster victims—Missouri—Personal narratives. | Floods—Mississippi River.
| Levees—Mississippi River. | United States—History. | Pinhook (Mo.)—Race rela-
tions. | Pinhook (Mo.)—Politics and government. | Pinhook (Mo.)—History.
Classification: LCC E185.915 (ebook) | LCC E185.915 .L39 2018 (print) | DDC
305.896/0730778—dc23
LC record available at https://lccn.loc.gov/2017057200

British Library Cataloging-in-Publication Data available

story supported by grant
Figure Foundation
when they blew the law

Dedicated to every person who ever
lived in and loved Pinhook, Missouri

Stories matter. Many stories matter. Stories have been used to dispossess and malign, but stories can also be used to empower and to humanize. Stories can break the dignity of a people, but stories can also repair that broken dignity.

—**CHIMAMANDA NGOZI ADICHIE,** "The Danger of a Single Story"

PINHOOK ANTHEM

—Faye Mack (former Pinhook resident)

When I was a little girl, living by the Mississippi,
I called it home, my way of life; it was far, far from the city
I love this place, this sacred space, where I always knew
I'd find peace and love, joy and happiness, unconditional for you.

The elders there they taught us much with little that they knew
They put in us a sense of pride in everything we do
Oh, I can hear them say, the Lord he gives and then he takes away
Oh, blessed by the name of God, just continue, child, to pray.

Home that is my home . . . that the Mighty Mississippi now calls its own
My family flee, they run from thee, this one thing I know
I love this place, this sacred space, I will never let it go.

The waters may wash away our land, our house, our farms
But it can never remove the love of God for it keeps us in his arms
So we thank you now God for what you've done and what you're going to do
Bring back peace and love, joy and happiness, that can only come from you.

CONTENTS

PROLOGUE: RIVER RISING

In matters of race, silence and evasion have historically ruled . . . the habit of ignoring race is understood to be a graceful, even generous liberal gesture. To notice is to recognize an already discredited difference. To enforce its invisibility through silence is to allow the Black body a shadowless participation in the dominant cultural body.

—Toni Morrison, *Playing in the Dark*

4.24.11 Mississippi River gage at Cairo, Illinois, at 52.5 feet and rising

April 24, 2011, was Easter Sunday. The religious celebration at Union Baptist Church in Pinhook, Missouri, was undoubtedly a grand affair. People came from far and wide dressed in their finest Easter suits and dresses. Men gathered around the front door catching up on farming news, the rain, and planting dates while the women hugged each other, laughed, and chatted near the pews. New babies were adored and passed around. Children in new clothes and shoes must have dashed about the adults, running back to the fellowship hall where they could play freely. Hats were everywhere in abundance, graced with ribbons and flowers. The service was filled with song and prayer, passionate testifying, and a sermon full of gratitude and joy. The Pinhook choir rang the rafters with their songs of praise. Everyone looked forward to good food and fellowship that would last far into the afternoon. A perfect Easter Sunday. Perhaps the only damper on the day was the rain that never seemed likely to stop. But Pinhook was accustomed to lots of water. No one likely suspected this time would be any different.

4.25.11 Mississippi River gage at Cairo, Illinois, at 54.5 feet and rising

On the Monday following the Sunday Easter service, a small family of African American women gathered to watch television in their mother's home in Pinhook. It had been raining for days. Aretha, Debra, Twan, and LaToya Robinson could not have been aware that within the next several hours their lives would change in ways they could not even imagine. These women, sisters and mother, had been neighbors and friends their entire lives. Nearly every day they gathered after work in one of their homes to cook, share a meal, tell stories, can vegetables, and enjoy each other's company. Over the evening, their small gathering would gradually accumulate other family and community members. Debra's daughter and her son arrived, as did their brother David and their cousin Larry and, likely, their long-time friend and neighbor George Williams. No one knocked on the door or called ahead that they were coming. Folks just arrived, parked on the grass, settled in, and continued conversations they had started the day before. Children, grandchildren, and neighbors' kids ran in one door and out the other yelling to each other, grabbing a bite to eat from the table, heading for the next house to snag something tasty there as well, finding another friend to tag along. The sounds of conversation and laughter surely could be heard from the road.

"Y'all hear anything about the levee today?" Debra may have asked as she lugged in several grocery bags and shut the door behind her with her right foot. The others may have told her no, they hadn't heard anything, but why did she ask? "I heard at work they're going to breach the levee if the gage at Cairo gets to 60 feet or higher. Did you all hear that?" She was not yet convinced this was actually true. Even by six o'clock, Debra wasn't terribly worried. There was nothing on the news, and the others sitting in her mother's living room did not seem to be concerned as they turned at least some of their attention to the television.

Debra probably kept an ear tuned to the television as she made dinner. She also started a cake to decorate later that evening for a friend's birthday, while she carried on several conversations at the same time. She had to move carefully not to bump into her mother, who was now wheeling around the kitchen in a perfect choreography of food tasks. No one was quite sure how many people would be eating tonight. They never did. David might leave and go home, or he might stay and eat before heading out. LaToya might actually sit down and eat with them, or she might trill her fingers in good-bye on her way to someone else's house, or head home. It was a fluid congregation of people at ease in the house together. Greetings were simple, "Hey, George, what's up," or "David, get your dirty boots off that coffee table," or "Aretha, did you hear from Miss Gertrude today? How's she doin'?" Life in Pinhook was often slow, noisy, and quiet in turn, always pleasant and comfortable. Debra loved this moment of arriving home, cooking, sharing food and talk and laughter with the people she knew best and loved the most.

The group thinned out as first one, then the others, made their way to the door, taking food with them, telling Miss Aretha goodnight, leaning down to give her a kiss on the cheek. They had to run to their cars; the rain continued to fall. "You take care, now," she told each one. "See you tomorrow." She got up to go to her room just as the clock passed the midnight hour. She was tired and sleepy, ready to go to bed. She may have asked Debra to turn out the lights as she left for her own house just a few doors away. But Debra might have stopped her to listen to the newscaster who was reporting that the Army Corps of Engineers had just announced a breach of the levee and were warning residents in the spillway to prepare to evacuate. "Did they really say that?" Debra must have questioned the facts of the short report. "When is this supposed to happen? Did they say that, Mama? When did they say they were going to breach the Birds Point levee? Evacuate? Really? Now? Are we supposed to evacuate tonight?" Certainly, Debra must have been worried by this fragment of news that could potentially devastate her small community. Aretha sighed at the thought of another invasion of water. Not knowing exactly what the morrow would bring, and trusting Debra to figure it out, she might have gone off to bed.

But Debra was wide awake, aware it was still raining outside in the dark. Within hours, she tried calling everyone she knew, including all the people who had just left her mother's home, telling them to turn on the news and let her know if they thought the town should evacuate. She tried calling county emergency services and even the Army Corps office, but she could not reach anyone for details. No one was answering the phones this time of night. But they should be, shouldn't they, if there really was a mandatory evacuation?

Debra began to take the television news seriously. As unofficial mayor of Pinhook, she expected to hear directly from the officials if she needed to evacuate the Pinhook residents. She knew they should call her, but her phone did not ring. She kept thinking surely someone would tell her what to do. The sheriff would come out and notify them about an evacuation. The emergency teams would bring trucks and ambulances to help get the elderly and infirm out of their houses. Right? If there was an actual threat of a serious flood, that would all happen, wouldn't it?

Debra got little sleep that night wondering what was going on, how she would be notified, and what she might do the next day. The television reports continued late into the night, mainly registering the flood levels across the river in Cairo. Higher and higher the levels rose throughout the night. Photographs of the Mississippi River near the Cape Girardeau Bridge showed waves cresting across the wide expanse of the normally calm river. The sheriff of Mississippi County declared a state of emergency. Debra knew she would get no rest that night. She began to gather together a few of her belongings.

4.26.11 Mississippi River gage at Cairo, Illinois, at 56.5 feet and rising

Tuesday morning, April 26, David was at his mother's door shortly after dawn. He knew Debra had never gone home. They talked about what needed to be done. He waited with her while she tried to call the various agencies again to get specific information. They really wouldn't flood the entire region, would they, without official notification? And they would help them evacuate, right? Debra wasn't sure, and David definitely had his doubts. They were often ignored, had been for years, either intentionally or simply out of blatant disregard. Either way, he did not trust the officials to help them. Finally, he could not sit any longer. He told Debra he was going to find trucks to evacuate their people himself. He would return when he had found some.

Debra continued to try and call for information and assistance. She could not get any answers. The phones rang and rang. What to do? It was raining outside again, and the morning was dark and dreary. She went in to wake her mother, telling her to pack a bag and go sit in Debra's car with the radio on to the local news.

David returned a couple hours later with a friend and two U-Haul trucks he had managed to rent in Poplar Bluff, more than an hour east of Pinhook. He began to drive the trucks through town, gathering people and belongings. Before long, other trucks arrived and cars followed. Other residents drove into town with empty box trucks ready to load up belongings. Debra walked between the houses making certain every house was checked and the residents safely in a car or truck. Trying to keep everyone in good spirits and calm, she encouraged everyone to pack small bags of essentials, still thinking this was a time just like all the other times when the flood waters would arrive in their yards, stay a few days, then recede. They could return, she told them all, in a few days. Just bring a few clothes, some shoes, your cell phone if you have one—and the charger, bring your charger so we can keep up with each other. People were deliberate in their efforts to gather a few belongings, their faces worried, their voices filled with dread. Not one to show panic, Debra no doubt began to call out the names of people she knew were in their houses to those in the trucks. She opened every door and checked each house. Taking control, she began to throw out orders to the young men who had arrived to help, telling them which house to check, who lived there, if they had a wheelchair. She carried her cell phone with her and continued to call every number in her address book. She got no answers, and she got no phone calls.

There must have been a point when Debra glanced up the road to the west of town. She would have seen the access road on that side of Pinhook was already flooded, two to three feet of moving water lapped up across the pavement. She had seen water on the road before, but that did not erase its urgency. It was moving quickly across the fields. The town was going to be under water in no time, how deep was anybody's guess. She must have watched as David turned the lead U-Haul toward the other access road and motioned for the other trucks, cars, and tractors to follow. Lady and LaToya gathered up a meager pile of Aretha's belongings and followed in Lady's car. Debra started her own car, wondering where they were going. But first, they needed to outrun the water that was following steadily behind them on the road. Nobody knew exactly what was happening, but it was clear now they needed to leave.

As the caravan of vehicles pulled up onto the last hill beyond the spillway, Debra and some of the others got out of their cars to survey the flood. None of them expected what lay before their eyes. As far as they could see there was only water. They all stood together stunned by the breadth of the water. But Debra did not have time to watch Pinhook get submerged in the steady waves that began to roll across the fields; she needed to get all these people somewhere—to Sikeston, Charleston, maybe East Prairie. As she drove, she called everyone she knew, friends and family, asking if they could take in one or two Pinhook folks for the night, or for several nights, surely no more than a week. She drove her mother to her cousin Larry's house in Sikeston and asked him if she could stay there for a few days. Debra tried to tell him just how serious this breach seemed to be even though she still had no details. Larry was angered to learn that the National Guard had not come to assist with the evacuation of the Pinhook residents. He shook his head when he learned that no one had warned Debra of what was going to happen, that the government officials had still not talked with her. He opened his home to his family.

4.27.11 Mississippi River gage at Cairo, Illinois, at 57.9 feet and rising

Wednesday night the now evacuated Pinhook residents listened to the news that all 230 residents of the spillway were under a mandatory evacuation notice, which most definitely included the residents of Pinhook. This seemed terribly late to Debra, given that the roads were already covered in

Pinhook. But she was relieved to know that all her people were safe in the homes of friends and family members throughout the Bootheel. Although she hears that the Mississippi county sheriff has ordered the evacuation and had requested the Missouri National Guard knock on every door to make certain no one was left in the spillway, she doubted seriously if anyone had knocked on the doors in Pinhook. How could they? The waters were already over the roads when they had pulled over the levee on Tuesday.

4.28.11 Mississippi River gage at Cairo, Illinois, at 58.7 feet and rising

Another day passed, but Debra still had not heard anything official about the flood or the evacuation. She and Twan went to work, hoping to hear more in town at their jobs than they were hearing in Larry's house. Finally, on Friday, she received an official notification from the sheriff's office by way of a fax to her workplace. A little too little too late, she must have thought as she read the order: "All residents in the Mississippi spillway must be evacuated by 4:00 pm TODAY, Friday, April 29." Were there still people down there? How could that be, she must have wondered. She drove to Larry's home to a solemn group of friends and family gathered near the television. They must have greeted her at the door with the news that Judge Limbaugh, in Cape Girardeau, had ordered a breach of the levee, primarily to save Cairo, Illinois, and the Illinois side of the river.

A breach? To save Cairo? Her shock was mirrored on the faces of those in the room. They were fully aware of the reputation of Cairo, a town that had seen better days but now was largely an expanse of deserted buildings and only a small population of poor folks. The town had battled gang wars and drugs for years, except for the rich folks who still lived in the mansions on the far side of town, clinging to their dreams of a former, richer time in this southern Illinois town once celebrated as the "Gateway to the South." Saving Cairo and that side of the Mississippi made no sense to Debra, her friends and family. But another question was perhaps uppermost on her mind. What would a breach mean for Pinhook? How much water could the area sustain? The spillway was already flooded. Why would they need to blow the levee? And when they did blow it, what would happen in the Missouri spillway? Suddenly, the worry about their land flooding yet again must have escalated to fear that this might be the end of Pinhook. Their homes could not withstand a breach of the levee. She knew that. The others in the room knew it, too.

Saturday was another gloomy day. The rain continued to fall steadily. It must have been hard to believe only a week had passed since Easter Sunday.

5.1.11 Mississippi River gage at Cairo, Illinois, at 60.5 feet and rising

It rained all day Sunday.

5.2.11 Mississippi River gage at Cairo, Illinois, at 61.7 and cresting

Monday night, May 2, found them again gathered at the television in Larry's living room. Their numbers had swelled with friends and neighbors, as well as family members staying in various houses in Sikeston. At 10:02 pm, KFVS TV in Cape Girardeau aired live video of the breach of the levee. No one said a word as they watched Colonel Walsh of the Army Corps of Engineers talk about how "this was the only thing they could do under the circumstances," that this was for the safety of all the people near the flooding Mississippi River. "Safety was their number one priority," he said. He thanked all the men standing in the rain there with him, as well as Congresswoman Joanne Emerson, for coming out to the levee.

The television screen was dark. The newscaster's voice was shrill, excited, as she announced the imminent breach. The listeners watch the black screen as they hear her voice: "Let's pause for a second." The darkness was punctured by several explosive blasts, orange and red and pulsing. "Wow! That was fast! Wow! We saw that line of fire just as it was described, strong enough to feel my insides shake, for the vehicles around us to shake! I'm sure it was a sound strong enough for you to hear! That was the intentional breaching of the Birds Point levee!"[1]

The broadcast ended.

By the end of the week, Debra, Twan, and Aretha were exhausted and drained. They continued to watch the television footage in dismay. Several white farmers were interviewed about the loss of their crops and the damage to their barns and equipment sheds. No one on the television ever mentioned the town of Pinhook, and no one interviewed any of the African American residents from Pinhook, the town that was slowly disappearing in the floodwaters. News coverage consisted mainly of video footage of the flood and the river as it raged near the Cape Girardeau Bridge.

Nearly a week later, the Robinson family members watched a video of the flooding in Mississippi County shot from a helicopter. While the visible roofs of houses could have been any town, the photographer reported he was filming the site of Pinhook, the first time their town had been mentioned. Debra, her mother, and her sister could not believe what they were watching. Houses were submerged in water up to the eves, only their roofs were visible in the ten

Pinhook residents walking on road during evacuation, 2011. Debra Robinson-Tarver.

to twelve foot water, and then, they saw the spire of their beloved church. Until this footage was aired, Debra, her family and friends, had no idea just how devastating the breach had been for Pinhook. She stared at the town that was no longer there, marked only by the shingles on the housetops in a sea of brown water. She probably knew at that moment that no amount of cleaning would recover their homes this time. As mayor, her brain was working overtime.

What would they do now?

Where would they live?

Who would take them in for weeks or months?

How would they recover without their clothes and precious belongings, including photo albums, cherished furnishings, heirlooms, letters, their dishes, pots and pans?

How could they live without all that they owned and had worked for?

If Pinhook was gone, what did that mean for those who had been living there?

We can imagine Debra sitting alone long into the night in the unfamiliar house, deep in prayer. She would be praying for guidance, and she would call on her best resources to help her figure out what to do tomorrow, and the next day, and a month from now, and even a year. Their beloved town was gone. What would they do now?[2]

WHEN THEY BLEW
THE LEVEE

ROAD MAP OF MISSISSIPPI COUNTY, MISSOURI

1939 Road map of Mississippi County, including Pinhook. Courtesy of the State Historical Society of Missouri.

INTRODUCTION: FINDING PINHOOK

If we found, as my grandparents and parents did, the scales weighted against us at counting time, we also knew we grew the crops ourselves, literally dining at our dinner table every single day on our own strength, innovation, and pluck. Around such a table we were less concerned with "the man" than with belonging, and with becoming a man or a woman. Such a rural, all-Black context—where all you can see is the land you or your neighbor or your kin own—or that you rightly claimed once, either through sweat equity or actual money—provides an experience familiar to many African American families. In such a space, there is a stability, humor, and scale of being not warped by the outside world.
—**KEVIN YOUNG**, "How Not to Be a Slave," *The Grey Album*

This book is about a historic flood that devastated parts of Missouri, Illinois, Arkansas, Tennessee, Mississippi, and Louisiana during the spring and summer of 2011. It is about how an intentional act taken by the U.S. Army Corps of Engineers during that flood destroyed the village of Pinhook, Missouri. On May 2nd the Corps of Engineers breached the Birds Point levee, flooding approximately one hundred and thirty thousand acres inside the Birds Point–New Madrid Floodway in Mississippi County in the southeastern corner of the state of Missouri. This intentional breaching of the floodway's front side levee was done according to procedures dictated by the Flood Control Acts of 1928 and 1965, both of which were guided by the "Jadwin Plan," a plan developed after the Great Flood of 1927 by Chief of Engineers Major General Edgar Jadwin. The intentional breaching of the levee was intended to divert the rising waters in the main channel of the Mississippi River whenever it crested over 61.5 feet on the flood gage at Cairo, Illinois.[1] This act of breaching the Birds Point levee, an entirely legal one, forever changed the lives of the residents of Pinhook, Missouri, a small, largely African American farming village located within the floodway. This book is about that town and the failure of government officials to acknowledge the town's existence, to effectively warn Pinhook residents of the impending breach, to assist the residents in their evacuation, or, in the years since, to help the now displaced residents relocate and rebuild their town. Our research follows the Pinhook residents to the various places they have been living in cities and towns throughout southern Missouri and elsewhere, assisted primarily by family and friends, awaiting word of restitution for the rebuilding of their town from FEMA and other emergency funding agencies. At the time of this writing, Pinhook residents have now waited seven years for this assistance to no avail. Recent meetings with federal and regional emergency management officials have confirmed that there will be no funding provided for the relocation of the destroyed town. Many residents had hoped that their entire town could be relocated and rebuilt outside of the floodway, but the most recent information from government officials has been that if financial assistance is to be provided, it will be offered to individual homeowners, not to the town as a whole.

✦ ✦ ✦

Our book focuses on two conflicting narratives about the flood of 2011—one promoted by the Army Corps of Engineers that boasts the success of the breach of the levees and the diversion of the flooding waters according to plan,[2] and the other gleaned from the oral narratives we heard from displaced residents of the town of Pinhook. Our research with the former residents of Pinhook reveals a long history of discrimination and neglect of the rights of these African American farmers from the time they migrated to southeast Missouri from the mid- and Deep South in the early 1940s—self-sufficient farmers who, for the first time, owned and worked their own land, built new homes for their families, and shared in the establishment of a town and church they had every right to own with pride.

Oral tradition regarding the beginnings of Pinhook suggests that in the years prior to 1940, African Americans were not "allowed" to buy land in southeast Missouri.[3] When African Americans and poor whites living in the Bootheel region of Missouri who had previously known life as sharecroppers were "allowed" to buy land, the only land made available to them were parcels of swampland within the Birds Point–New Madrid Floodway.[4] From the beginning, African Americans were subjected to discrimination both in terms of the land they could buy and the difficulty of living on land that was plagued by consistent backwater flooding. Although those African American farmers believed that the decades-old levee system would never be "operated" and that their homes and land in Pinhook would remain safe from a devastating flood caused by an intentional action, when the river rose to historically high levels in 2011, the Army Corps of Engineers breached the levee and Pinhook residents lost everything.

Through our field research in southern Missouri, we have come to know well the former residents of Pinhook. Their personal stories relate what it has been like for them to be displaced, living in other small towns in southeastern Missouri with relatives and friends while continuously filling out and filing all the paperwork required for FEMA and SEMA (Missouri State Emergency Management Agency) funding. Although their stories do not always point to race as a factor in their failure to obtain assistance before the flood or disaster relief following the flood, after seven years many have come to recognize that their plight most certainly has to do with the fact that they represent a small number of African American farmers who are not of interest to anyone in the state or federal government. They have been systematically ignored in their efforts, while other disaster sites in Missouri have been fully supported. Our argument in this book is that the poignant stories of loss and trauma experienced by the Pinhook community provide a significant counter-narrative to the celebratory "success" story posited by the Army Corps of Engineers, one that should be told and heard. More than merely documenting what happened to Pinhook, we join them in calling for restitution and justice.

In addition to stressing the importance of the personal and collective stories of the now displaced Pinhook residents, our book also offers an in-depth discussion about the power and resilience of this African American community in maintaining their close bonds and collective strength as they continue to fight for the right to rebuild their town on higher ground. The people in this study have been ignored and discriminated against, yet their spirits are not diminished, nor has their faith or cohesion been destroyed by what has happened to them. Remarkably, they have not identified themselves as powerless victims, but rather as survivors who place their faith in God and in each other, ever trusting that they will be assisted and will begin the process of restoring their community in a new physical place. Throughout our research and interviews with the people of Pinhook, we have come to share in their belief that they are due assistance from the government and that decisions not to restore their town deny them what is rightly theirs; however, their sense of community resides in a space separate from the physical location of their town. We have come to understand this, also, as an important part of their collective story.

Researching Pinhook

The authors of this book, Todd Lawrence and Elaine Lawless, first met on the campus of the University of Missouri in Columbia in 1997, when Todd came to the university as a doctoral student in African American Studies and Folklore Studies. Elaine was one of his professors, and it was in that context that we grew to know each other quite well. Following Todd's graduation, he left Missouri to teach at the University of St. Thomas, in St. Paul, Minnesota, but kept close ties to Missouri, where his parents still reside. Both of us grew up in Missouri—Elaine in the Bootheel region of southeastern Missouri, and Todd in central and then southwest Missouri. We identify strongly with Missouri, perhaps in different ways, and we are both committed to doing the work necessary to document the destruction of the town of Pinhook and the residents' efforts to successfully garner financial assistance, even in the face of governmental indifference.

Elaine first learned about the destruction of Pinhook in late 2011 when she read an article about Debra Robinson-Tarver and the other displaced residents of the town in the *Sikeston Standard Democrat* while visiting her mother's home near Benton, Missouri. At that time, she realized she had grown up only about thirty miles from Pinhook but had never heard of the small African American community before she read the newspaper article. That article featured interviews and photographs of Debra, her sister, Twan, and their mother, Aretha, as they settled together, following the loss of their homes, in a very small house in Sikeston owned by their cousin, Larry Robinson. In the article, Debra Robinson-Tarver's comments to the news reporter focused on the despair of the Pinhook residents when their town was destroyed, but Robinson-Tarver also emphasized the town's determination to tell their story and seek FEMA and SEMA funding to rebuild. Robinson-Tarver invited anyone reading the newspaper article who wanted to know more about the story of the community to contact her. Lawless took down Robinson-Tarver's phone number and called her a few weeks later. At Thanksgiving, six months after the flood, Elaine visited the site of the flooded town and talked with a few people who were there to survey the damage and visit Lynell Robinson, the only Pinhook resident remaining in Pinhook. He was still living on the second floor of his severely damaged home with his wife in the deserted town in the fall of 2011, seven months after the flood.[5]

Remembering that Todd's family had close ties with Pennytown, a small historic African American town in central Missouri, Elaine shared her concerns about the treatment of the Pinhook residents with him at a conference later in 2011. We agreed then that we were both interested in pursuing this story and researching why the town had been destroyed and why restitution funding was lagging so far behind other disasters in the state and region. At the time, we knew none of the particulars of the story. We did not know why the levee had been breached, how many people had been affected, and what was being done to help them. The facts were stark, but to us they suggested a story of possible racial discrimination, neglect, and disregard for the African American residents of this small farming community. At the very least, we wanted to find out more.

The fieldwork for the Pinhook project has been difficult in many ways. The town we wanted to research was gone; the people were dispersed; neither of us lived in the area; and both of us had jobs and families at some distance from southeastern Missouri's Bootheel region. These realities meant that our work would be largely accomplished by interviews of the former Pinhook residents during relatively infrequent visits to the area and by attending gatherings of the entire community, such as the annual Pinhook Day celebration. In every way, most of the people we sought to interview were generous and accommodating. While some were more hesitant about our interest at first, in time we were able to speak comfortably with many of the displaced residents of the town and record a number of interviews. We have visited Pinhook many times over the years now, and we have attended four Pinhook Day celebrations, documenting them all with photo, video, and audio recordings.

Much of the footage we recorded during our field research made its way into a film we completed in 2013 that documents the Pinhook flooding and its aftermath. Our film, entitled *Taking Pinhook*, is available on the website we share with Pinhook residents, ReBuildPinhook.org, as well as on YouTube.

In some ways our fieldwork with the former residents of Pinhook was hampered because the Pinhook residents were dispersed over such a large area and because often we simply could not find where someone was living. Over the past several years, we have interviewed as many as thirty people who at one time or another had lived in Pinhook, or their extended family members had lived there. We have had informal conversations with many more. Whether named or not, the voices of all these people are present in the pages of this book alongside those of the extended Robinson family and other Pinhook residents we were able to interview.

Without a doubt, the members of the Robinson family were highly vested in the town's history, largely because of the deep ties of their father and grandfather, who, along with Lewis Moss and a few others, migrated to Missouri and established the community in 1941. The Robinsons had heard, and told, the many oral stories about the origins of their town all their lives and were eager to share them with interested listeners. The Robinson family constituted

Elaine Lawless listens as Debra Robinson-Tarver speaks about Pinhook at the State Historical Society of Missouri in December of 2012. Darcy Holtgrave.

a good part of the contemporary Pinhook community as well; many members of the Robinson family chose to continue living in Pinhook well into the twenty-first century even when other residents had left. Following the flood, many of the Robinson family and other long-standing residents of the town relocated to nearby towns, including Sikeston, Charleston, and East Prairie, which made it easier for us to continue our field research with them. Those who held Robinson family ties, and those who stayed close to Pinhook, were further invested in our work because they were the ones most involved in seeking restitution for their homes and the town. Along with Debra Robinson-Tarver and her sister Twan Robinson, a number of former Pinhook residents were committed to doing the work necessary to gain funding to rebuild and relocate their town. Certainly, the Robinson family and the Pinhook community at large rallied to help us in our research. They supported the idea of our documenting what had happened to their town. At every turn, they assisted us in our efforts to find displaced residents for interviews, they helped us make the film *Taking Pinhook*, and they connected us with the organizations that promised to assist them in their efforts. Several of the Pinhook extended family joined us on various occasions when we screened the film and made presentations about the story of Pinhook in various locations in Missouri and Illinois, eager to be involved in informing the public about their experiences.

As folklorists trained to do field ethnography, we wanted to talk to the people involved, hear their stories, and share them with the general public. We honor the people's stories as legitimate counter-narratives to the more officially recognized narratives published by the government entities involved. Ultimately, we hoped our attention to their plight might illuminate their situation and assist in getting them the help they needed to rebuild their town. That was nearly seven years ago. We have traveled to southern Missouri many times, talked with the residents, recorded their stories, and made numerous public presentations emphasizing the lack of assistance they have received from state and federal agencies. But it has made no difference. While we hoped that this book might end with a coda describing the triumphant rebuilding of Pinhook, when this book goes to press, it is unlikely that will have happened. Recent conversations with Debra Robinson-Tarver have led us to believe that the town will never be rebuilt in its entirety. Some people may get new houses, but not a new home and community of houses in a safe location. The destruction of Pinhook was given scant attention in 2011; certainly, since then, even less attention has been given to the fact that the town has not been able to rebuild. We share their frustrations; we share their anger; we are appalled at the lack of concern about the lives of these rural African American citizens. We will continue to document the efforts of this small town and its residents until somehow justice is done and their lives are restored.

Finding Pinhook

The first time we visited Pinhook, Missouri, together, it had been several months since the U.S. Army Corps of Engineers had intentionally breached the Birds Point levee. In the spring of 2012, as we drove east on rural road VV looking for signs of the ruined town, we were struck first by the beauty of the country. Both fallow and cultivated fields lay on either side of the road, cut through by trees framing them into the quilted patterns that we often see below when we fly overhead in jet planes. As the gravel road changed into blacktop, we began to see damaged houses out the right window of our car. At first the homes didn't look to be completely destroyed, but closer inspection revealed the devastation that resulted from being submerged under twenty feet of river water for nearly two weeks. Siding was ripped away, exposing interiors through both large and small openings, revealing bathroom toilets tipped over, couches thrown against walls, curtains blowing out the broken windows, and everything covered with hard-dried mud. Because the residents of Pinhook had to leave their homes without effective warning, they

Destroyed Pinhook home in 2012. Elaine J. Lawless.

Interior of Aretha Robinson home, 2013. Emilie Sabath.

were unable to salvage the majority of their belongings. They took only what they could load into cars and onto tractors during an evacuation period of less than twenty-four hours. When the two of us ventured into what we would later learn was the former home of Aretha Robinson, we found many of her family's possessions still there, including clothes, blankets, plates and silverware, furniture, pictures, framed diplomas—soggy belongings scattered all around the house as though spun like a washing-machine tub. We found precious pieces of the Robinson family's life—the very lives they would later tell us about—amidst the disarray of that house. We witnessed in that moment the destructive power of the raging water as well as the indifference of the government that had unleashed it. This was plainly evident in the strewn debris left behind, in what had been submerged by the water's depth, and what had been torn apart by its force. It was clear to us that we were witnessing the aftermath of something terrible. We stood trespassing in their homes, but there was no one there to greet or admonish us save the whisper of the wind and the occasional sound of a bird. The town was empty; what was left were only broken memories and the scattered evidence of nearly a century of living.

Over time the Pinhook residents became collaborative, interactional, and participatory in our fieldwork and in the ways we, and they, could articulate what had happened to them and why, employing what might be called both "deep" and "just" listening. With other ethnographers, we have recognized the value of friendship as ethnographic method and practice (see Tillmann-Healym 2003). During the seven years we have visited the Pinhook residents, now displaced, we have maintained close relationships with many of them through telephone calls, Facebook connections, and text messaging. We consider them friends, and we know that care and concern has become reciprocal. Recently, we learned the Pinhook people often refer to us as "the guy with dreads and the white lady," with some amusement and plenty of affection. We could ask for no more apt description, and we have come to treasure the relationships we have developed with them through this work.

The accessibility of the Robinson family to us when we traveled to southeast Missouri was enhanced both by their proximity in the vicinity as well as their open generosity to us. They welcomed us into their homes and fed us many delicious meals. At various times, they spent endless hours with us sorting through the names of former residents, the relationships of kin, the history of the town, historical photographs, the town's relationship with the other towns in the area, and their dealings with the government agencies that have been negligent in assisting them when they most needed it.

Although we thought about how we might apply Elaine's concept of "reciprocal ethnography" to our work with the Pinhook residents,[6] our attempts to ask them to read the chapters in our book as we wrote them and give us feedback did not actually result in the kind of response we had hoped for. Like the traumatized survivors of domestic violence Elaine encountered in previous research working at a women's shelter, the displaced Pinhook residents were far too busy collecting themselves and their belongings (at least what was left after the flood), supporting each other, and filing papers to engage in the kind of concentrated reading and response that reciprocal ethnography in its earliest conceptions had advocated (Lawless 2000). Our work with the displaced residents of Pinhook actually assisted us in rethinking how reciprocal ethnography can actually work "on the ground" when the collaborators are fully invested in the project and their various perspectives become the core of the ethnographic approach. In this way, the objectives of reciprocal ethnography can become the basis for including participants in studies where they share the articulation of their own intellectual and social history.

✦ ✦ ✦

This book is not only about the time immediately before and after the Missouri flood of 2011, or even the months between the breach and when we first visited Pinhook. Our book is also about a much broader range of time and issues—the decades before the breach ever happened and the more than six years since. It is also about the issues of race and discrimination that intersect with the stories of the African Americans who built and lived in Pinhook. It is true that we were compelled to find out what had happened—how something like this could have happened to a small town of mostly African American citizens—but more than that, the time we spent with the displaced residents of Pinhook hearing their stories showed us how a group of people who had been treated unjustly for many decades had survived and grown stronger in spite of many floods and the final terrible disaster that had displaced them over the years. We learned how the intentional breaching of the Birds Point levee had destroyed a town, but we also learned how a strong community had been built and how it has continued to survive injustice and disaster through the strength of their long-standing traditions, practices, and values. Therefore, this is also a book about resilience, determination, and the collective power of a community to resist the institutional desire for them to just "go away."

As folklorists, we often align our work with that of cultural anthropologists, social historians, oral historians, and sociologists. Indeed, our research for this book intersects with ongoing conversations about environmental racism, racial discrimination, cultural ignorance, violence, and general disregard for the lives of African Americans taking place around the country. Importantly, the work of Derrick Bell and other scholars aligned with critical race theory (CRT) remind us that racism in the United States is systemic, even necessary, to maintain the fabric of life enjoyed by most white Americans. Bell argued the U.S. was founded on racial difference and that difference persists regardless of all the post-racial discourse that insists it does not. With Bell and others, we recognize the foundations of race and class hierarchies that were established in an American slave state and that persist to 2018. Through our work with the destruction of Pinhook, we find ourselves face-to-face with the reality that change for race relations has been very slow indeed in southern Missouri. We had hoped to find this was not the case, but the story of the destruction of a town and the continued disregard of the residents of Pinhook offer little possibility for more hopeful analysis. Certainly, some African American scholars see great change in America for black citizens since the civil rights movement, yet others see small steps toward full equality and respect, with much more work to be done. In our work, we strive to acknowledge both the reality of discrimination many African Americans face daily in a white dominant society, while also recognizing the importance of a continued commitment to what Ta-Nehisi Coates has called "the beautiful struggle" for equal rights in this country (2008).

By doing on-the-ground field research in the Bootheel region of southeast Missouri immediately following the flood of 2011 and continuing to talk to many of the participants in the story for several years following, we have come to a much greater understanding of what happened to Pinhook, and why. We argue that government and institutional programs and policies perniciously failed to take into account the successful endeavors of one group of African Americans, who had been living quietly and quite successfully for nearly a century in the place they had carved out for themselves, their children, and their extended families in southern Missouri. To destroy the town they built and loved was an unwarranted act perpetrated by entities that felt they were under no official obligation to take the town of Pinhook into account when making vital flood control decisions during the spring flood of 2011. For those in power, the African American community of Pinhook was invisible, unimportant, and dispensable. The town this community built was literally washed away by the indifference of individuals and institutions that refused to "see" them or recognize the importance of the town to the people who lived there.

While it is true that the physical buildings of Pinhook are now long gone, we also intend to highlight how the community of former residents has survived without any governmental support or intervention. The essence of this community continues to thrive through the bonds of the people who created the town and those who lived in and cared for it. Miles and distance have not reduced this community to tatters; rather, they continue to talk amongst themselves on a daily basis, gather for face-to-face meetings to discuss their future, and often worship together inspired by the music of their gospel choir. Pinhook has modeled what resilience in the face of destruction looks like. Their strength in unity has kept the spiritual and emotional walls and rafters of their town in place. It is their hope, and ours, that the power and spirit of their resilience and persistence will serve, in the end, to successfully rebuild the material aspects of their town as well.

As trained folklorists, we come to this study with an argument for the importance of attention to the power of the oral word and the people's stories. We have learned to trust actual people's stories to reveal both the history and the contemporary reality of their lives. Certainly, for many African American communities in the United States today, the oral history of their lives and their communities has far more vibrancy than whatever meager written words have been included in the nation's history textbooks. The importance of the oral tradition in many African American communities attests to the vibrancy of this singularly American culture through our continued understanding of the beauty, value, and influence of the blues, gospel, jazz, storytelling, and a myriad of material aspects of both urban and rural African American life. Folklorists and oral historians continue to record the many aspects of culture on the ground, while our finest literary writers and artists celebrate that culture in their artistic endeavors.

In addition to our respect and love for the power of the word and the creative artistry often located in African American communities, we acknowledge the importance of the study of community in our cultural studies. When concepts of folklore are discussed, terms such as "folk," "group," and "tradition" are always included, but often the concept of "community" is assumed without being examined. This study demonstrates why and how community should be of greater concern in our studies. In the same way that scholars have recognized the importance of context to the study of text, we seek to emphasize the importance of community to the understanding of groups. By itself, "group" does not identify the interplay of ethnicity, religion, love of family, food, and the shared traditions of working the land, building homes, and raising children in peace and harmony. When discrimination and disregard for a community are also a part of its shared experience, the roots of community may further connect the people involved. Oddly, we might never have known anything about the community of Pinhook had the town they built not been destroyed. Perhaps even more odd, we have built our study of Pinhook solely on the remembrances of those who lived there. This is the study of an erased town, but not an erased community.

Pinhook's persistence in claiming their right to rebuild their physical town stands as a testament to the power and significance of the community they had already established and maintained over time—whether they lived there in the immediate past or years before. For the people of Pinhook, the town and its surrounding fields were proof of what one group of African Americans had accomplished in the mid-twentieth century through tenacity, determination, and the will to create a place for themselves in a world that refused to accommodate them and their dreams, either in the American south or in the urban north.

While it is true the Pinhook residents were appalled and angry that they were not assisted when the levee was breached, they were perhaps not surprised by the government's ability to just "forget" their town was down there in the spillway. In some ways the history of African Americans in Missouri must have prepared them for blatant disregard by the officials who failed to discuss the breach with them, neglected to effectively warn them of the evacuation or assist them in their move to higher ground, and, subsequently, refused to provide assistance to help them rebuild after the destructive flood. Many of the residents of Pinhook would prefer to believe that it was not racism and discrimination against their community that allowed the Corps of Engineers to flood and destroy their town, yet most will acknowledge that, in fact, they are keenly aware that the concerns of the white farmers in the area were taken into account long before and after the levee breach.

There is no apparent reason why the town of Pinhook was not of concern during the early discussions of the intended breach of the Birds Point levee. Incorporated as a village since at least 1955, the town has appeared on maps of the state for decades.[7] In Missouri, incorporated communities are classified as villages when they have a population of fewer than five hundred people. Ironically, one can still find it even on more recent maps of the state. Yet, the town was ignored when the U.S. Army Corps of Engineers diverted the Mississippi River in 2011 in order to save Cairo, Illinois, and protect farmland on the Illinois side of the river.

What we have witnessed since the destruction of the town of Pinhook is actually the truest testament to the importance of community even in the face of blatant discrimination and callous disregard. The flood occurred in May, 2011, and by the following May, on the first anniversary of the destruction of the town, its "mayor," Debra Robinson-Tarver, had rallied displaced community members to meet in East Prairie, a nearby town, for a Pinhook celebration. In the depths of their despair, Debra insisted that they gather to celebrate. In so doing, she was intentionally relying on the continuation of a long-standing tradition in Pinhook to celebrate "Pinhook Day." For years the community had come together once a year for a homecoming, inviting every person who had ever lived in Pinhook as well as their extended families to return to the town for a day of good home-cooked food, companionship, introductions of new babies and spouses, the renewal of family ties, gospel singing, church services, story-telling, and an auction that often displayed the best of the talents of the community—exquisite quilts as well as signature pies and cakes prepared by the best cooks in town. Debra, her mother, her sisters, and others worked tirelessly following the flood to re-create the Pinhook Day celebration even though there was no longer a physical town of Pinhook to celebrate. This fact alone isolates the single-most important point in this study—although the place-specific site of the town is now gone, erased from the earth and the map, the *community* of Pinhook persists—which is to recognize that *community* resides in the collective, shared connections between people far beyond the physical buildings that mark a site. This work expands upon and interrogates our perceptions of *community* in new and significant ways.

Our work argues that community should be central to any discussion of folklore and folklife. Specifically, in this case, the community of Pinhook came to stand for what one group of African Americans valued in life—the ownership of farm land, the right and privilege to work that land together and harvest from it what they could for their own well-being, the opportunity to build a church and worship as they wished, and the responsibility to raise their children in an atmosphere of lovingkindness at a distance from the streets where racism and discrimination continue to be a part of ordinary life for people of color in middle America, especially in the Missouri Bootheel region.

Broadly speaking, we attempt to accomplish two goals in this book: to explain and theorize the destruction of Pinhook, Missouri, as a disaster that was enabled by a number of factors, not the least of which was the refusal of institutionalized structures of power to recognize the value of a community whose existence was defined by non-institutionalized traditions, beliefs, and practices; and to offer an extended counter-narrative to the official accounts of what happened in April and May of 2011, composed of orally-transmitted origin stories, oral histories, an account of the breach and the aftermath, and a collective testimony to the lack of assistance provided by government agencies for over five years.

At different times during the course of our research, the former or the latter have been more important to us. When we began, we were focused on answering the question of how something like this could have happened to a town in the heart of America. We have engaged cultural geography, critical race theory, critical rural studies, and cultural theory for answers to this question. Ultimately, we have arrived at a way to understand what happened by describing the workings of a system that systematically denies the humanity and existence of rural African American citizens by devaluing the traditions, practices, and beliefs of their communities, especially if they do not adhere to popular perceptions of what African American culture and communities are or should be. Not only have the displaced residents of Pinhook, Missouri, struggled with this in the years before this disaster, they have had to deal with it in its aftermath as well. As we have spoken about the destruction of Pinhook across the country, as well as internationally, we have consistently been asked questions such as "How many people lived in Pinhook?" or "How many people actually died?" These questions illustrate how our audiences' ability to comprehend the Pinhook situation initially depends upon institutionalized metrics (population size; number of deaths) rather than the factors we have come to recognize as more significant: the traditional belief, practices, and values that have helped to make and keep this community strong, as well as the government's willingness to flood and destroy all they have accomplished.

The Chapters in this Book

The chapters of this book reflect that emphasis. In the first chapter, we begin with the origin stories of the town of Pinhook itself. As we mentioned above, Pinhook was a town that was settled by African American sharecroppers who migrated from the mid- and Deep South to the Missouri Bootheel region looking for land to buy and a chance to make a fair living for themselves. This chapter contains stories told to us by George Williams, Aretha Robinson, and Larry Robinson, as well as parts of an older interview with Jim Robinson Jr., the son of Jim Robinson Sr., one of the five men who first came to Pinhook from Tennessee. Jim's story, which was recorded by Will Sarvis of the Missouri Historical Society in 1998, is important in relating how Jim Sr., then Jim Jr., became leaders in the town, speaking on its behalf in the county, the state, and all the way to Washington, DC. Aretha Robinson, Jim Jr.'s widow, and Larry, his nephew, also add important perspectives on what they know and remember about the establishment of the town. George Williams, a current respected town elder shared his account of arriving in Pinhook as a teenager. The stories of all of these individuals provide a foundational understanding of the kind of place Pinhook was, the extraordinary challenges its citizens encountered during the process of building and developing it, and how they came to live where they did.

Chapter two, "Living in Pinhook" focuses mainly on an evening, like many, we spent talking to members of the Robinson Family—Twan, Debra, David, and their mother Aretha—about what it was like to grow up and live in Pinhook in the years before the flood and levee breach. Debra Robinson-Tarver was one of the first people we met on that first day the two of us visited Pinhook together. We called her up out of the blue, dialing a phone number we found in the newspaper. She agreed to meet with us at Pinhook after she got off work. That day, she walked through the town with us telling us who had lived in each devastated house. After she showed us the ruins of the town, she invited us to come to her house where we met her sister Twan and her mother Aretha, displaced Pinhook residents living in a small house owned by their nephew and cousin, Larry. We stayed and spoke with them for a couple of hours that first night. We would spend many nights like that one with them over the next few years. Our almost instant connection with the Robinson family is part of the reason they play such a prominent role in this book. They were as personable and welcoming to us as we could have ever hoped. As we got to know the Robinson family better over those first few months, we recognized how central they were to the town of Pinhook. Jim Robinson Sr., Aretha's father-in-law, was one of the original group of African American men who brought their families to the area in the early 1940s. His son, Jim Jr., her husband, became an important figure in the Pinhook community as well as in Mississippi County where Pinhook is located. As Aretha told us, "He was into just everything, just everything you want to name from Kiwanis to Mississippi County board things." Jim Jr.'s three brothers, all of whom lived in Pinhook, were also important figures in the development and success of the town over the approximately seventy years of its existence.

After the breach, Jim's daughter Debra became the unofficial mayor of Pinhook, spearheading the effort to relocate and rebuild the town outside of the floodway. Chapter three, "Debra 'Steps Up' to Save Pinhook," explores how a quiet, unassuming woman became and continues to be the community's relentless voice for justice for over six years following the breach. Debra is, without doubt, one of a handful of women who have been essential to keeping the community of Pinhook from fracturing during the difficult years of displacement. Debra has led the charge in seeking restitution from the government; these women together have helped to preserve the community by working diligently to sustain the bonds that still hold it together.

One of the most important traditions that has survived primarily through the work of women in the community is Pinhook Day, an annual celebration in the model of the African American homecoming. Chapter four, "Pinhook Day: An African American Homecoming," centers on that celebration, one which has taken place as long as anyone can remember, and still continues to this day over six years after the breach. Detailing the celebration itself, this chapter explores the importance of this annual tradition in helping to reconstruct the idea of home and to shape memories of the collective history of the community and its residents. This kind of gathering is particularly important in light of what was lost in the aftermath of the breach. Many Pinhook residents, faced with very little time to move and store their belongings, lost precious keepsakes—pictures, family bibles, certificates, books—that marked important events among families and in the larger community. An important aspect of Pinhook Day has been the opportunity to share what residents were able to save and what they still do have—whether those are materials objects or stories and memories. Together, each year, the extended family of Pinhook and their extended families work to reassemble the collective record of memory that constitutes the foundation of their connections to each other. Positioning Pinhook firmly within the recognized tradition of African American Homecomings, this chapter seeks to explore the sustaining role this tradition has played in the community's ongoing survival.

One of the main tensions this book interrogates is the interface between institutional and folk frameworks of understanding. We argue in chapter five that this man-made disaster is about legibility and erasure. To explore this idea we analyze two narratives about the levee breach. One narrative comprises the official version of the U.S. Army Corps of Engineers, an entity of the federal government, and the other is comprised of the oral narratives related to us by the displaced residents of Pinhook. The "official" narrative of the government has an advantage for its position within print and social media. Yet, the stories shared with us by the displaced residents of Pinhook offer a reliable counter-narrative to that fashioned by the government and legal entities, one that did not acknowledge Pinhook's existence in the spillway at the time of the flood, does not acknowledge the government culpability for the destruction of Pinhook, and has not shared in the responsibility for restitution to the African American farmers who lived there. On the other hand, the oral counter-narratives we have heard numerous times over the past several years and recorded for this book, function to fill in the facts from a different, on the ground, perspective and serve to disrupt the carefully crafted dominant narrative that serves to justify the Corps' actions, which were operated with the federal court's legal sanction, one that denied the existence of the Pinhook community and continues to blame the victims for being there, even on the rare occasions when their land-owning presence is acknowledged. Those who preferred to erase the residents of this African American town are willing only to acknowledge the existence of the community if the narrative includes the proviso that those who were living there should not have been there in the first place. Including the displaced Pinhook residents' stories in our book allows us to take into account, perhaps even privilege, the black people who lived in Pinhook and the stories that continue to be told in southeastern Missouri by them. Without these stories as a part of the permanent record, the town of Pinhook might disappear from public consciousness altogether, despite the efforts of Debra Robinson-Tarver and others in her large community. The destruction of Pinhook was made possible because the people who lived there were rendered invisible by agencies who did not bother to take the town and its occupants into consideration. What happened to Pinhook is a story that intersects squarely with current twenty-first-century concerns about race matters, the importance of black lives, and public discussions that argue African Americans do not enjoy equal citizen rights in our country. Remarkably, this is not a story about clashes with police, incarceration, or drug and gang wars; yet, prejudices against and disregard for African Americans that stem from these national concerns allowed for the abandonment of the Pinhook residents in Missouri's Bootheel region. We offer the Pinhook stories as the counter-narrative to the "official" record that needs to be told and honored.

In our final chapter, "Why Home Means So Much and Why Its Loss is So Traumatic," we turn to a discussion of Pinhook as place. While we emphasize the importance of community independent of place in this work, we cannot deny the massive importance of place to the displaced residents of Pinhook. We refer to those residents consistently in this work as being "displaced," a usage which obviously points to the importance of their being moved from their home place against their will. This reality plays a significant role in the traumatic nature of this disaster. While the oral histories of Pinhook present a picture of the Bootheel region as an inhospitable, fetid swamp, early Pinhookians transformed that space into highly productive farmland that became home and a source of prosperity for this community. This chapter explores the importance of place in the story of Pinhook and why the loss of that land has affected the displaced residents of Pinhook so deeply.

We offer the story of Pinhook to the general reader in the hopes that this specific case study provides evidence of our civic commitment to engage with the issues of politics, race, class, erasure, and overt and covert discrimination against African Americans in this country. In dialogue with the people we have come to know well, we have engaged in collaborative meaning-making that goes beyond simply documenting the fate of this town by providing a better understanding of the significance and depths of community they embrace. Unlike many other disciplines, folklorists become implicated in our advocacy stance. We welcome the implication that we stand with the people in this study—not at a distance from them serving only as observers, but with them in their struggles. Our work has convinced us of unjustified actions on the part of state and federal governmental agencies that ignored the importance and value of this small African American community in southern Missouri. These citizens deserved better in 2011, and they continue to deserve attention and restitution for what they have lost. While we can attest that the concept of community in this case reaches far beyond any specific place on a map, we also recognize the reality that this strong community deserves a specific place they can call home—one that in some way resembles the Pinhook that was destroyed through no fault of the residents.

Ultimately, we argue that the government has failed the citizens of Pinhook largely because they are black and rural. The attitudes that led to Pinhook being rendered invisible to the various players in this situation, the attitudes that meant no one would effectively warn them of the impending flood or help them evacuate, and the attitudes that persist in the continued denial to provide them assistance are examples of how black people are ignored, discriminated against, and oppressed in the twenty-first century. Yet, it is also our argument that this strong African American community whose bonds were developed over time and through shared traditions was not rendered helpless and ineffective in this time of disaster. While they were certainly vulnerable to the whims of the institutions that did not recognize their existence and they were victims of an intentional flood that destroyed their homes, their continued strength in the face of adversity demonstrates the power of community to resist all efforts to erase it. Over seven years after the intentional breach of the Birds Point levee, we now know that the people of Pinhook are not going anywhere. They will rebuild as they can, and they will continue to live in southeast Missouri and farm their fields. Whether any federal, state, or local agency comes through with funding and assistance for them or not, the community of Pinhook will survive. How we have come to know these significant truths is the story of this book.

CHAPTER ONE

Origin Stories of
PINHOOK

This is your country, this is your world, this is your body,
and you must find some way to live within the all of it.
—TA-NEHISI COATES, *Between the World and Me*

In 2016, the Wikipedia entry for Pinhook, Missouri, read:

> There has been a lot of mystery about the founding of Pinhook. Many people
> believe that it was founded by sharecroppers in the 1930s. This largely African
> American colony was expanded to nearly 250 people at one time. During the
> Summer of 2011 the Mississippi began to flood, [and] Pinhook was destroyed on
> May 2, 2011. The Birds Point–New Madrid levee was blown to save Cairo, Illinois
> from flooding. Everyone in Pinhook lost their homes that they had lived in for
> many years. Many are devastated because they loved living in a small community,
> knowing everyone. These people fled to family or apartments, until they could
> find a new home. There has been talk of relocating the community as a whole,
> but the funding is the only issue.

We might call this a typical public narrative of the town of Pinhook, with
some wording added that suggests the entry was edited by folks sympathetic
to the losses suffered by the Pinhook residents in 2011. Even though this
account refers to the town as a "colony," the incorporated village of Pinhook
has appeared on maps of Missouri for more than fifty years. Furthermore,
the first-hand accounts of the people who founded and actually lived in Pinhook offer a counter-narrative to the dubious claim that there has been "a
lot of mystery about the founding of Pinhook." The story of the founding of
Pinhook itself is not that mysterious, thanks to the memories of those who
helped clear the land for the town and the fields. What may need explanation, however, is how and why Pinhook emerged following the 1939 Missouri
Sharecroppers Demonstration. These demonstrations of the plight of farm
workers, both black and white, created new spaces for African American
farmers to settle in Missouri. Although Pinhook was not developed by the
Missouri farmworkers who were involved in those very visible demonstrations of poverty and despair, their story intersects in significant ways and led
to the possibility of an African American town near the Birds Point levee.

Farmworker's Lives and the Sharecropper's Demonstration in the Bootheel

In the late 1800s and early 1900s, following emancipation, many African
Americans in the American south were limited in the kind of work they could
do. Without education or the means to acquire it, farm work was what they
knew best; thus, sharecropping and tenant farming had become a way of life
for many African Americans. In the South, the vast fields of cotton provided
sufficient work for the farmworkers for many years, but when the boll weevil

began to decimate the cotton crop,[1] the cotton workers migrated north to states like Missouri as landowners there began to plant cotton in an attempt to supply the country's increasing need for cotton products.

Sharecropping was a horribly difficult life, one that many African American farmworkers were desperate to escape. Southern Missouri, specifically the Bootheel region, had factored in a national story about how this way of life could not be sustained. The 1939 Sharecroppers Demonstration revealed the precarious social and economic position sharecroppers found themselves in following the Great Depression. In fact, the "Demonstration" was just that, a demonstration of the sharecropper's plight, not a workers "strike" at all. Rather, as Thad Snow, local landowner and writer, put it, the "lid came off" when the system of unpaid servitude imploded on itself (Snow 196).

Farmworkers were never paid in wages, but rather participated in a complicated system of credit the white landowners developed. Year to year, the farmworkers could never pay off their debt, which they accrued for the bare necessities they required including soap, clothing, coats, and shoes. Children wore adult castoff clothing and shoes; babies were wrapped in old sheets; the families rarely received adequate flour, sugar, beans, meat, and salt to cook their own meals. The farmworkers were housed in substandard shacks with no heat or insulation. No medical attention was provided to the workers, and many children died. As a result, some governmental agencies sought to relieve the poverty that sharecropping and tenant farming generated for hundreds of Missouri farmworkers. A series of "grants" were made available to assist the large landowners to develop their land for cotton production. These grants also provided funding intended to improve the lives of the farmworkers as well. While the intentions may have been laudatory, the manner of distribution rewarded the landowners handsomely, but miserably failed to assist the poor farmworkers. Unfortunately, the funds were distributed to the landowners with the instruction that they were to distribute a share to the farmworkers.

Snow claims tens of thousands of "cotton workers" migrated to Missouri over a thirty-year period, most of them African Americans from the Deep South. During this time, he reports that, "in the biggest cotton county [he is referring to the county in which he lived, Mississippi county] of the Missouri Delta, thirty-five men came into the ownership or control of seventy-five percent of the farm land" (198). These landowners, according to Snow, were intent on keeping as much of the profits of the new cotton crop for themselves. As it turned out, the landowners, including himself, devised a semi-lawful plan to ensure that the landowners got most if not all of the government funding for cotton production, a plan that also ensured the cotton croppers, the actual field workers, were kept as poor as possible. Any evidence that the workers had money to spend irked the landowners and suggested the workers were not working hard enough. This "set many of us to thinking: really now, were the croppers entitled to receive the government payments that the law seemed to apportion to them?" (199). The landowners "re-examined the law with great care" and found that others in their situation had devised enterprising ways to adapt the law to their own benefit. The most devastating of these manipulations changed the farmworkers from year-round worker status, tied to their farms, and, in effect, determined to treat them as "mere day hands, either in fact or on paper, in order that the so-called 'cropper payment' might be taken by the owner-operator." (199) This action served to sever whatever relationship the field workers had with the large farms they worked and forced them to move several miles away, often in the least hospitable areas of the swampy Bootheel region.

By 1935, as this change in the status of the farmworkers had become the general rule in the Bootheel region, Snow claims "the croppers appeared to take the loss of their status and payments meekly enough." But too late, the landowners came to realize the workers actually were not happy with their situation at all and, indeed, "were talking amongst themselves." Snow and the other landowners discovered their workers were also talking with outside agitators and unionizers who urged them to reject this reading of the law and demand their rights as workers and their government funding. "Naturally," Snow writes, "we were surprised and outraged." (199) Snow defends the actions of the landowners claiming "it was hardly out-and-out fraud and thievery of a magnitude and purity comparable to many time-honored practices of big business and finance." (199) After all, he asserts, "chiseling croppers out of their cotton money was embedded deeply into the tradition of cotton growing, and the tradition had more or less come along with the crop when the boll weevil sent it on up north to the Missouri Delta." (199) The fault, he writes, "lay in the wording of the law," which was "really framed to invite all the fraud that inevitably came out of it." (200) The landowners were not prepared for what happened next. "When the lid blew off and the croppers took themselves and their belongings to the roadsides in January of 1939," the landowners knew things had changed (199).

Certainly, any account of the cultural changes in the Bootheel during this period credits the whims and ravages of the Mississippi River as contributing to the difficulties of farming and for bringing out the worst in human nature. Snow wrote: "Unavoidably, we are dredge-ditch and levee-conscious. We have had things to think about and problems to deal with that do not come within the experience of upland rural people." (200) Certainly, Snow credits the woes of the fourth decade of the twentieth century to "the icy January flood of 1937. . . . More and colder water came down the two great rivers than ever before in the memory of any living person. Thousands of croppers were caught almost helpless and suffered hardship, exposure and danger as never before. This awful flood of 1937 is undoubtedly a part of the background of the great sit-down-strike of '39" (201). In truth, the farmworkers were helpless and had suffered immeasurable hardship both before and following the flooding. The combination of the loss of the government funding intended to improve their situation and the intentional breaching of the levee, created the worst possible situation for the workers. Theirs was not a "sit-down-strike," but rather an organized demonstration to the world of just how bad their situation had become.

In every account of the period, the story of the beleaguered farmworkers continued to be integrated with the ravages of flooding in southern Missouri (See Cook). Living with water became a way of life, for landed and not-landed farmers alike. Natural flooding was expected every five years, at least. Snow blamed the Army Corps for the "mess," but his account is tainted by his position as a landowner. Snow's home was on a hill overlooking much of the Mississippi spillway land. While the situation was certainly a mess from his vaulted position, it became an impossible situation for the farmworkers who lived in the lowlands where the flood waters might stand for weeks and even months, regularly destroying the meager shacks they had to build for themselves.

The final blow to this already despicable situation was the intentional flooding of the Bootheel region by the Army Corp of Engineers in 1937, the first time the "operation" of the levee system was ordered. In an article published in 2010, historian Jerod Roll claims that possibly as many as ten thousand sharecroppers and their families took up occupation along the intersection of state highways 60 and 61 in southeast Missouri in 1939 in order to get the nation's attention to their dire situation (Roll 2010). The destitute farmworkers, both white and black, camped out on the roadside demonstrating their plight to everyone who drove by on the road. They had nowhere else to go. Union organizers sympathetic to their cause began to visit their camps and rally for regional, state, and national support of the farmworker's story. Their efforts succeeded largely because of the visual documentation by WPA photographers that accompanied this volatile story. The accounts of the farmworkers' impoverished situation, accompanied by the now iconic WPA photographs of their desperation, reached as far as the White House. Eleanor Roosevelt's concern for the families sitting on the road in the freezing January rains resulted in the president concluding that action needed to be taken to alleviate "as much suffering as possible." While President Roosevelt actually called for the Secretary of Agriculture to do "everything in our power to assist

the families of the sharecroppers, farm tenants and farm laborers in southern
Missouri who 'went out on the road,'" this directive was translated to the local
sheriff and lawmakers as an order to get the people off the road and out of
the public view.

Roll argues the operation of the floodway served as the catalyst for union
organizers' efforts to generate resistance among landless farmers toward their
working conditions. Certainly, 1939 was not the first year the farmworkers
had suffered deplorable living conditions and lack of basic necessities; but the
intentional flooding of the spillway exactly where they were living created an
untenable situation. In fact, Roll's account of the floodway operation eerily
foreshadows the events that unfolded again in the floodway in May of 2011,
even to the details of flooding the Missouri spillway to "save" Cairo, Illinois:

> The story of how the demonstrators "went out on the road" begins two years
> before with the Mississippi River flood of 1937. On January 21 that year, the U.S.
> Army Corps of Engineers announced it would deliberately breach the levee that
> protected the richest cotton land in the Missouri Bootheel in order to relieve
> pressure on the levees guarding the city of Cairo, Illinois. The threatened stretch
> of Mississippi County had been cordoned off by a sixty-foot high setback levee
> following the disastrous flood of 1927. The setback levee created a flood zone that
> could provide the river an outlet if waters rose again. When the army announced
> that it would use the spillway, it gave the twelve thousand tenants and share-
> croppers who made up ninety-five percent of those who lived there three days'
> notice to rescue household goods, tools, and livestock. On January 25, the Corps
> dynamited a gaping hole in the riverfront levee, rattling windows in Charleston,
> twelve miles to the west, and sending a cascade of muddy, icy floodwater across
> the land.

According to Roll, it was this act that led to increased attention to the
sharecropper's plight, intensified resistance, and led to the "demonstrations"
on the roadways, eventually resulting in the sharecroppers being relocated
behind the levee in the spillway itself. Roll documents in detail what happened when the authorities removed the demonstrators:

> The protestors were distributed in small groups throughout the area following the
> removal. The largest of these new "concentration camps," called "Homeless Junc-
> tion" by its inhabitants, was on a swampy piece of land in the spillway near the le-
> vee in New Madrid County—ironically on the very same ground that the federal
> government had flooded two years earlier. The land provided no better health
> safeguards than did the roadsides, but it was out of press and public view and

Sharecropper relocation camp inside Birds Point-New Madrid Floodway in New Madrid County, Missouri, 1939. Library of Congress, Prints and Photographs Division, FSA/OWI Collection, LC-DIG-fsa-8a10366.

under police control. "They took us eighteen miles back in the woods," protestor Booker T. Clark recalled, "and dumped us. We didn't have nothing." To maintain control, the sheriff ordered local officers and "deputies" to guard the camp around the clock to keep visitors out and demonstrators in. Rothstein [photographer] left the area after the removal. Save for a few distant photographs from atop the setback levee, he did not document life inside Homeless Junction. Few additional photographs of the protest or its troubled aftermath appeared.

It was clear to sharecroppers and organizers that the government had "flooded the poorest people on the land in order to protect others from a bigger flood." Roll concludes, "This apparent injustice seemed to capture in microcosm the problems poor people saw on a regular basis in the rural South." By physically removing the farmworkers from the roadways and out of sight, the government agencies involved ensured many more decades of misery for the African Americans who had moved to Missouri to work the cotton. Very little evidence remains about what happened to the thousands of farmworkers, once they were removed from the road. What remains clear, however, is that they were dispersed to the least hospitable areas of the still swampy Bootheel region.

Even though the demonstrators were moved out of sight, and perhaps out of mind, national attention to the Bootheel had brought the region a modicum of relief in the form of a few housing projects such as the "Delmo Homes," a model community built near Charleston that was intended to provide a much-improved house for a few hand-selected workers. Perhaps more importantly, subsequent social justice campaigns led by the Southern Tenant Farmers Union in the early 1940s led to the influx of outside money that enabled residents of some government housing projects to actually, for the first time, buy their land and homes and establish communities in safety and relative security. As might be expected, the land sectioned off for sale to the farmworkers was, for the most part, the least productive land available, land that had not been cleared, bottom land that was at the mercy of the regular floods in the region. Much of the land available was, in fact, squarely in the middle of the spillway of the Mississippi River. Thus, while the increased access to land and opportunity that resulted from the 1939 Missouri Sharecropper Demonstration contributed to the perception that southeast Missouri was a preferable destination for hopeful African American farmers, what might not have been clear at that moment was that the land available for them to buy was the land most likely to be flooded on a regular basis, much of it was still the "swampland" Thad Snow had described thirty years earlier.

This is the historical moment when the narrative of poor farmworkers in Missouri's Bootheel intersects with the arrival of several African American men from the Deep South who had traveled north intent upon buying land and clearing it for themselves to farm. Although life in the American South certainly had not been easy for African Americans who could find little work beyond sharecropping and tenant farming, they undoubtedly were not aware what attitudes they might find in Missouri. Their enthusiasm for their migration to the new state was fueled by their dreams of leaving the servitude of the plantation-like existence forever and raising their own children with all the benefits of landed farmers. For a time, their dreams were fulfilled, but in time the story of race relations and the battles with the flooding waters would emerge again and serve to destroy everything they built between 1941 and 2011.

A Town called Pinhook

The origin stories of the community of Pinhook now exist only in archived historical documents, deeds of sale, and in the vivid collective memories of the people who lived there at one time and those who continue to return to visit, all of whom claim Pinhook as a shared "home place." Because the town of Pinhook emerged in fairly recent memory, we are fortunate to have first-hand and repeated oral accounts of how this African American town began.

Elaine Lawless taking photo of fields just before arriving in Pinhook, 2012. David Todd Lawrence.

It is impossible to know how much the founders of the town had heard about the 1939 Sharecroppers Demonstration and the strained relations in southern Missouri. What they had heard was that land was available for blacks to buy in Missouri. That was incentive enough to cause them to travel north.

Even with the detailed histories of the region available to us, when we first started traveling to Sikeston, Charleston, and East Prairie in southern Missouri to begin our field research on the destruction of the town of Pinhook, we had little to go on. We wondered if the town of Pinhook had been populated by some of those dispersed farmworkers who had participated in the roadside demonstrations. Had the town originally been one of the projects sponsored by the Southern Tenant's Association? We certainly had more questions than answers. Who founded Pinhook? Who had lived there for nearly a century? Where had they gone? We returned several times to the site of the now-deserted town, taking photographs, walking between the houses, and, once, sitting for hours in the car next to the crumbling church writing in our journals our separate responses to what we could see, and what we could not imagine. There were no people left in the town, and the buildings were in total disrepair, moldy, smelly, and unsafe to examine. Occasionally we would see a farmer on a tractor who might wave and carry on with his work in the fields. But the town was silent.

We were sad and frustrated by turns, both of us dismayed by the implications of the Pinhook story, wondering how we might research a town that was gone, and how we might approach the African Americans who must feel their town had been sacrificed by governmental dictates with no regard for them, their town, or their livelihood. But there were no stories to hear out here at the corner of routes FF and VV, only the songs of a few birds and the wind blowing through abandoned houses warped by water and sun, soaked and baked into empty, moldy shells. The open windows invited us in, but the devastation offered us no information we could use.

Based on the newspaper articles that had been published following the flood, we created a possible list of people with whom we might talk. We determined to contact all of the Pinhook families scattered throughout the Bootheel, interviewing anyone who could tell us about what the town had been like and what the former residents planned to do now. In general, we were welcomed by people saddened by the loss of their town but eager to talk about Pinhook with anyone who might take the time to listen. But we faced caution, too, from those who felt they had been wronged and their trust worn thin. Certainly, there were many awkward moments on the telephone, or when we first arrived to visit with people. We carried around the Sikeston article that had featured Debra Robinson-Tarver; we called her, and set about to learn more about Pinhook. Guided by her good will and directions, we headed for Sikeston, where we hoped to find people willing to talk with us about the devastating flood of 2011, the origins of Pinhook, and its destruction.

By the time we arrived in the Bootheel in early 2012, it was clear to the people of Pinhook that the reality of their lives in Pinhook had not been recognized by those making decisions about what to flood and where. The "operation" of the floodway, the decision to breach the levee, was done without regard for them or for their beloved town. Our questions and our evident concern for them became an opportunity for them to articulate what had happened. As a group, they determined to tell their story, not only to emphasize how critical FEMA funding would be for them to rebuild their town but also in order to tell the story of their town. It was obvious that the founding and development of Pinhook, Missouri, had not been adequately documented before the 2011 flood. In fact, it might be argued, the lack of knowledge about the town, and a total disregard for its history, led easily to its being invisible, ignored, and destroyed. Only a fully-formed, fleshed-out, narrative about the history and importance of Pinhook would enable them to advocate for restitution.

✦ ✦ ✦

Early on in our research on Pinhook, a helpful oral historian who worked for the Missouri Historical Society archives located an interview with Jim Robinson Jr., son of the founder of Pinhook, that had been recorded in 1998 by an oral historian who worked for the State Historical Society. Will Sarvis traveled to Pinhook to interview Robinson in his home on October 26, 1998. In his lengthy and informative interview, Mr. Robinson admits that much of what he knew prior to his own move to Missouri was based on the stories from his father and other men who had been traveling around trying to find land to buy where they could farm for themselves.

Fortunately for us, Sarvis placed the full transcription of the interview in the Western Historical Manuscript Collection in Ellis Library at the University of Missouri.[2] Sarvis drove to Pinhook largely because Robinson had become something a political celebrity in the Bootheel region and had earned the respect of some of his neighboring white farmers and businessmen in the area towns of East Prairie, Charleston, Benton, and Sikeston. He had also been recognized as a consultant for the Extension Service at the University of Missouri in Columbia and had a framed document on his home office wall to commemorate this honor. Mr. Robinson was 65 years old when Mr. Sarvis visited him for this interview in 1998, nearly sixty years after Robinson, his father, and his uncles had migrated to Missouri.

The oral historian might have been surprised when he arrived in Pinhook that day and located Mr. Robinson's stately stone house on the outskirts of the town. The house was quite elaborate, with two gable ends, a two-car garage, a beautifully landscaped yard and garden, and a back patio area that was his wife's favorite sitting area. They sat in Robinson's office, just inside the front door, to the right, where the walls were covered with framed documents of all the boards and governmental honors Jim had won and accomplished, as well as framed newspaper articles about his success in politics, education, and the University of Missouri. The office was neat and efficient, complete with several filing cabinets, a desk, two or three folding chairs, and Jim's own swivel chair behind his desk.

We might add that this was all still in evidence when we first visited the flooded town in fall 2012, although the interior of Robinson's was a wrecked scene of ripped and moldy curtains, chairs, and rotten floor boards. Gingerly stepping around the holes in the floors, even dodging snakes in the collapsing ceilings, we entered the abandoned Robinson home in 2013. Although some of the walls and the floors were badly damaged, Robinson's framed documents were still on the walls, as was a wooden clock, frozen in time. The effect was eerily disconcerting. All the furniture was still in Robinson's office, although the chairs were ripped and turned over. All of the Pinhook houses, including Robinson's, remained in much the same condition through 2013, but by 2014, when we returned to the area for the annual Pinhook Day, we were shocked to find the Robinson home had been leveled. Nothing marked the house site save the concrete slab where it had sat, a neat stack of bricks to the back of the lot, and a basketball hoop without a net standing silently on the driveway.

When Sarvis visited Aretha and Jim Robinson in the fall of 1998, he asked Mr. Robinson to tell him what he knew about the origins of Pinhook. The story Robinson tells that day lays a firm foundation for the beginnings of the town his father and friends built and loved until the day they died. The details retained in his memory include many historical facts that add to our understanding of the economic features of this critical time in Missouri development, as well as the verification of a landed African American presence beginning in 1940. Robinson Jr. was nine years old when he accompanied his father to southern Missouri.

"I was born in December of 1933, December 12, to be exact, in Arlington, Tennessee, that's in Shelby County, a big county [that] takes up all of Memphis. It adjoins Fayette County on the south side, sort of, and that was all the famous domain of Mr. Crump down there. In fact, my dad knew Mr. Crump personally. He made whiskey for him. Yes, sir. The still belonged to Crump and other law enforcement officers, and my daddy carried it out in the woods and made whiskey for them.[3] At that time I was a baby, of course. I was in diapers. Now, you know this has got to be hearsay because in 1934, I don't remember that much because I was so young.

"We lived there for about nine years after I was born, then my dad moved to Missouri, and I've been here ever since, with the exception of being two years in the service, in the army. When he moved us up here he said he wasn't moving any further north. This was as far as he was going to go. Besides, he found out there was land black men could buy in Missouri. That's what brought him here.

"I remember distinctly when we moved to Mississippi County, in Missouri, it was December the 9th. There was a group of five or six men that had bought an eighty-acre block of land together. They had an equal share of sixteen acres apiece. How many is that? That would be five men. One of the men died. And maybe one went back to Tennessee.

"One of the men that came with my daddy was Lewis Moss. When the other man died, Mr. Moss knew that my daddy could come up with enough money to take this other guy's place, which was very little. They were paying like to the tune of $16 an acre for the ground. They managed to hook up with some shyster that lived here, and by the time they got it paid for, he actually

Jim Robinson Sr. From Robinson Family Personal Collection.

charged them $28 per acre. But my daddy bought the sixteen acres of the man
that died, and from that it just grew block by block.[4]

"I loved hanging out with my daddy and his buddies. My mama let me
come up here with him and the other men early that summer, when they were
looking to buy the land. I was only nine, then, but I was already a farmer. As
soon as I was big enough to walk out there and catch a mule, see I was already
a farmer, which was very young. And if you notice my stature, I'm very short
anyway. But I used to crawl up the mule's leg to put the bridle on. And it
worked. I know this sounds like a joke, but I didn't have nobody to catch my
mule for me. Daddy said, 'Do it,' and you had to do it. There was no if's, and's,
or but's. Catch a pair of mules and hook them up to the plow.

"When we lived down there, my grandmother would come periodically
and spend some time with us. She was Indian and very hellish, very mean.
She could never get along with nobody, so she went from place to place to
place to place until her death in about 1959 or '60. She passed on. She was pure
Indian, by the way. My mother's ancestors were pure white, and Grandpa was
white. So, ha, ha, I'm kind of mixed. I don't know much about my other grandparents, just a wee bit. My mother was born in the hills of Mississippi—that
was down there at Macon, in that general area. My dad was born at Jackson,
Mississippi. They both ended up moving to the Delta, or what they called the
Delta, which was around Inverness, Greenwood, Itta Bena, places like that,

and Morehead, Indianola, all of that area around Clarksdale, what they called the Delta, right on up to Yazoo City.

"Somehow or another, my parents met in that general area and got married. They stayed there about one or two years, but not very long because of mistreatments to my dad and some other things—some ways they treated my mom that my dad wouldn't go for. Like, for instance, the boss wanted Mom to clean his house. But my dad said, 'Well, who's going to clean mine?' And, so, they got into it, because it wasn't a 'you can if you want to' kind of a deal. They demanded certain things of us [blacks] then. This is how my dad explained it to us. And my dad wouldn't stand for that, to be treated like that.

"For a time, they moved to Arkansas, and they began to clear land by hand for some people. They made share crops. My dad drove an old iron wheel tractor which had killed a man. It had slipped back over and fell on him and killed him, so nobody would drive it. But, my daddy wasn't afraid of nothing. In fact, he turned over several more of them himself, ha, ha. He got the job driving that thing.

"Eventually, he ended up over in Tennessee with the Gillespie brothers. They were pretty good-sized landowners at that time and very fine fellows. And, my daddy became a renter. He rented, oh, I guess, three or four hundred acres—farming by mules, you know, that's a lot of land. This landowner had both sharecroppers and wage hands. The sharecroppers, as you know, got half of a crop and they furnished all of the labor. The wage hands worked for $100 a year or one bale of cotton, their choice, whichever one they wanted at the beginning of the year. And that's all they earned, was one bale of cotton. [And] they got a meal from my family, because my mom used to love to cook, like cooking for a levee camp or a big group of people. And so they always had a dinner meal. And they just kind of went lacking for supper and breakfast. This was how people lived. All the sharecroppers and wage laborers that worked for my daddy were all black. There was nobody white but the people who owned the land. We couldn't talk to whites the way me and you have talked here without fear of reprisal of some sort. This was another reason why my daddy wanted to get away from Tennessee and come to Missouri. My daddy didn't bow to nobody, you know, and I'm similar to him. We always believed that we should treat people fairly, but we're just as good as anybody, and we're no better than nobody else. So we dealt with that all our lives.

"That's part of the Tennessee story that moves up to the time we moved to Missouri. And he knew things were better in Missouri. He had a brother [in law] that worked for Shannon Logging Company. We called it just Shannon Camp. And they helped to cut logs for Peco Valley and Manglewood Box & Company. His name was Major Butler, and he was a brother-in-law to my dad.

He married my dad's sister. And they lived just up the road from where we are now. They never knew that we bought land right where they lived, because they died before we got there, but they were right here in the area. In fact, we met people who knew them. He was supposed to have been one of the best timber cutters in the business. During the time he was up here, he contacted my dad. At that time land was selling for 50¢ an acre. Can you imagine that? An eighty-acre farm for $40. And he was trying to get Dad to come and buy some land because he knew Daddy was a farmer. But we didn't get in on the 50¢ an acre. We got in on the $16 an acre, which later cost $28, because the man beat us out of the money. The lowest going price was $8. Oddly enough, it doubled every time it went up. It went $8 to $16.

"Well, we paid $28, and that didn't quite double, but it was close. This land was just freshly cleared of the timber. It had never been farmed. This is what you would call virgin land. We called it cutover land. That means that the three big timber giants had cut all of the big virgin timber, all the good timber, and sold it off. So there was no immediate use of the land anymore. That's why it sold so cheaply. And they were getting rid of a tax burden. That's the beginning of this Pinhook area. This was a low area and it flooded, like it still does. My daddy worked until his death trying to get the people of the higher-ups [in charge] to see how bad we needed flood control down in this area. I, too, argued that right behind him. I've been working and digging and trying to get this levee completed down here at New Madrid and this general area. If we ever get that done, we won't get backwater in here and this land will be just as valuable as any land in the state of Missouri. It's good land. It just floods. We lose crops. And when you lose crops, you lose your livelihood. But we've hung tight. We've been here ever since I was nine years old.

"But at that time, the land was all water and we had to clear it all for farming. Thad Snow called it 'Swampeast Missouri,' and that kind of stuck. I knew him. You better believe it! During those times, we were always fighting about this project to drain the backwater there at St. John's Bayou. If we could get that done, we wouldn't need nothing. It's something to keep you working at, all the time. But they put that levee—what I call a spillway levee [there]—[it] followed the river on out to New Madrid. They got down to New Madrid, [but] they stopped and left a blank space of about a quarter of a mile, a half or quarter, or whatever. So when the water gets up so high, instead of just coming on [into] this ditch like it normally would, it's got this whole open area. [So, if] you turn loose a quarter of mile of water coming up in this area, [then] where you're sitting now you could see water from my back door. The deer got run out of the woods. We sat right here on this porch this spring and just sat here with field glasses and watched the deer play. They couldn't go in the woods. Water was [everywhere] out there. You could get on a boat from way over here at this hill and ride all the way across to this other hill before you got to land again. If they shut this off and put in a pumping station, any rain water collected in there would be lifted over the levee and into the river. And when you had high water everybody else would suffer right along with you. They'd have to go down river instead of in this whole area.

"They look at the economics of things, and that's understandable. They say, 'We're losing x-number of dollars for certain crops because we can't get them planted in time; we can't get them harvested; we can't do all of this.' So that hurts us. And then we start talking about the hydraulics of the thing, and I get so sick of all of those big terms. And I'd say, what about my feet? I got up, when I lived right down the road, and my feet went in the backwater, on the floor! It had gotten up in my house. I'm talking about people's butts, their lives! They're far more important than economics. I ain't worried about how much money we lose. I'm worried about losing a child, losing a family, losing your life, ruining your home, ruining all these things. All they have to do is plug up this levee and they'd stop that stuff. But they just can't see helping— and I always kind of say, 'We've got too many minorities that they'd end up helping.' They just won't do it.

"That was the Army Corps of Engineers. I spoke with them, by the way. I went and spoke on the boat. I got a chance to speak to the Mississippi Colonel or somebody, I don't know what it was. I thought they listened to me. I don't know if I done any good. I know we're still fighting the battle, and I'm just kind of praying that somewhere down the line somebody will see what we're hollering about. They already see where they can go ahead and take care of this. If they plug that up, put in some pumping stations, some lift stations, that's all we need. That's all we're asking for. I just pray that I could live to see the day when that levee's plugged up. To know that my family would be protected. That's an eerie feeling—when you wake up, and you know the only way out of here is a 40-40 diesel tractor; or else a twelve-foot jon boat. Or something like that. That's the only way we can get out. When the water comes up, all of this across there is knee deep to a young giraffe. You just don't get across there. So we take my tractor and hook a flatbed trailer behind it, and we run taxicab-like, myself and my brother, until the water subsides, until it goes down, which sometimes is three weeks to a month. We start running and bring people back. Because you saw the town up there. It's kind of a nice place. People would rather be at home than be anywhere. We help them out. We never charge them a quarter. When the water gets low enough, we park the tractor and put a piece of cardboard in front of the truck, which pushes the water, and we get them out like that. The same way with the children going to school, we take these kids across that levee, and they catch the bus on the other side.

"See, this is Pinhook Ridge. All of this ridge is ours. If we had to call it in acres, we'd say about 5,000 or 6,000; maybe 10,000—that doesn't get under water at all. But you can't get in and out because it has cuts like this ten mile point bottom that goes right across over there.

"When my daddy first got involved with farming here, we had our own share croppers. Just like down in Arkansas. The ground that I farm now, at one time, there were twenty-six families farming my ground; the ground that I'm farming now. Twenty-six families. Now it ain't nobody but me. So you see what has happened. But see, at that time, we had one mule going down the middle, and he was taking a half a row. Now I carry fifteen rows, one way. While we were walking behind a mule, I [could only] go so fast. Now, ha, ha, they're going to get me for speeding. We move right along.

"When you hear them talking about the 'good old days,' they can have them. I worked too hard with mules. We cleared land by hand and mules. When you cut down a tree like this, we'd line up the limbs and make a pile and put a chain around the tree and hook a mule to it and drag it up to a pile. Everything we did was with a mule. There was no tractors. In fact, the first tractor that was bought in this area by a black man was my daddy—a iron wheel John Deere, 1937 model. And it was a man killer. You'd go ride a road, and it'd just shake the snot out of you. But there was no roads. All you had was field(s). You had a little road going towards the store and all that, but it was dirt also. When it rained you got stuck. You couldn't go down it.

"But I come from the lowest up to where we are now. And I don't want no more parts of the 'good old days.' No kind of way. I had heard about the supposed intelligence ratio of the mule, and all this, blah, blah. And I didn't believe none of it. He was still a mule or a horse or whatever. He's still a—oh, I wish I could say, ha, ha, what I want to say! He still was a mule. I didn't care for him. When I get down off of them, I like to turn a key and be done with it. I worked too hard with mules.

"My daddy used to tell me all the time, 'Jim, you'll always do greater things than me.' And I couldn't see it, because I thought he was the greatest. But I see it now. I see the things. He didn't see my home. When Dad died, I didn't even have a car. I had nothing. And I've moved up pretty good. I've got a yard full of cars and just about anything I want. But he taught me. I'll never forget that.

"My dad got into politics, and then so did I. It was important to get both whites and blacks into the government, for protection. We had a thing in Charleston where every Saturday night a black person died; sometimes two or three. My wife's brother went through World War II and didn't get injured.

Jim Robinson Jr. and Aretha Robinson. From Robinson Family Personal Collection.

He come right back to Charleston, and they busted his head. And he hadn't done nothing; didn't do nothing. He just had a couple more girlfriends than some other dudes had. So they said, 'Let's get him.' And they got him. They didn't go to jail. They didn't do nothing [to them].

"Daddy and them was looking for prosecuting attorneys, judges, et cetera, that would jail them folks and make them pay for the crimes that they done. And that's what started the breakup of the Charleston Badlands. And now it's kind of tightening back down again. Every time you turn around somebody is getting wasted up there. We try to do the best we can. I'm not saying that all of the law enforcement we've got now is that good, but they try. They try their best. I work with them. I don't just guess at what they do. I know what they're trying to do. But it's hard.

"Down in this area, in Pinhook, it's kind of nice. And I try my best to keep it this way. Because I don't let too much go on by me unless I'm going to be right on top it. There's a key in every vehicle sitting in this yard. You can get down in one of them vehicles, and there's a key in it. You can go anywhere you want to go. My house is unlocked. You don't want to lock no house.

"I never drank nothing in my life. I'm a teetotaler. Never drank a bit. I just stayed away from that sort of thing. Alcohol, I make some eggnog once a year for Christmas for the kids. My grandkids, my kids. They like my recipe.

I do it out of memory. I don't know why they don't [make it]—I've got one son can make it, now. But, I just make it for them. I taste it and make sure it's right. And it's with alcohol. I put that hooch in there, man. It tastes good, but I don't want it. My wife don't drink. We just don't touch nothing. I'm not against drinking, at all. By no means. If you like it, fine. I just don't want it. I'm already silly enough as it is. If I get something that would make me silly, I'd sure enough be messed up.

"But, speaking of segregation, the graveyard up there at Charleston is segregated. What in the world is some bones going to do? The whites are buried here, the blacks are buried here. That is so ridiculous and so silly. But segregation goes on and on and on. It will live forever. Well, it would be [there] past my time."

◆ ◆ ◆

Robinson's oral history provided much information we needed to begin our research on Pinhook. We were delighted to locate such a thorough, first-hand account of the founding of the town. As we talked with many of the Pinhook residents over time, we learned just how important the Robinson family had been throughout the history of the town. Robinson's description of the culture of the Bootheel region when his family first migrated to the state fleshes out the accounts by white historians of the time, including writers like Thad Snow.

In Mr. Robinson's oral account, race appears several times as a factor in the African American men's decision to move out of the Deep South into Arkansas and Missouri. According to his son's narrative, his father announced that he "did not intend to travel any further north." This, in itself, is a significant historical statement. At a time when so many southern African American people were traveling to the north to find work and better lives in urban areas, this group of men chose to go no further than Missouri, recognizing that the Bootheel of Missouri was the furthest from their homes they could go and still live within what they endearingly called "The Delta." These men sought to improve their lives by taking their skills as farmworkers into a new life as landed farmers themselves. Their intention was to buy land and farm it, choosing, unlike so many others, not to travel to the urban areas, but rather to stay and work the soil.

In order to get out of the indentured sharecropping life most African Americans in the South endured, this group of men travelled to Missouri, where they had heard "black men could buy land." Jim Robinson Sr. had heard through family members that farmland was selling for $.50 per acre in Missouri: "Imagine that, an 80 acre farm for $40." This seemingly simple statement elides several systemic failures for African American citizens. If, in 1940, "black men could buy land," this statement implies that prior to 1940 black men could not buy land in southeast Missouri. The language of most of our study participants verifies that until this time, blacks were not allowed to buy land. According to oral accounts, in the early 1940s blacks were finally allowed to buy land. In truth, these statements may hold several possibilities: that white landowners would not sell land to people of color; that farmland was too expensive for most African American farmers to buy; or, exactly what it says, that blacks were not allowed to buy land in Missouri prior to 1940, which would have been illegal. This does not mean it was not true. Certainly, the efforts of the Southern Tenants Association following the 1939 roadside demonstrations factored into the story that land was available for blacks to buy.[5]

By the time Robinson and his group had arrived in Missouri, the brother-in-law who had told him about the availability of land was already dead, and the price per acre had increased. Even as the men were bargaining for certain plots of land together, the price doubled and quadrupled, raising questions about the intentions of those who were selling the land. Certainly, the buyers were gouging the black farmers as much as they could, ("because the man beat us out of the money"), and possibly they were loath to sell blocks of land to a collection of black farmers who might then own and operate a rather large acreage in the region. Most important for this discussion is that the land the African American farmers "were allowed to buy" was the least desirable land in the area. Some of the timber had been cut, leaving swamps full of low-lying dank water, not at all suitable for human habitation. Certainly, it was not farmland. It was swampland and lay deep in the Mississippi River spillway which was always prone to flooding—either by the whims of the river or the decisions of the Army Corps of Engineers. The land they bought was described by Robinson Jr.: "So there was no immediate use of the land anymore. That's why it sold so cheaply. They were getting rid of a tax burden. That's the beginning of this Pinhook area."

Significantly, the black farmers buying the land were told: "This land will always seep with water, and you will have to live with that water all the time." And the Army Corps of Engineers told them, in essence: "This land is in the spillway and the Corps can breach the levee at any time and flood out your land and whatever you build on it. By signing these papers, you are acknowledging that you know you are buying land in the spillway that can be flooded at any time by the Corps if they deem it necessary to engage the levee system." Having no alternative, the African American farmers bought the swampland in the spillway and proceeded to clear it, digging ditches to drain the water.

It might be noted, as well, that the white landowners owned all the acres on higher land. Although that higher land did flood occasionally, the result was not destruction, but rather the accumulation of a rich layer of silt on the bottomland that added nutrients and ensured an even better crop the following year. Perhaps more importantly, the white farmers were protected eventually through the crop insurance they could buy which provided them with reimbursement if their crops failed because of flooding. Of course, many of the smaller black farmers could not afford insurance, and even if they could, they would not be able to buy insurance for land squarely within the spillway.

In addition to his desires to leave the sharecropping life, Jim Robinson Sr. explained to his son his intention to find a less racialized place to live. In the Delta, he recalled, his own father had had difficult encounters with whites over some things he and his wife did not want to do for them: "And, so, they got into it, because it wasn't a 'you can if you want to' kind of a deal. They demanded certain things of us [blacks] then. This is how my dad explained it to us. And my dad wouldn't stand for that, to be treated like that." Robinson takes time to identify his own genetic make-up. He tells Sarvis that, according to family history, his grandmother was full-blooded Indian, that his mother was "pure white," as was his Grandfather. He knows little about the other side of his family, but concludes that he is, of course, of mixed race, which means he was treated as a person of color. In the Delta, he grew tired of the fact that all the sharecroppers and tenant farmers were black and all the landowners were white, and race relations were strained. Black people could not even talk with whites without fear of "reprisals": "There was nobody white but the people who owned the land. We couldn't talk to whites the way me and you have talked here without fear of reprisal of some sort. This was another reason why my daddy wanted to get away from Tennessee and come to Missouri. My daddy didn't bow to nobody, you know, and I'm similar to him. We always believed that we should treat people fairly, but we're just as good as anybody, and we're no better than nobody else. So we dealt with that all our lives." Robinson's father was seeking to buy land where black people would be treated as equals rather than as inferiors to their white neighbors. While many of Robinson Sr.'s experiences in Missouri did not meet with his expectations of being treated fairly and with dignity, Missouri did offer him at least the semblance of a voice concerning the politics of the region. The politics in the Bootheel near Birds Point were about water and flooding. Mr. Robinson Sr. knew early on that the levee system was not adequate to the flow of the Mississippi River after spring rains in the north. Robinson Jr. recalls how his father immediately saw the problems of the levee construction and began to take his concerns to those in power.

Robinson Jr. explains how he has continued to fight for a more just levee system that could protect both the white and black farmers: "My daddy worked until his death trying to get the people of the higher-ups [in charge] to see how bad we needed flood control down in this area. I, too, argued that right behind him."[6]

It is ironic to note that Robinson Jr. is speaking with Sarvis in 1998, telling him the problem has not been resolved at all. Farmers in the spillway are still battling the water on their land and in their homes, but the levee system has not been improved. He points out, "I've been working and digging and trying to get this levee completed down here at New Madrid and this general area. If we ever get that done, we won't get backwater in here, and this land will be just as valuable as any land in the state of Missouri. It's good land. It just floods. We lose crops. And when you lose crops, you lose your livelihood. But we've hung tight. We've been here ever since I was nine years old."

Robinson points out that if the levee system had been improved, backwater flooding would have been eliminated, and that's all the African American farmers were arguing for. His words are prophetic. Because the people in power would not improve the system to eliminate backwater flooding from the Pinhook area to improve the lives of the black farmers, the lack of support for this rather simple solution kept the black farmers agitated and frustrated all the time. Not only were they constantly fighting the water, they were also constantly fighting the policy makers. The result was the utter waste of their capabilities on things they could not control: "It's something to keep you working at, all the time." Both Robinson and his father knew what the problem was and how it could be fixed. No doubt those in power understood this solution was rather simple as well but preferred not to improve the system in order to help the African American farmers in Pinhook.

But they put that levee—what I call a spillway levee [there]—[it] followed the river on out to New Madrid. They got down to New Madrid, [but] they stopped and left a blank space of about a quarter of a mile, a half or quarter, or whatever. So when the water gets up so high, instead of just coming on [into] this ditch like it normally would, it's got this whole open area. [So, if] you turn loose a quarter of mile of water coming up in this area, [then] where you're sitting now you could see water from my back door.

Water was [everywhere] out there. You could get on a boat from way over here at this hill and ride all the way across to this other hill before you got to land again. If they shut this off and put in a pumping station, any rain water collected in there would be lifted over the levee and into the river. And when you had high water everybody else would suffer right along with you. They'd have to go down river instead of in this whole area.

Robinson clearly understands the rationale of the policy makers, even in 1998, as systemic racism based on the supremacy of white privilege. The economics they proffer support only the needs of the white landowners and ignore the daily influx of water onto the black farmland and into the black farmers' houses. Robinson notes who the policies are aiding and who continues to suffer. He is correct in his assessment that helping minorities is not in the best interest of those in power: "They look at the economics of things, and that's understandable. They say, 'We're losing x-number of dollars for certain crops because we can't get them planted in time; we can't get them harvested; we can't do all of this.' So that hurts us.

"And then we start talking about the hydraulics of the thing, and I get so sick of all of those big terms. And I'd say, what about my feet? I got up, when I lived right down the road, and my feet went in the backwater, on the floor! It had gotten up in my house. I'm talking about people's butts, their lives! They're far more important than economics. I ain't worried about how much money we lose. I'm worried about losing a child, losing a family, losing your life, ruining your home, ruining all these things. All they have to do is plug up this levee and they'd stop that stuff. But they just can't see helping—and I always kind of say, 'We've got too many minorities that they'd end up helping.' They just won't do it!"

Aretha Robinson's Story [Jim Robinson Jr.'s widow]

When we visited southern Missouri in our efforts to hear the stories of Pinhook, we often headed first to a small gray house on the cul-de-sac off John R. Road in what is often referred to as the "Sunset" area of Sikeston. Although it is not clear why this area was called by this name, it may well have referenced an earlier time in this southern Missouri town when African Americans were required to be off the streets "after sunset." To this day, Sikeston remains an economically depressed, racially divided, and contentious community. The Pinhook residents who had to move into Sikeston were not happy with the notion of living there very long.

In May 2013, two years after the flood, we visited the house in Sikeston now occupied by Aretha Robinson and her two daughters, Debra and Twan. Their cousin, Larry, owns this house and had invited his family members to live there after Pinhook was destroyed. Although we had visited several times before and come to know the Robinson family fairly well, we were arriving

Aretha Robinson at Pinhook Day, 2014. Elaine J. Lawless.

today for an extended visit. We had mentioned to Miss Aretha that we wanted
to get her recollections about living in Pinhook. It must have been about 3:00
when we got to their house. We pulled our car onto the grass just as the others
had parked and pulled out all our recording equipment. It may have been a
bit daunting for Aretha to watch us lug it up to her door. She sat quietly waiting in a wooden chair that squeaked every time she rocked, which was all the
time. Her smile was sweet, and she leaned forward so we could each give her
a gentle hug. Todd kissed her cheek as she looked him over, and before long
they were chatting about Todd's third cousin who had come to Charleston, a
nearby town, many years before from Central Missouri—an undertaker, well
known to the Robinson family, perhaps even kin somewhere in the unofficial
records of African American families in Missouri. Soon, Elaine was explaining that she had grown up not far from Pinhook, near Benton, although she
confessed she had never heard of the African American town before she read
about the flood in the Sikeston paper at her mother's house. Todd's African
American ties and Elaine's recollections working in the fields only a few miles
to the west of Pinhook helped us all to relax. We set up the cameras and audio
recorders and then sat down ready to listen to Miss Aretha. Everyone in the
room seemed poised to enjoy Aretha's stories as well. We were creating an

historical record—filling out the story of Pinhook based on the stories of those who had lived there.

Todd was prepared with our most important question: "So, Miss Aretha, can you just tell us what it was like to live in Pinhook when you went there to live?"

Without hesitation, the matriarch of the Robinson family began to rock with intention, gazing out the window as though she could see the place just outside the glass.

"It is just so peaceful out there. People were loving and kind toward each other. You could get help—you could always get help. Something could happen and the community was always there for you, to help you. It was just a great place to live. Peaceful and quiet. You didn't have to worry about the noise and robberies and stuff like that. We had some, of course, but very little, not like in town. And I really enjoyed living there.

"I went there in '55, and I have lived there ever since, except for a year and a half that I lived in Dalton, Oklahoma. My husband was stationed out there, and then we were back to Pinhook again. And we were farmers, farmed there for years. We finally sold out our land when his health got so bad. So, then, we were just living there. Just enjoying living there. All the children graduated and were gone from home, except Bert who often stayed with us on his runs. That made us a little lonely, because we were there by ourselves, but that was okay because we had never been alone by ourselves, you know, because, we've always had people living with us. Always. And it was just great, it was great, it was just a great thing. We loved living there.

"Pinhook was his home, really. They, he and his brothers, moved to Missouri in 1941, to this area. I moved to Missouri in 1940, just five miles north of Charleston in a little community called Texas Bend. I had never lived in the Bootheel area down that far. And I met him, and we were married, and then I moved there, in '55.

"And he always asked me, he said, 'What kind of house do you want?' And my baby daughter had just been born, and I was still in the bed. And he said, 'What kind of house you want?' Because all of his brothers, you know, had built their homes there. And I said, 'I want a home with two of these things—I want two of those on my house, you know, they go like this' [she gestures to indicate a gable end.] He said, 'I've never seen a house with two of those on it,' and I said, 'Well, that's what I want. You asked me what I want, and that's what I want.' And he said, 'okay.' And he sat down with the Etch-a-Sketch, one of the children's Etch-a-Sketch, and he drew that house on the Etch-a-Sketch, and we started building that house from his drawing on that Etch-a-Sketch. And then he said, 'Well, where're we going to get stones?' And he drove all around, all over, trying to figure out where we can get the stones. And, then, over to Marble Hill, Missouri, he found a house there that had stones, and they told him they went to Crosby, Tennessee to get them. And we went all the way to Crosby, Tennessee with that baby, and found those stones. And it was amazing to me, because I had never seen stone like that. I thought they made stone up like you do bricks. But it's in the ground, and we bought it. And I love that house. That's what I always wanted, was a stone house. I would just love it if they would build me another house, and I would just love to have at least the front in stone. It doesn't have to go all away around like that one. If we did just this front half, that would be okay. I would love to have that.

"Have you seen it?" At this point Aretha turned to Elaine to ask her if she had seen her house. She was pleased to hear that we had seen it just that week.

"Oh, I just love it, girl. I loved it. I used to just love it. I used to sit in the yard. It was just so peaceful there. And there was another house, you know, down below me about half a mile and we were good friends. And he would always raise a garden, and he'd call us up after I got to where I couldn't raise garden, he'd always call, and he'd say, 'Aretha, the greens are ready,' or the 'green beans are ready. You can come down and get whatever you want.' And we'd walk down, we just walked down and get them, because all the people were just so close. We were also so close together there, and if someone grew something and they got a flush of something, or an overflush of it, they'd call the next person and say, 'Would you want this or can you use some of this?' It was always really nice like that. I just loved it. And it was just so nice because we had our church up there on the hill. It was just great.

"And if somebody got sick, we were there to help. And if they needed somebody to wait on him and help 'em out, maybe this family would cook today, and another family would cook tomorrow, you know, rotated. It was just good. And we would have Pinhook Day once a year just like we had this year. Every year we would have it, every Memorial weekend, we would have Pinhook Day and the people, all the people would come back. It was just wonderful. It was great! We did it, my family did it for a long time until my husband got older and we had to cut back, because he was having trouble with his heart. And he had heart surgery. He had two open heart surgeries, and we had to kind of back off a little bit, you know, we couldn't do all of that any more like we used to. But he enjoyed doing it. And I was hanging in there with them, then all the children picked it up and we'd all do whatever we could.

"It was so easy living there. That's what we used to always talk about, you know. Somebody would come in, the kids would come in from the kitchen, and our kids would ask, 'Can we go a piece of the way? Can we go down there a piece of the way with them?' And we'd say, 'Yeah you can go a piece of the way.' So, they'd go down there a piece of the way, you know, to the other house, and then they'd turn around and go a piece of the way with them, and then they'd turn around and come back to our house. It was wonderful. I enjoyed it so much.

"I have talked about it so much. I talked about it before the flood and I talked about it after the flood. One time there was a guy came down wanted to talk to my husband about Pinhook, because Jim knew more about it than I did, 'cause, you know, he lived here at first and I didn't. I married him, and then I came here, so he knew more about it. When I came to Pinhook, it was already there and he knew a lot of history about Pinhook that I don't know. From the time he was nine, he lived in Pinhook, until he was 71. He came to Pinhook way before George. I think they came like in the 50s like '52. And Jim had already been there 10 years, twelve years earlier.

"It's hard to say exactly when Pinhook actually started. His dad [Jim Robinson Sr.] came there way, way back, maybe '39 or '40 they came out. Five men came out and they cleared up all the land there and started building homes. They could buy an acre of land there for little or nothing. So they bought the land, you know, and Mr. Robinson brought his family back. Those that bought the land—one was a Mr. Lewis, Mr. Lewis Moss, and the other three guys I can't remember their names but there were five of them. Two of them stayed, and then three of them left. They went back to Tennessee, or something, because they didn't like it. But they all cleared it. It was just trees and brush out there. They cleared the land with their hands, mules and hands. And that was way back in the early—early, like in '39 and '40. That's what they cleared the land with. And the three guys that left, the others bought their land when they left.

"But down there, that was the only place we could go, because they wouldn't sell land to blacks nowhere else down there! So, that was the only place we had, that was the only place we could buy land, the only place that we had to live. And my father-in-law would go to Jefferson City and whatnot to argue to get the levee fixed so we wouldn't have all that backwater every year. And they had maybe 10 or 20 acres like that, but it had to be cleared, because it was all those woods, before it could be farmed. First, it had to be cleared. Jim Sr., my father-in-law, and Jim Jr., my husband, and his brothers, they all worked out there and cleared it, cleared the land by hand, mules, using axes and whatever.

"Even when I got here I would come behind and pick up those chunks of wood. I just hated that. I picked up those chunks of wood and I run and I would cry, because of those lizards, you know. Now, the snakes were fine with me, but I didn't like those lizards. And they are running from the snakes, they were afraid of them. But I'd run and cry from those lizards. [She is laughing; we are, too.] I would just kill a snake, but those lizards they moved too fast.

Oh Lord! [laughter] That was a hard job picking up those chunks. That was really hard.

"First I had Debra. Then, I had four boys straight in a row, and the doctor said, 'Aretha are you going to quit?' And I said, 'No, I'll have one hundred until I have a girl, until I have another girl.' Then, I had another girl, the one that is sitting now outside there with her brother. And then he was born, that is David. And after David was born, I had another girl. I had three girls and five boys and I lost my oldest son in 1996. [She gets real quiet rocking in her chair.]

"And I enjoyed every moment of it. Having all those children. Everybody would say, 'You're so crazy girl, having all these babies.' But they were all, you know, like two years apart or whatever. But my oldest son was like a year, a year and four months apart from the next boy. And, then, they were like two years apart, and three years apart. They were just spaced out just right. I didn't just have a baby every year. But I enjoyed every moment of it, and I raised them all up on the farm. They all worked on the farm with us and, Lordy, we had some times on the farm.

"Sometimes I just stayed in the kitchen, and to this day I just stay in the kitchen. All the time. They tell me, 'Mom, you don't have to cook all the time. You cannot cook no more, you just cook too much.' But I just love cooking. Like this morning, you can't think what I did this morning. I got up this morning and I was working on the ads, the stuff we were going to do for this walkathon, you know, for Pinhook Day. And I went into the kitchen and I got my little Cornish hen, and just split her in half and seasoned it real good, and then I put it on the stove and fried it and then put some gravy on it and then put a top on it and just let it sit there. And my grandson came to pick me up and he says, 'Oh, Grandma, I just have to have a taste of that that Cornish hen, because everything you cook just tastes so good.' Everybody come here! You should have seen it this Saturday. Lord, all of us were here, just family.

"But I don't think I ever cried. I never did. I wanted to, but I didn't cry. I just want to go back. I'd just rather move on. You got to go on a-living. I'm just thankful we all got out alive.

"Everybody was checking to make sure nobody was left behind, when everybody was helping everybody else get out. They were checking to see if you were out or did you need help. And, Lord, I swear, a lot of people were trying to help us out, because they brought people from their jobs to come out and help us get out of there. We didn't have any trucks or nothing. And my son out there, David, he had to go all the way to Poplar Bluff just to get two rental trucks. That was all they would let us have. And some people knew me from Charleston, some youngsters there, and they had known us for years, you know. We knew people around there since they were babies, and they brought an 18-wheeler out there and that's what helped me get some of my stuff out. They brought an 18-wheeler down there for me and I put some of my stuff on there. And she had put everything that she could get into her car but even still I left all my stuff in my utility room, all the stuff on the patio. I left worlds of stuff out there. Just worlds of stuff.

"Now they been talking about snakes. They said to beware, because they say there's lots of snakes down there. David, you remember after the flood they warned us they said there lots of snakes down there and they're very— what did they say, Lady, when the water came up? They'd tell us, 'They're very aggressive. They were very aggressive.' And you'll see one picture, there is one picture of my house with a bobcat on top of it. He was trying to be safe up there, trying to stay alive. You know, the flood killed so much of the wildlife. There is not much of that down there anymore. We had deer and turkey, all kinds of wildlife—bobcats, rabbits, and now they say don't see anything down there. It killed off everything. But my granddaughter said that the deer are doing okay, 'cause she hit two of them there, messed up her car. And I think we had another picture in there, I think, where the deer were just up on the mound. They got up there thinking that that was high enough.

"Oh, they were just stealing us blind after the flood. They were going in with trucks and trailers and taking the people's stuff. You know, I went up to the Sheriff's Department and said you know they're stealing our stuff and he said, 'Oh, we're patrolling, Miss Robinson, we're patrolling.' But I don't know what they were patrolling because people were just stealing in broad daylight. So, they weren't. There's no way they could have been.

"I only had one thing in there that I really cared about that was stolen. I had an old iron pot like the ones you used to wash in a long time ago? They stole that. It might be worth $50 or $60 maybe more than that now. But I had that old iron pot and they stole it. And I had told the cops, we had pulled it up out of the mud, set it up on its legs, and we were going to come back and get it. But before we could come back and get it, they had stolen it. And that really hurt me, because I really wanted to keep that pot."

We were aware that Aretha had stopped talking. Her gaze out the window seemed lost in the memory of what she had lost. We decided to stop recording for the day. Debra had already gone into the kitchen to prepare the evening meal. She enlisted our help shelling peas. Soon, Twan and David had come back into the house, and we all began to gather at the large table in the kitchen. Debra asked if one of us wanted to offer thanks. We were embarrassed and mumbled something totally indistinct, so she said a prayer thanking God for all that he had done for them, for keeping all in the Pinhook community safe, for the food on the table, and the new friends who were there to hear the stories of their beloved town. They all echoed her concluding "Amen." We wondered at their faith and their resolve, their ability to thank God for all his blessings when, in fact, they had just recently lost pretty much everything they owned, their homes and most of their belongings. But they were thankful for life and for each other. That seemed to be enough to be grateful.

In subsequent conversations with Miss Aretha, we learned more about her early life and her marriage to Jim Robinson Jr. Aretha was "brought up" to Missouri as a child of two, moving first from Tennessee, then from Arkansas, into Missouri's Bootheel region. She remembers her family working the Renard farm, five miles north of Charleston, for nearly 15 years. Also, like most other sharecroppers, her parents could never get out from under the economic servitude that sharecropping imposed on most farm laborers. They were given a poor shack on the Renard land and expected to work dawn to dark, the entire family in the fields chopping cotton, beans, whatever they had earlier planted. In the fall, they would complete the harvest, picking the cotton and corn, the men driving the tractors, sometimes rotating through the night using the dim lights to stay within the crop lines. The children learned early how to handle a hoe, their primary weapon against the encroaching weeds that threatened to take over Mr. Renard's crops. Aretha remembers taking care of the babies when she was only five so her mother could join the others in the fields. At the end of the year, the sharecroppers had little time to feel satisfaction over the payments they received for the season's work—without exception, they ended up giving most all of it back to Mr. Renard for the groceries they had bought through his office, the doctor's visits that could not have been avoided, the birth attendants who risked the horrible roads and bad weather to help Aretha's mother deliver her babies. The sharecropper's lot was to simply begin again, knowing full well that at the end of the next year's hard work, they would not have gained a penny for themselves or for their children's school shoes. At a young age, Aretha knew she wanted a better life than that of her parents, although she could not imagine what that might be.

Eventually, Aretha's family moved to a better farming situation closer to Charleston, Missouri. She remembers her family as not quite so destitute, but as thriving in some small ways. Her mother gave birth to six children and not all of them had to do the grueling farm work that she had had to do with her own parents in Arkansas and Tennessee. Aretha grew up, in fact, loving the farm. It was work she enjoyed; she and her sisters helped their mother with the enormous garden she was able to till and plant, and she learned how to improve their house and paint the walls new, vibrant colors.

When Aretha was 14, her parents allowed her to go to the movies on Saturdays with her older sisters and the neighbors' daughters. The group of girls giggled through the streets of East Prairie, bought ice cream cones, and sat in the front rows of the cool, dark theatre with smiles on their faces. One Saturday a nice-looking young man, sitting in the back of the theatre, asked Aretha for her name as she walked by him heading toward the exit. She smiled at him and said, "Aretha." "Well, Miss Aretha," he replied with more cool that she could imagine, "Would it be okay if I called on you on Sunday?" Trying to stand taller than her 14-year-old frame would allow, Aretha agreed that he could come visit her at her parents' home. As the boy (he really was a boy), walked away, Aretha got scared and gasped, "Oh, Lord, they are going to kill me!" as she and her friends walked away from the theatre and down the road toward their homes. Sure, enough, (she is not quite sure how he found their house), the young man came to visit the following Sunday. At first, Aretha's mother was amused, thinking the young man was there to visit her two older daughters. But no, they claimed, he's not here for one of us—they giggled, he's here for "Retha." Aretha? Oh, mercy, Aretha felt herself growing smaller and smaller as she tried to vanish from the room and her mother's glare. Her mother was not pleased to hear this news, but she was an elegant woman, respectful of her daughters and the young men. She would never embarrass her girls, Aretha claimed, even when she was displeased. So she graciously told the young man and his accompanying friends, "You may come here to visit, but my daughters cannot leave with you. But you are welcome to visit." And he did visit many times during the following year. When Aretha was 15, Jim Jr., asked for her hand in marriage. Aretha's mother was not surprised, but she told him Aretha was too young to be married that he would just have to wait. All right, Jim Jr. told her, I can do that. And he did. When Aretha was 16, he asked again for her hand in marriage. This time, Aretha looked at her mother with pleading eyes. And this time, her mother agreed. She told him yes. He was 21 to Aretha's 16, and they were married the following Christmas Day, in 1955.

During the two years that Jim Jr. courted Aretha, she learned a great deal about his family. He would sit in the parlor and tell her stories he had heard his own father and uncles tell long into the night. They were proud to be "landed" blacks, he told her. After arriving in Missouri, the men who had traveled there waited for weeks as the cost of the land kept changing daily. They watched as some of the wealthiest landowners were ordered to make some of their land available to African Americans in the region. They were deeply discouraged, but not surprised, to learn that the land being made available to them was all swampland and deeply within the heart of the floodplain. To buy that land did not guarantee in any way that they would soon be "landed" farmers. What a bitter joke. In fact, to buy that land meant they would have to spend years clearing the trees, brush, and water from the land long before they could even begin to think about farming it. The choice was both simple and terribly complex. That was the land available for them to buy at prices they could afford; but the land was far from ready to plant. Jim Sr. also knew that building a town and farming this land in the floodplain was a dangerous move to make. He had read the reports that made it clear that this land would be subject to constant flooding from the whims of the Mississippi River, and he felt they could deal with that each year as the waters rose and receded, but he also knew that in some ways, this was a "deal with the devil." Building in the floodplain meant they could not buy insurance against any future disastrous flooding, and, in 1954, they all knew that the Army Corps of Engineers could intentionally breach the levees along the Missouri side of the Mississippi if needed to "save" Cairo, Illinois, and other towns further south on the river. This meant the residents of Pinhook and the farmers in the floodplain would not have any recourse if the Corps determined the levees needed to be breached. They were required to acknowledge they knew they had just built their entire enterprise within the floodplain. But what choice did they have? This was the land they could buy. This was the land they had worked so hard to clear. This was where they lived and farmed. They would stay—regardless of the pitfalls and possible future destruction. They took the chance and for sixty years, a full generation, they were happy in the spot they carved out of the wetlands. Pinhook thrived and the residents loved living out there. This was their home. They could not imagine living anywhere else.

George Williams's Story

While it is true that the Robinson family knew perhaps the most about the founding of the town of Pinhook, we wanted another perspective from someone who did not arrive in Missouri with the Robinson group or marry into the Robinson family. We found the perfect person to talk with when we finally located Mr. George Williams. Mr. Williams lives in Granite City these days, but before he retired, if you wanted to find him, you would have had to go to the school bus garage for the East Prairie district. Mr. Williams prides himself on being the first African American bus driver in the East Prairie district (and perhaps the entire Bootheel region) after arriving in Missouri in the early 1950s. Nearly every interview we did with anyone from Pinhook contained a story about Mr. Williams, the school bus driver. He has become a kind of Pinhook legend, and he is quite proud of his legacy. He would drive

George Williams at Pinhook Day, 2014. Elaine J. Lawless.

the bus to Pinhook and pick up all the Pinhook children and get them to their schools in East Prairie or Charleston, always on time. Not only was he a good bus driver, he was also a kind of surrogate parent. If the children arrived on the bus poorly dressed or missing shoes, George often had a few available for them to "borrow." If a child climbed on the bus with bad body odor; he would spray them down with Lysol (much to the chagrin of all the children nearby); if they were rowdy he would move them to the front of the bus to sit on the step and turn the heat on high right over their head and roast them into good behavior. Aretha's daughter Twan told us about this on a different occasion. The women remembered, too, that if their "monthly friend" arrived unexpectedly, George would either find a dime for them and drop them off to go buy a necessity or, sometimes, he kept a box of "personals" on the bus for just such emergencies. The stories told about George were entertaining, but always told with deep affection. Although George rather begrudgingly admits he loved living in Pinhook because it was a quiet, pretty place to live and he loved having good neighbors, his own arrival story in the area tells a different story than that of Robinson Sr.

In April of 2012, we drove to East Prairie to interview George Williams. As expected, we were directed to the school bus garage, where we were assured George could be found repairing the old buses. Driving through East Prairie,

Missouri, is a rather bleak proposition, as the town has far more boarded up businesses than open, thriving ones. We passed one boarded-up ice cream stand, several car parts stores, a farm machine dealership, a whole string of empty warehouses, a flower shop with broken windows, and a tiny house just off the main road down a side street with incongruous rows of palm trees on three sides (we wondered if they were artificial). The bus depot seemed to be closed; we passed a large water tower with the weathered words "E ST P ARI" (EAST PRAIRIE) painted on the side in fading red ink; obviously, some of the letters had disappeared altogether. One row of abandoned shops sported a rather brightly colored mural about East Prairie being in the Bootheel; a skate boarder whizzed past us and slid into a concrete wall, got up, brushed himself off and disappeared down the street on a side-walk that was more cracks than concrete. The roads were full of holes and most houses were somewhat hidden behind giant political signs for various local politicians in long-gone elections.

Turning the corner, we realized we were already on the grounds of the school bus station. The parking lot was empty, so we found a place to park away from the exit of the garage, where the buses might emerge, gathered our recording equipment, and headed for the side door of the garage. Todd led the way into the gloom of the building that smelled of grease, gas, tar, men's sweat, and hamburgers. One man stood alongside the buses immediately in front of us and nodded with a murmured, "Hey" to Todd. Todd responded with a friendly, "Hey," as well, greeting whomever was in earshot, saying we had come to talk to George Williams. We were startled by a man sliding out from under the bus nearest to us on a mechanic's creeper who informed us that "George ain't here." Disappointed, Todd asked when he might be back, or could we wait around for him? "We just want to talk to him about the destruction of Pinhook. We are from the University of Missouri, not the newspapers, but from Columbia"—with that the man at our feet grinned, stood up, put out his hand for Todd to shake and said, "Well, in that case, I'm George." He nodded to Elaine without making eye contact, laughed at his own joke (as did Todd and the other men in the garage) and indicated we should follow him back into his "office." No one said a word until we were in a back room, an airless space about 6' x 6' with a table, a chair, and a second slanting chair that suggested it might not hold a person. Elaine gently leaned against what was sure to be a dirty wall, carefully holding the camera on the tripod she carried.

George sat heavily in a torn swivel chair and asked Todd how he could help. Todd delivered our usual explanation that we were doing research on Pinhook and its recent destruction by the breaching of the levee. He also let George know that everyone we had talked with had suggested we talk to him. This seemed to please George, as he chuckled to himself. Actually, we knew that he had been the subject of at least two fairly lengthy newspaper articles already and that he just might be getting tired of being sought out for yet another interview about Pinhook. But Todd continued with hope: "And from what we hear, Pinhook was an all-black town, is that right? And—oh, before you begin, do you mind if she turns on that recorder so we don't have to write all of this down?" George looked over at Elaine against the wall, waiting to set up the tripod and push the button, then nodded and told Todd, "Yeah, I guess that will be all right." He waited until Elaine said she was ready, then he looked at the floor before he began talking. "Yeah, there were one or two of them there then. And, yes, it was an all black community in there. You had 10 acres or 20 acres, and they took their axes in there and cleaned it up. Debra's granddaddy [Jim Robinson Sr.], he came up there in 1940 or 41, 42, or something like that, and him and some more guys, they cleaned up some of that ground. And they took axes and they cleaned it up and that's how he started there.

"Eventually, her granddaddy passed on and then her daddy took over and there were four of those boys, but there are only two of them living now. That's the baby boy, and the other one lives over in Sikeston, and they had three sisters that were related to those kids, but the older sister died. And that's how he got started there. He was a big farmer down there. I sharecropped down there, but I never did own no [farm] land down there. And I went to work for the school then. I went to work down there in '62 and worked down there at the school down there, then I moved up here and I've been up here ever since."

Thinking George might be finished, Todd asked, "So, where did you come from before you came to Pinhook?" George perked right up with this question and seemed eager to continue talking. "Well, I migrated out of Mississippi. I was born in Lincoln County, in a place called Morgan City. There was a cotton gin and two stores. That's where I was, right there." With that, George stopped talking again and the dark, smelly garage seemed to close in on the three of us in this musty room.

Todd couldn't let it go. Thankfully, he just kept asking questions. "So, what made you come up to Missouri?" George seemed a little surprised by this question, but mustered an answer. "Well," he paused, perhaps to sort out the familial connections that had been at play so many years ago. "My wife's mother and Debra's grandpa's wife, which would have been our grandmamma, they were sisters. And he came down there [to Missouri]. And I'd just been married five days, were married five days, and then I came back with them, up here, and that's how I got up here. [Apparently, Jim Robinson Sr., had come back to Mississippi for George's wedding.] At this point, George pondered more about this part of his life aloud: "I grew up down there in Mississippi. I left there when I was 18 years old."

Todd jumped right in with a new question, "So, what was it like when you came up there to Pinhook?"

At this question, George begins to chuckle, his head low on his chest, his eyes on the floor. "Well, when I got to Pinhook, I wish I had stayed [in Mississippi]! It was rough, boy! Working those rows up through there in the hot sun. It was rough. You couldn't even see, from about here to that shed over there, you couldn't see nothing. They've cleaned it up a lot in the last forty years. One guy, he finally drove some Caterpillars in there and cut out some of those trees. He helped cleaned that up, but there was stumps all across those fields."

Todd is eager, now, to hear more, "So, when you got there?" George picks the narrative right up, "When I got there, it was about 3:00 on a Saturday morning and I woke up and walked out onto Debra's grandpa's porch, and I looked around and thought, 'Oh, Lord, what have I done now?' George is shaking his head with such force, all three of us begin laughing. "It was rough, I tell you, it was rough!"

Todd is laughing as he finally asks, "Well, how long did it take before it got to the place where you thought, well, this might work?" George finally looks up at Todd, even looks over at Elaine before he blurts out—"Humm, about 20 years." Again, we are all laughing. "That's right, about 20 years." Before we left that day, George reminded us that although Pinhook grew into a really nice town, where he loved to live, at first it "wasn't no paradise. No, sir, it wasn't no paradise."

Larry Robinson's Story

From all our conversations with the third and fourth generations of the original Pinhook families, it is clear that the "origin story" of Pinhook has been passed down orally through the generations. The younger people seem to know most of this story, even if they do not remember all the proper names or the exact places particular things happened. Larry Robinson, Aretha's nephew and Debra's first cousin, talked with us at length one night. He had come over from his house to visit while we were recording the other generations of Robinson women. He knows, and loves, the story of Jim Robinson Sr., and Jim Jr., first coming into the area from Arkansas and Tennessee. In fact, his own father, Jerome, Jim Jr.'s brother, was in that original group that migrated into the Missouri Bootheel region in the early 1940s. He told us that the clearing of the land for the town of Pinhook and for the fields for farming fell to the men who first arrived.

"Really, when you look at that time in the 1940s and the '50s, Pinhook was actually woods. And it wasn't the farmland that you have now, it was actually woods. And those were the place—that was the only land where African Americans could buy. That's where they could buy land cheap, and in fact it was considered to be some of the worst land because it was mostly swampy woods, so, they lived in the woods until they got it cleared. But those men, they ended up clearing the land, and it ended up being some of the most profitable land because of its location, being right off the river there where the Mississippi and Ohio River merges. So down there was that ground was rich with a lot of different minerals in the soil. And not only that, it had had an extra layer of moisture and where even with a drought, like we're having now, there at the top of the crust of the ground it was dry but underneath this portion, it was moist." He explained to us that ironically the land turned out to be quite rich for farmland, yet the fact that it continued to flood every year—whether just a little or a lot, as in the flooding years of 1927, '37, and certainly in 2011, the land and the town were doomed from the beginning.

"I think it's important to note that African Americans have had to be—we have to be like 'stoics,' steady and strong. We are people who would share bits of information about the family and then they would pass it down to their children and they'd pass it down to their children. The elders, the stoics, would share different things that they knew. And we have to keep our history alive, even with some of the younger kids, they had to let them know. Things that we take for granted, like Pinhook photos, videos, all of these things become relics later in life. You wish that you could have held onto all of those things, but the floods have destroyed most of that. A few weeks ago Debra and I had some photos that we had of our grandparents. These are few and far between, like who has some of these photos any more?

"We actually lived there. Pinhook was a way of life to us. For my daughter it was different, although we would visit Pinhook all the time, that still doesn't have the same significance to her as it would to me, because you know it was a part of my life, for those of us who lived there, it was a tightknit community.

"And you know, if you're an African American farmer and you're farming back in the 1960s and 70s, there was not a lot of money out there for minorities. And you could not go to the tractor dealership and say, 'why don't you come on over and fix my tractor,' it didn't work like that. They wouldn't help you. You had to take the time to learn how to fix it yourself, and time was of the essence. So there are a lot of things that they learned on their own. They learned on their own just through trial and error, whether it was building, or plumbing, and what have you, it had to be done and you had children, so you had to learn how to do it. And I can also remember that my uncle had some cousins who would help them out. They were electricians in Jackson, Mississippi, and he went down and spent some time with them, and they were instrumental in showing them how to wire things. And so then he came back, and he'd be showing everyone how to wire a house, and it was just a way of exchanging information."

✦ ✦ ✦

Larry's words bring us full circle to Aretha's opening remarks about how important Pinhook was to the people who lived there because it was a town "where people were loving and kind toward each other." Both Aretha and Larry remember it was a close-knit community where people relied on each other for everything: "You could get help—you could always get help. Something could happen and the community was always there for you, to help you. It was just a great place to live. Peaceful and quiet."

The oral traditions that have kept the story of Pinhook alive among the people who lived there tell a story that stands apart from the chaos and heartbreak that had kept the Missouri sharecroppers destitute and unhappy for so many years. This was a new and different story. The lure of land to buy and farm, the idea of building a self-sufficient town of African Americans that would not have to rely on government funding or the disregard of white landowners, and a spirit of enterprise and hard work created the foundation for a new era of African American life in Missouri's Bootheel region. While the people of Pinhook relished the idea of being out in Pinhook subject to no one's authority but their own was compelling. Yet, in the end, nearly a century later, the town's isolation and lack of integration into the larger Bootheel culture created a situation that allowed the Army Corps and the waters of the Mississippi River to sweep away all their dreams and the material reality of their lives in Pinhook.

CHAPTER TWO

Living in
PINHOOK

People carry with them the blueprints of memory for a place. In time, the landmarks of destruction and rebuilding will overlap and intersect the memory of what was there—narrative and metanarrative—the pentimento of the former landscape shown only through the memories of the people who carry it with them.

—**NATASHA TRETHEWEY,** *Beyond Katrina*

Over the years from 2011–2016, we were able to visit with many former residents of Pinhook and glean from them a kind of oral portrait of their town and gain a sense of what it might have been like for them to live there. Race was rarely mentioned; any comments in that direction were largely confined to the fact that Pinhook was an African American town or to the fact that because they were African Americans no one really cared about their town—before or after it was flooded. As that was the case, over the seventy-plus years of Pinhook's existence, the family and friends who lived there came to regard their entire community as family.[1] Many residents were, in fact, kin, as Twan would say, "by blood or by marriage." The town was founded by African Americans who owned the land they cleared, built the town, and farmed the fields. When the town was thriving, the residents claim the population swelled to more than 250 people; at one time the town sported a gas station, a store, school, and a church all run by African Americans. Former residents of Pinhook often refer to how easy it was for them to live and be happy in Pinhook, as opposed to living, or even shopping, in area towns. Jim Crow laws, traditions, and policies remained in Missouri's Bootheel region long after they were outlawed in other Midwestern areas. African Americans from Pinhook were often hassled in town, were refused services, had difficulty finding employment, and could not afford to buy land or a house because of high prices. In contrast, living in Pinhook was rather like living in a small enclave. Former residents describe the town as pleasant and comfortable; people were easy-going, generous, and caring. Everybody knew everybody else; conflict rarely emerged among the population and crime was virtually nonexistent. Except for the farmers who continued to work the land, nearly everyone in Pinhook had employment outside the town. Thus, they had to interact with other people at work, but returning to Pinhook each day made their lives quite enjoyable. Few residents had money to spare, but they had enough to buy and keep up a home, own a car, buy groceries and clothing, and pay for all the normal amenities a small town could provide. For rural African Americans whose parents and grandparents had endured sharecropping and tenant farming following the emancipation of African Americans, Pinhook seemed a kind of paradise: good friends, good food, good relationships, good music, and enough love to go around.

The following is a narrative piece composed from transcripts of conversations we had with the Robinson family over the course of a late afternoon and evening in 2014. It was fairly common for us to arrive in Sikeston to visit, drop by the house of the Robinson women, and stay for several hours. We learned a great deal about their experiences in Pinhook from the numerous stories they told us during those visits. These are the stories of one family, but each family of Pinhook has similar stories to tell. We hope that their stories can provide a sense of how much Pinhook meant to all the displaced residents of the town. Hearing the stories of living in Pinhook provides a palimpsest of images that evoke the sense of family and community that embraced all the people who lived there. Whatever was owned was shared with all; whatever was cooked was shared as needed; whenever tragedy struck, it was felt by all. Like the population of the town, the community was fluid. Houses were not locked; knocking was not required; homes, gardens, and yards were seamless, stitched together by conversation, work, and practice like the quilts the women worked together on room-sized frames.

✦ ✦ ✦

When Jim Robinson Jr. married Aretha Myles in 1955, all he could think about was bringing her to Pinhook. She shared his excitement about taking her to live there. He wanted them to have a house in the town alongside his father's and his brothers' homes. He hoped to farm the land he had helped them clear and claim his place in the Pinhook family of farmers. Both he and Aretha wanted a large family, and he planned to build her a stately home in the town. But when Jim turned 21, the government began to hassle him about military service. He preferred to stay in Pinhook and farm. So, he and Aretha made a game of trying to get her pregnant. However, every time she went to the doctor for a checkup, they were disappointed when the news was "No, she's not pregnant." Eventually, he could not avoid it any longer. He did his duty, signed up, and was sent off to Fort Leonard Wood and then Fort Still, Oklahoma. Both of them loved to tell the story that neither of them knew then that Aretha *was* pregnant when he signed up. She had intended to follow him immediately, but the impending birth of her baby girl kept her in Pinhook for several more months. After Debra was born, Aretha left Missouri with her baby to join Jim Jr. in Oklahoma. When his service duty was completed, they were delighted to be able to return to the growing community of Pinhook.

Over the years, Jim Jr. and Aretha had several other children, eight in total, and Jim managed to build nice houses for them as he had promised. Aretha tells us she loved it there. Almost the first thing she said to us when we sat down to interview her was that she loved to garden. "I just love to garden, always have. We would plant, then chop beans and greens, the whole works. I loved it. I would love to do it all the time, because *I was able.* I had all them kids and they all had a *hoe.* We were always working; if you are on the farm, you had a *hoe.* But now my kids say they don't want to garden, they are tired of the hoe. I really don't understand that. I loved it." Aretha knew hard work, and because she was strong and able to work and feed her family, she appreciated the work in her garden and all the food she could can and store for the winter. She was also willing and able to join Jim Jr. in making a place for their family within the Pinhook community. Aretha's garden fed not only her own children and family, but others as well. Aretha has always loved to cook, and she was so proud that she could feed her entire family, as well as share with others. She talks about feeding anybody who happened along who was hungry. Like us. If you show up at Miss Aretha's—then or now—she is going to feed you. She tells us that if her family would be at the table eating dinner and someone, anyone, even traveling salesmen, stopped by, she and Jim Jr. would say, "grab a chair and sit down." And later they'd tell her "Oh, thank you for this meal. I haven't eaten such a good home-cooked meal like this in days, weeks." This continues to thrill Aretha and give her such pleasure. "We just had fun like that. I loved it."

Today, Aretha's health is not as good as it once was and her legs, she says, "don't work so good." So she slides around the kitchen on an old office chair that Debra brought home for her. The chair helps her roll over to the stove top and stir the pots, slide back to retrieve items she needs from the refrigerator, and reach low into the oven on her way to the table with plates full of steaming food. Aretha is in her seventies and is a fury to watch in the kitchen. We murmur our protests as she tells us to grab a chair and sit down to eat. We have been recording Aretha's memories for two and a half hours. Now, she rewards us with food that melts in our mouths, corn bread with sweet butter piled on top, and beans she and her daughters snapped the night before we arrived to record the siblings' recollections of growing up in Pinhook with Jim Jr. and Aretha as their parents. We, too, thank her for the delicious home-cooked meal and she beams. She is happy to feed us every time we visit.

Miss Aretha enjoys telling us about their life in Pinhook and the various houses Jim Jr. built for her over the years. But these days, Aretha seems despondent. She and her daughters, as well as the other former Pinhook residents, are homeless. They do not want to seem ungrateful, but they are tiring of life in the small bungalow in Sikeston courtesy of her husband's nephew, Larry. Luckily, he owned a house he could loan to them for what they hoped would be a short time before FEMA and SEMA stepped in to help them rebuild their town. But two years, then three, then four, five and now, seven years later, they are still in Sikeston and no closer to rebuilding their town than they were in 2011. As Aretha sits in her squeaky rocker to talk with us about Pinhook, she often gazes out the front window of her house, and, now, her eyes fill with tears. This is not where she had planned to live when she was older. Aretha is pretty certain she will not see the day Pinhook is rebuilt and she can return.

After his stint with the Army, Aretha, Jim Jr., and their toddler, Debra, returned to Pinhook. During those first years, she had to help Jim in the fields more than she did later when she could devote herself to the house and the gardens. When Debra was five and six, Aretha told us how she would have her stay in the house to watch the babies as they came along. On those days, Aretha would climb aboard a tractor and pull the disk through the dark soil with Jim Jr. following behind with the harrow, as they readied the land for planting. Aretha's descriptions of those times are poignant; she talks about the relationship she and Jim Jr. had and how working the land brought them closer together. She liked sitting on the tractor; she preferred it to working in the fields alongside the other farm workers. But even as she proclaimed to enjoy this life, she also admitted it was very difficult. "Yes, it was rough—it was rough raising eight children, you know, trying to farm and raise them up. You have to work; you've got to try and help, and it was rough at first." As Debra got older, Aretha could go outside more often, explaining, "We had a cotton crop right outside, and I could go out and chop cotton and leave her in the house, you know, something like that. I didn't have to stay out there in the fields."

Clearly, Aretha loved the land, the farming, her home in Pinhook, and she took great pleasure in her children and raising them in the country. What she was not prepared for was the water, always the water. This woman who was not afraid of snakes and would kill them with her hoe or stomp them with her foot without hesitation (while her frightened children watched from a safe distance) hated the water and what the water did to their homes, how it disrupted their lives every year. The water was a constant character in the story of their lives in Pinhook.

Several times every year, the backwater would flow through the levee opening and creep into Pinhook during the night. By morning, Aretha would stand on her porch and watch the slow, dirty waves lap up her front steps. She knew it would recede, but every time the waters came into town, life was altered. The farming couldn't continue if the fields were flooded, and Aretha could not leave her house as she liked to do to tend her garden or visit a neighbor, go to church, or send her children to catch the bus. In fact, Aretha knew her husband would have to put all the children up on the tractor and slowly drive through the water, or if the water was too high, Jim Jr. and the other fathers would collect all the children into a boat and paddle them to higher ground where George Williams sat patiently in the school bus ready to take them to Charleston and East Prairie for school. The first few times this happened, Aretha was dismayed, but year after year it became merely one fact of living in the floodway. But, she tells us, she never got used to it—the water was the only thing that marred Aretha's love of Pinhook.

When Aretha and Jim Jr. built their first large home in 1973, Aretha was so proud. Folks came around, she says, to walk through her house to exclaim their pleasure in this large house Jim Jr. had built for her. She was careful not to be too prideful, but she did love her new house and enjoyed sharing it with others. We detected a bitter tone in her story when she told us how "a month to the day" of them moving into their new home, the water passed over the steps and quietly lapped across the threshold, ruining her beautiful new walls and floors. When we asked Aretha about the constant flooding that year, her anger and frustration were clear. After the waters invaded, she recalls what it was like to clean up her house, revealing the darker side of living with the water. That particular year, their home was nearly destroyed by the flooding waters, but she and Jim Jr. and their children went back when the waters receded and rebuilt it. Her memories were painful: "That's the awfulest thing anybody would ever have to go through. I'd hate for anybody to have to go through that. After the flood, people would come in and steal things, too, you know. We had to go live in the church while it was being rebuilt, but that left our home to vandals. They took lots of my things, and the stuff they didn't want they just rip it out of the wall, like my intercom system and my lights. And in all the stuff we left in the house on the shelves—it was just terrible, it was just awful."

In 1978, she tells us, it happened again. Aretha was exhausted in both mind and spirit: "Then, it began to happen more often, every 10 months or so. I think it was the second or the third time, we just had to go in and rip everything out it was so bad. We had to take in water hoses and scoops and shovels and just scoop the junk up off the floor and put it in a wheelbarrow to haul out." As she tells us this story, Aretha begins to pat her hair as though she is distressed recounting the losses of her homes to us: "We had to get it outside and dump it. Then we had to turn on the water hoses and just spray it down. You'd have to rinse it down first and then you'd have to come back with your disinfectants and stuff, like Purex and Lysol, anything that you could use it to disinfect the rooms. Then you would just have to throw your doors and windows open and air the place out and let it dry." Fixing the house after the various floods put Jim Jr. and Aretha in debt. It was a big house, she told us, with four bedrooms. But it wasn't as large as the house she lost in 2011. That was her biggest house, five bedrooms, and built with Tennessee stone they had hauled up to Pinhook in truckloads.

In Aretha's mind, the floods and the houses are distinct, yet the story of their common destruction became both familiar and heart wrenching. She dreaded the waters. This was new for her; she and her family had never had to deal with constant flooding. She hated the hard work of clearing out the houses of their precious belongings and starting again—over and over. Now, she tells us, she cannot smell paint or disinfectants because they make her sick. With pride, she remarked that before the floods she had excelled in creating beauty in their homes: "I did almost all the woodwork, the staining and the woodwork until it bothered me a lot. And the doctor told me to try not to smell it anymore." Even now, recalling the bitter times of flooding and rebuilding, the pride Aretha has reflects their sense of independence, because *"We built it ourselves.* We didn't have nobody to come in and rebuilt for us, we build our home. We did it all ourselves. Oh, I wish I had some of my picture books, my photo albums, to show you. Folks would stop by just to see how nice we had done it, rebuilt it all ourselves. I wish I had my photos, but they are all gone in the last flood, the one in May. That was the worst."

At this point in Aretha's sharing her stories with us, Todd asked her if they had ever thought about just leaving that area and building somewhere else. Her answer surprised us at first, but her reply helped us understand Aretha's commitment to her husband, her family, and her community. "No," Aretha told Todd, "I don't think he ever thought about leaving. He thought, now, we're going to live through this. That was the way he was. For a while we lived in the church and every morning, we'd get up and I cooked breakfast for them all. And he'd climb on the tractor and he'd work till 12:00 noon, come in for dinner, and got back on the tractor and work until six in the evening. Then we'd all get our hammers and our aprons, and we'd go back and work on that house. At night, in the church, we would just open up all the doors at night for the breeze, and it had the windows on the side, so at night you could get some air. It wasn't so bad. But we didn't move back in that house until July, and that was in '73. That's terrible if you have go through that. It's a terrible thing. It's way worse than a fire." We noticed that Aretha's extended response to Todd's question relied exclusively on what her husband, Jim Jr., thought about moving. She tells us he did not even entertain the idea of leaving. He and his father and brothers had cleared this land; this was *their* land and this flooding would also pass. They would clean it up and go on. That's what you did; you climbed back on that tractor and kept on working; that's what Jim Jr. thought.

Regardless of her own despair at having her homes ruined by water, Aretha has fond memories of living in the church. At that time, the church was one big brick building, the pride and joy of Pinhook. They had not yet built the community center attached to the back of the church, so Aretha put up sheets on ropes to designate different rooms in the church. Sometimes other families lived there as well—those that stayed to rebuild their homes or clean them out. So, she created a "living" area for everyone and "private" bedrooms for adults and children. The church had a kitchen in the back, so Aretha continued to cook large meals and feed everybody. They had everything they needed, she claimed, "heat, the kitchen, a bathroom, and hot water." It wasn't easy, but they did it for "maybe four or six months, something like that. Jim Jr., he was determined to stay, because they had been there, you know, since the '40s and he'd seen a lot of flooding and stuff like that, you know. But, you know, for me—I was afraid, I'll say that. I was so nervous, I had never been around water, and all my life, you know, that was new for me. That was my first time. I'd never been in water, you know."

Elaine couldn't resist asking Aretha again about whether or not *she* had ever wanted to leave. "So, when Jim Jr. never wanted to move away each year, did you ever say, 'Honey, it's time to leave?'" At this, Aretha laughed a deep belly laugh, leaning forward over her knees. "No, I never did, because I had told him wherever he could make me a living, I would stay with him. And he could make a good living. He was really good at that. He was a good provider, a good husband, and a good dad. He was all that." So, she stayed and worked hard after each flood, but she does admit she grumbled about the waters that ruined her homes year after year. She grumbled, a little.

The stories Aretha told us about living with the water certainly confirm her ambiguity and fear about living in the floodway. We had been with her for quite a while when we asked her if she wanted to take a break. She agreed to stop and eat, but before she rose from her chair, she chuckled and said, "Oh, let me tell you a good one before we stop."

When we were living in the church and Reginald was just a baby—we called him "Ducky," and one night I was looking for Ducky and they were all outside playing. So, I went out there and I called and called, and I said, "Where's Ducky?" And they said they didn't know, they hadn't seen him. Oh, Lord, that scared me. And I said, "Lord, where is that child?" And so we looked and we looked. I called, "Ducky!" I called and called. And we looked and looked. Everybody was calling him. And some of the people they were running up and looking for Ducky. Jim Jr. was on the tractor in the field, and they wanted to go get him because we needed the tractor, you know, to drive around and look for him in the water. But I knew it was going to scare him to death. And I was looking everywhere, and the neighbors were looking everywhere, for Ducky. And we'd go to the edge of the water and try to look in. I was so worried that he had fallen into the water, you see, and drowned. And they looked at me, well, I'm just so nervous. I'm so nervous and I'm a wreck and I'm about to pop. And here comes Ducky. And, I said, "Ducky, where have you been?" And he said, "Down the fence row." And he just looked at me. And I'm thinking down the fence row where there was nothing but snakes. He was only five, or he was about four, or five. And then I said, "Ducky, oh, I'm going to whip you, boy. Why did you go down that fence row?" At this point, Aretha is laughing, tears running down her eyes, bent over her lap. In fact, by now we're all laughing. I said, "go get me a stick," and that little kid was just looking at me, just looking at the way I was talking. And the other kids are saying, "Mom, why you going to whip him? He hasn't done anything." "Well," I said, "he went down the fence row, and some snake could have killed him, and we would never have known it. Or he might have been drowned in the water."

Later in the evening, we were gathered again in Aretha's living room, and this time we were joined by some of her adult children, Debra, Twan, and David. The women were busy shelling peas as we talked and laughed. David declined to participate in the shelling, but he was holding his own telling stories. We were also given pans of purple-hull peas to shell, and the entire family was entertained watching us try to compete with the women's mastery of shelling peas. We referred to the story Aretha had told us about Ducky disappearing and her worry about him drowning in the water. We asked them if Aretha actually spanked the boy for disappearing and scaring her so. They all looked at each other and said in unison, laughing, "Oh, yeah, Mama just tore him up." We all enjoyed a good laugh with Aretha. "Ducky would always tell that story—that Mama 'whopped' me near to death because I went down the fence row and went to sleep. And we would all fall out laughing at him for riling Mama so much," Twan explains. After the laughing dies down, Aretha has the last word. "I didn't hurt the boy a bit. But it scared me to death," she told us quietly. "It just scared me to death."

We asked the family gathered in Aretha's living room about where they had all gone to school. This discussion revealed some history about Pinhook we had not heard before. Apparently, the men who cleared the land and developed the town of Pinhook named the town after a previously named area nearby. "Pinhook" was a name that echoed back to an earlier era that may have included both African American and white families. Debra brought out some historical photos of several schools and identified those she could remember. One photo of a small one-room church labeled as built in 1929 is far earlier than anything else we had heard about in Pinhook. Another photo appears to be this same building labeled as "Pinhook School," built in 1929 (perhaps first as the church) and "rebuilt in 1939" (as the school). A fourth photo identifies the "Lower Pinhook Colored School," built in 1946. The caption indicates the church is nearby but just out of the photo.

Debra remembers going to school in Pinhook. For a while her elementary school had been in the church, but later a schoolhouse was built, or rebuilt, in the town. At this point, Aretha remembers there had been an "all-white school" somewhere in between "Pinhook One" and "Pinhook Two" for a time. These photos and this discussion led us to understand that "Pinhook One" was also referred to as "Lower Pinhook" and may refer to the area where Aretha and Jim Jr. built their first house. At the time of these photos, the races were clearly segregated, and it makes sense that the area on higher ground, which belonged to white farmers and their families, was "Pinhook One," or "Upper Pinhook."

Aretha reminds David that he was in Head Start in Pinhook. "That's right," David agreed. "Yes, they started up a Head Start class there in the church at Pinhook, so I was one of the first graduates of Head Start, and there were about 12 or 13 of us at that time." Aretha remembers that more than twenty children graduated from the Head Start in the Pinhook Church. She and David began to name all the Pinhook children who graduated with David from the Pinhook Head Start Program. Debra and Twan helped them remember the names, counting them off on their fingers. David comments, "One thing I can tell you is that all those people, all those black kids, that went to Headstart in Pinhook, we all graduated from high school. That's right, from start to finish. We all graduated from high school." Because she is younger, Twan remembers that she and the other Pinhook children were eventually bused to Charleston and East Prairie following school desegregation in 1954.

When we ask the adult children what they remember about growing up in Pinhook, David is quick to reply. "Man, it was work! That's all I remember; I remember a lot of work. Period." But Debra interjects, "It was work, but we had fun." David barely nods when Debra says this about fun and continues, "Don't get me wrong, that's all we did, we worked. But we didn't know nothing else, you know? It was hard-core living. My daddy believed you always needed something to do, and he made sure we had something to do—from policing the yard to everything else. We planted the rows straight and they had to be kept up. From riding tractors and combines, planters, harrows, what have you, to picking watermelons, picking strawberries, whatever he could come up with we did. And every day we'd have to slop the hogs, build a fire, whatever. You know my older brother used to say Daddy never left us inheritance, but the best inheritance he gave us was that we know how to work hard. I guess it kept us all out of trouble. Our dad was really good at that, too. And, killing hogs in the winter, oh, Lord, when you kill hogs you've got to get everything ready; there was always something. And you didn't throw anything away, like the brains and everything. If it was part of that hog, you had to clean it."

Twan follows David's memories of life in Pinhook with some of her own, like how hard it was to shell the popcorn, saying, "We had to rub them together, you remember, that would just ruin your fingers. And us kids had to go into the corn fields after the combines, collecting left-over corn for the hogs." David jumps in with his own remarks here, "We really didn't have feed for the hogs, you know, so we just gave them everything—all the scraps and everything. Anybody cut the corn, then we'd go out there and go behind them and get what they left, all the stuff the combine didn't get. And we'd pick it up and throw it in truckloads for the hogs, come back and pitch it into their pen and then go back and get some more."

✦ ✦ ✦

Oddly, telling these collective memories of working together to get the various chores done seems to have a positive effect on David. By evening's end, he has tempered his remarks about Pinhook being nothing but hard work by agreeing that he, too, loved growing up there, despite the hard work: "I just didn't want to go home sometimes when we would go visit family who lived somewhere else, because I knew I'd have to go home and work, but, you all are right, it was a good upbringing. I wouldn't ask for no other—actually— no other upbringing. And, Mom [he gestures toward Aretha sitting in her rocker by the window], she was the very best. We grew up eating three meals a day and not just three meals a day, but three *hot, home prepared* meals a day. Every day, amen, amen. Not once or twice a week, not just on Sunday, but every day. Every day the Lord let you wake up, there were three hot meals a day." Twan echoes David's recollections, adding, "And she was home, she was always home when we got there. And she was there when we left, and she was there when we got home. And I never remember having to look for her. She knew where we were at all times, and what we were doing, and she was always there for us."

Throughout this evening of shelling peas while listening to David and Twan tell their stories, Debra has mostly sat quietly on the floor. Now she adds what is her assessment of the value of living in Pinhook, "The best thing about Pinhook was the community gatherings and all the good food at the church, and sometimes different houses, [where] we had picnics. We ate everywhere. People would come just come 24-7. It didn't really matter, they'd come in and we would feed them. People ate at the church, and some of them coming in later, they would come and eat with us. Dad would bring men and we'd feed them. They'd come to help him get a start in the fields, or whatever. It was always like that on Sunday, I remember the table would always be set for 20 or 25 people. Every Sunday she cooked for them and we never ran out, we always had enough for everybody. I can never remember a time we ran out of food. We always have plenty of food and lots of people came."

Miss Aretha laughs and adds, "Their cousin, Billy Ray, he would call every Sunday, until he got of age, he would call the house and say, 'Grandma did you fry chicken?' And he knew I did, I cooked fried chicken every Sunday. But he would call and ask if I'd cooked chicken. And it didn't matter if his own mama had already cooked dinner, he would call us and come down. We called him "Diffie," and he'd come down every Sunday. And then Jim Jr., he was always teasing, he'd play the devil and he'd say, 'Can Ms. Aretha cook better than your mama?' And Diffie'd say, 'Yes, Sir, she sure can.'"

At this point in the evening, Twan asked if we had talked to George Williams, the bus driver. We told her we had and that he had told us about being the bus driver for all the Pinhook kids. "Oh, that was a riot," Twan tells us. "I can remember kids run all over town, and there were a lot of kids, you know, I remember all us kids running to the bus. We'd all get on the bus about seven, and we'd be on the bus until we get to school or whatever. We always had the most people on our bus. We were also crowded on the bus, but we had the best bus in the area. Anybody will tell you that. And George Williams was the bus driver, and he was a good bus driver. He was *in control on that bus!* We had assigned seats on that bus, David, do you remember that? First day of school, you get your assigned seat; the bus driver would assign you a seat. And he'd say, 'Now don't get out of your seat.' And he'd know. He would know where you are supposed to be, he remembered. And the older you were, he'd put you in charge of the younger kids. Like my junior and senior year, I was in charge of the young ones who are in the back. So you have four or five kids in the seat in the back, so you could accommodate the other kids on the bus." David is both laughing and talking now, interrupting Twan, "And sometimes he'd put two big kids in a seat with a little kid in between, like Ducky had to sit in the middle. There was always the case when a little kid didn't want to sit in the middle and say, 'I want to sit on the end,' but that didn't go over well, with George."

Not to be outdone, Twan counters, "George was a great bus driver. He knew the schedule really well, and he knew our families and such. And he had a paddle you know and stuff like that and he'd use it on us, you know, and he would always tell our parents if we got into any kind of trouble and they would just tell George to go ahead and paddle us if we needed it." Both Twan and Debra are laughing and crying hearing this story of George's bus. Aretha joins in the laughter, and we do as well.

David is leaning back in the sofa pillows slapping his knee with delight. "And if you get on the bus all funky and stuff, he'd just spray you down. If your hair was nappy, he was going to comb it. If we needed to get our face washed, he'd wash it down with a cloth he kept just for that."

Twan cannot contain herself, "Yes, if a kid would get on the bus and they just had body odor really bad, and he knew that you were old enough, you know, to take a shower, he would stop that bus and he would, he'd say, 'There is no reason for you to come on this bus smelling like that,' and he'd reach under the seat and spray you down with Lysol. And to this day we are just sick of the smell, we hate the smell of Lysol. But that's what he did. He'd stop that bus and he might sit there for five or 10 minutes until the smell went away, that's what he'd do."

David can hardly talk for laughing so hard, "I remember that one kid—what did he do to that one kid? He said, 'Boy, you smell like—what was it?—you smell like two fornicating London dogs, so to speak,' and he just sprayed him down. And he said, 'I'm just going to defog you today myself.'" Twan could hardly speak for laughing so hard, "Whatever kid got sprayed would be just like to die and everybody would just about die, and everybody would just do like this at this point" [she pulls her shirt up over her face to show how the kids would cover their faces when someone got sprayed with Lysol].

By this time the room is rocking with our laughter. When she could speak again, Twan added, "So much fun. We all just had so much fun. Ask anyone. It was really like this. George was wonderful. He was like the black 'go-to' person in town. If something was going on with one of us kids, we knew that we could get to him quick even if we couldn't call somebody at home, you know, for instance, girls who needed, you know, like personal hygiene stuff or something like that, and if we didn't have money, he'd have it and help us out. He'd give us money for the machines."

David finishes that thought: "AND—if you were not ready, *he would leave you!* He would blow his horn at the house one time and if you don't come out, you'd hear the sound of the bus taking off, and he'd be gone."

Twan laughs and agrees, "One time he left his own daughter, you hear me? He left her and Maxine, he ended up leaving both of them. And we laughed all the way to school. Me, I was always eager to get George on my side, you know, butter him up, so to speak. Like, we weren't allowed to have food on the bus, but I'd get on and say, 'you need part of my sandwich?' And he'd take part of it, and I just got so used to sharing with him, I'd put together the sandwich stuff and I just get on and hand him part of it. So, he was funny, too."

With that, Debra brought us back to what was important to her: "What I love the most were the holidays in Pinhook, the cooking, the food and the families and the fun. We always had games, you know, boy's games and girl's games and games we made up. Things like that, things you don't see anymore, stuff like that. We did all that in Pinhook all the time. It was fun, and unless we work really hard to make it happen, those times don't happen anymore.

Sometimes we play silly games on Pinhook Day. That was what living there was like every day."

Aretha, agreed, "Especially at church and out in the yard, like hearing about the memories, listening to the old folks talking when we'd gather at the church or they'd sit out under the trees talking."

Elaine is taken by their sense of community: "What amazes me is that even though Pinhook is no more, you all landed fairly close to each other. You did that on purpose, right? We have noticed, if you call Larry or David, they're here in three minutes flat." Debra replies, "That's what family has always been about for us and *family meant everyone in the town*. I mean, we see David a lot of times, but if he calls us at 2 o'clock the morning and needs help, there will be somebody there to help them. So it's togetherness and the love that everybody has shown toward us, and we will in turn show to someone else, and we try to pass that on to our kids. And while we're working on a new Pinhook, we want to stay together so we can work on that together. So, we can meet and talk and work together."

Twan begins to talk about how important the church was to all of them. "One of the most important things, I think, that we were really blessed with was our singing, our choir, and in music—having the talent to have music, to express our joy together, and I think we do it well." Debra continues, "And the way they would teach us, you know. I miss that. Sunday school was just like this," and she gestures around the room. You didn't have to dress up. We would just gather and pray and worship, sing and pray some more. We laughed, we cried, and we weren't, you know, like jumping all over the room, jumping over the benches, and all that. We didn't worship like that. But the word got taught and it got taught in a way you learned it. They did it in a special way. And then it was very interesting, and there are lots of things that you remember that you learn when you were a kid, and hopefully we can get that back together again."

They all talked about the importance of church and how strong their father's faith was. Twan remembered, "We would always tease Daddy, we would tease him because he would cry in church. He would just cry and cry."

Aretha nods, "He did that. He would just cry in a heartbeat." Twan adds, "And Daddy would say, 'You just don't know how good God is.' But we do, we know that God lives, and we know God loves us. And he has been here for us." Debra finishes with, "And he *is* going to help us raise up a new Pinhook."

Twan agrees, "People loved each other and they had this mindset about what Pinhook was, what it meant. I grew up there and then I built a home there. Over the years, we still had the love and respect for one another. And when we were kids and we lived there, we were all related by blood or marriage, all of us. I think all this brings up all these good memories. And over the

years, different people came there—there were other people who came into
the fold. And we loved and cared for them just as much as we had loved and
cared for our own family. And we still had that connection, and we had the
burdens of living in the country, trying to make sure that people got the kinds
of assistance they needed. In some ways, I feel kind of bad for those people
who have this memory stuck in their brain of some place like this because, in
fact, it probably never will be the same. It's never going it to be like that, quite
like that, again. You want to keep it, hang onto it—you want to hang on to that,
hang on to that memory."

At this point in this discussion of living in Pinhook, Debra wants to bring
the conversation back to how strong the Pinhook community was and still is,
coming from a slightly different place than her sister. She, too, knows it can
never be "exactly the same," but she holds tenaciously to the idea of rebuilding Pinhook, not in the floodway, but on higher ground. She explains, "When
all this stuff started with flooding Pinhook in 2011, we all helped each other.
David was at work and got the news from his supervisor who was watching the TV. And I got a call from our brother in New York. He was the one,
the first one, to tell me they were evacuating Pinhook. At first, I was saying I
hadn't heard anything about evacuating, but then I got this call. My brother
had heard it on the radio, there in New York City, but I hadn't heard anything
on the radio and I called Mama and I'm telling her we need to get out. And I
said, 'Mama, I'm on my way home and you get in there and start packing your
stuff.' And, David and them had to drive to Poplar Bluff where they only let
them rent two trucks to come back into Pinhook and get all the people and
some of our stuff and get out. And even though we were out and had lost our
homes and everything, my brothers came, both brothers came, the one in
New York and the one in Iraq, he came back, too. They let him come. He came
here to make sure that we had got out, that we were all okay. And we all stuck
together, we made sure that everybody was okay not only us but all the other
people in the village. They were keeping in contact with everybody, then, and
we still do."

It was past nine, but their cousin, Larry, who owns the house the women
now live in dropped by and joined our conversation. He, too, had many stories about living in Pinhook and wanted to share them with us. Mostly, he
wanted to talk about Jim Robinson Jr. and the women were eager to share
the storytelling with Larry, especially if he wanted to talk about their favorite
subject, their dad.

"I'd like to talk a bit about Jim Jr. He was a special guy. He was the second
to the oldest child, because my dad was the oldest of the brothers. But he was
the one that was probably the most productive in getting out, getting outside

of the norms. He didn't mind a bit going out and being part of any kind of activity, if that was going to better the community or better his family. So, these were some of the things he was involved in. I would say he was like one of those individuals who . . . kind of ran the town. He was the sheriff, the Marshall, and all of the above, and that's just kind of who he was. But I think what I remember about him the most was what was really, really significant to me was that it didn't matter who you were, what your ethnicity was, he was the same with all people. It didn't matter if you were an adult, or a kid—he would just as soon to take a child, if a child was eating candy, he'd get down with that child and lick off the same lollypop as the kid was eating, just one of the silly things that he did, and that was his way of winning over that child. All the kids they loved him, too, that was just his personality. And, I think, when you see some of the siblings and some of his children and some of us in our community, those same core values are in our families. It even spills over into our family even now.

"He was a pretty witty fellow, you know, I remember he went to Washington DC, and they would have all these meetings and he would go. And, he was simple. He would say to them, 'if you just put some mud in that hole [speaking of the levees], you could take care of that problem.' They were talking about the levee, and he had seen that problem, like, a long time ago, and he would just tell them, 'you just take a little mud and that would fix the problem.'

"Now, something that we didn't touch on was my grandfather. At some point, I'd like to talk more about my grandfather, Jim Robinson Sr. He came from a large family. And, that's something I would have liked to have gotten more information on, was his siblings. I know there was uncle Jack, uncle Joseph, Gertrude, and Mr. Robinson Jr. That was six or seven—so, you take these huge families where there are seven or eight siblings, and they have children and we want to keep that history alive. That was another thing my uncle, that was Jim Robinson Jr., was really, really good about. He was the glue that kept everything together. He made it a point to go and visit relatives and make those connections, this one is related to this one, like that. So, if you wanted to know who somebody was and how they were related to us, you'd just have to go ask uncle Jim. He could tell you that and how they fit into the puzzle. He could do that. He was a people's person, he could make the connections. And if he couldn't, he could point you in the right direction, where you needed to go to get such information.

"Or, if there was a problem that needed to be addressed, he'd figure out some way to address that. That was true of most of the people in Pinhook, that if something needed done they'd figure out how to do it. Yes, sometimes I get with my cousin, Bert, and we talk about the lessons that we learned and that we're just now incorporating into our own life. You learn to make those things a part of who you are. I think we should train our children to do what's right. Not just religious issues, but just doing the right thing.

"I think when you read some of the letters that were written about how much people loved the town of Pinhook, we wrote letters to go with the block grants we were filing, one of the letters was really impressive to me. She talks about what Pinhook meant to her even though she lived in town by 2011. In Pinhook, everybody worked together and everybody cared about one another. If there was a little guy that was doing something he should not be doing, then there is a little 'tweety bird' and he's out there telling what he's been doing. They knew your parents alone could not have all the answers and the solutions. That's really a good saying that Hillary used for the name of her book, 'It Takes a Village,' that's a really good thought.

"Even though we now live in Sikeston, when I found out about the flood, found out that it happened, it wasn't just despair—instantly, I mean like your mind kicks in and you ask what can I do to help my own community? We can let them live here in this house, although we all know there's nothing like your own space. That's something my cousin and I talk about a lot, Reginald, that is 'Ducky,' we said that—you know, Mama needs her own space. Debra and Twan, they need their own space. We know that. But that night I was glad that I had this particular house here, and I utilize it for this kind of the guesthouse. This is where the missionaries stay when they visit. But when the flood came I said to them, 'Just come on and come over here, live in this house over near where we are, and stay with us.' So, one thing that my aunt here said was 'What do I need to bring,' and I said, 'the only thing you need to bring is yourself.' Some of the others had never been over here, they never been in this house. So, I think, when they came, how it was just interesting how we worked all that out. Even like for me. I had an idea; I bought a house so that I could fix it up. I had no idea how I would actually utilize it. But I knew I didn't want to rent it out, because that's not a good idea. I was very glad to be able to utilize it for this purpose, for the community."

✦ ✦ ✦

After Larry left, we asked Aretha if she wanted to go back to Pinhook. Before she answered, she nodded to Todd and asked him to go stir the pots on the stove and check the cornbread. He did and reported back to her that everything was just fine. "He's a good boy," Aretha smiled at Elaine and they both laughed at Todd's antics.

When Todd sat down beside her, her answer was realistic, yet sad. "I don't want to rebuild. Why would I want to rebuild down there in the floodplain again? I wouldn't have any help and now I am handicapped. So that would be kind of crazy to go back to build back down there, at my age, so far from the hospital. That would be a big risk." Aretha's response was clarified as we continued to talk with her that evening before supper. What she meant was that she did not want to rebuild in the floodway. She hoped her adult children, who were working so hard with the government to rebuild Pinhook, were talking about rebuilding the town on higher ground. Going back to the floodway meant just more grief from the whims of the water. And the new rules were ridiculous to her. She had heard that anyone who did choose to rebuild in the same place had to build their homes on 12 to 15 foot stilts and still had to live there with no insurance or reassurances about future floods: "So, how could I do that? How could I get up and down from a house like that, on stilts?" It just doesn't make sense to Aretha to return this time to the same place where Pinhook had always been. Jim Jr. is gone; he had been dead for several years when we interviewed Miss Aretha, and now she is firm that she will never go back to Pinhook as it was before. She was done with the water invading her life and her homes. A bit later she quietly added, "They say this isn't about race, but sometimes it sure feels like it."[2] Aretha knows she may not see the day Pinhook is rebuilt and she can return to her own community. But Aretha is a survivor. "You just have to go on," she tells us, "you have to just keep on."

✦ ✦ ✦

On a different evening, we sat once again in the Robinson women's living room and talked about the effects of the 2011 flood and the destruction of their homes. Our conversation went long into the night and continued over fried chicken and greens in their cramped kitchen. This night, Twan was vocal and willing to express her anger: "You know, after the flood, people were going on Facebook and they were saying things like 'why were you even living in the floodplain,' you know, and saying stuff like that. They were saying you shouldn't have lived there, you shouldn't have chosen to live in a floodplain, you should have built your house somewhere else. But, you know, people have to understand—I had the newest house in Pinhook—they have to realize that there was no other place that we could afford. Mine was the youngest house in Pinhook, and it was 13 years old. Prior to my buying land in Pinhook, I had checked out lots in Sikeston and Charleston, and the outlying area. A building lot for me would have been anywhere from $6,000 to $60,000, just for a lot. Between Charleston and East Prairie, a lot began at about $6,000 and went up to about $10,000. And I was like, I can't afford that. But in Pinhook, I paid $1500 for my lot. That's easy math. So, I told them I want that one, the plot

Twan Robinson home, 2012. Elaine J. Lawless.

on the end of the road, on the corner. And, you know, it's really frustrating if you're single, you know, trying to have your own place. And every which way I'd turn there were always obstacles. But Pinhook provided everything that I could've wanted as far as my house went. And I'm so glad that I ended up buying there. But nonetheless it hurt to know that all that you did to try to build yourself up, to get educated—I'm getting my masters in social work—and get something for yourself, and working that out in building my house there, and you had no say in it being gone. I had no say. For me that's been the hardest part for me. I know the Corps did what they thought they had to do, but *put me at the table.* Engage me in conversation. Let's talk about it. But every time there was a meeting, it was with the farmers, the white farmers, those that owned so much land. When I read those articles now about the flood, it's all about the 180,000 or more acres of farmland that got flooded. They report about those big farmers losing so much and then there's mention of 'a few homes, crops ruined, and a few homes'—that was us! Those homes were us. That was Pinhook!"

Debra joins Twan in this conversation. "Never do they mention the village of Pinhook, a town that was destroyed."

Twan, interrupts. She isn't finished: "And if they do mention it, it's very insignificant. Nobody noticed we were there! We were there! And I'm just

Interior Twan Robinson home, 2013. Emilie Sabath.

saying that some people had options, and other people didn't have options. As far as I know, those farmers who were displaced, some of them had another place to go to, most of them have two houses, and they got funding to help with that relocation before they could go back into their house. They could buy insurance. We didn't have those options. Every one of us, every one of the community members in Pinhook, had to go live with family because there was nothing provided for us, no housing provided for us, and we would ask, 'Are you for real? Are you for real?' I remember they offered some of us bleach, you know, to go back in and clean our houses, after the flood. But this time, that was not enough. I can't go back in there and clean what was left in 2011. I've got walls missing—like most of them! So, now, what is bleach going to do for me? So I'm just sitting there looking crazy like because they were offering me a cleaning kit. I'm not going back in there. We had to deal with stuff like that. It was just so frustrating."

These remarks caused us to talk for quite a while about how long the Corps had known they were probably going to have to breach the levee. Todd suggested, "They must have known. They must have known this was a possibility three weeks before, right?"

Debra agreed with him. "In fact, I've had this question. Since 1937 and 2011, what were they doing? All those years in between, all those floods every year. Why weren't they trying to figure something out about the levee, long before then?"

Twan adds, "They weren't doing anything, because it wasn't imminent *for them*. The Corps of Engineers lost nothing. As a matter of fact, they had already approved the breach, the legislators had already approved the funding needed for them to build the levee back. We went to a meeting with the Corps after the flood, and the meeting lasted at the most twenty minutes. Some of the farmers were mad and wanted answers, as we did. Then the head guy, the guy that was running the meeting said, 'We did not come here to answer any questions. We only came here to tell you how to file a claim. Good evening.'"

Twan and Debra learned all they could about filing a claim. Twan explained the procedures to us. "That's right. We can file a claim. We have up to three years to file a claim against the Corps of Engineers. If the Corps decides, okay, you've got a valid claim, *then* you basically have to get a lawyer and fight for your claim. And if [she laughs as though this is really ironic], IF you win the claim, whatever money you get from the claim, whatever you get from the Corps, you've got to give that to FEMA. See what I'm saying? Because they are both government entities. So, why would I do that? If I can get FEMA money, why would I sue the Corps? But that's what they want you to do. It's a run-around and it's meant to keep us busy. But all of this is really difficult for us. You know, you have to spend all that money getting a lawyer, going through all that. And that's the frustrating part with FEMA, because FEMA's job is to help you get back on your feet and get back into your home. But if I cannot move back into my home, you can't give me any money. If I'm not moving back into my home, the way I understood it, was then we can't help you, we can't reimburse you, if you're not going to go back into your home. Well, I *can't move back into my* home. None of it makes any sense. At least, I ask them, 'pay for my storage unit for the few things I dragged out of there.' But they won't do that either."

✦ ✦ ✦

Since May of 2011, Debra has taken on the job of filling out all the paper-work. She tells us how difficult it is to read all the directions and comply with the various requirements for submission of claims: "And they're making it so impossible week after week, we take one letter and they say, 'We can't accept this, you go to such and such and get another letter with another signature' and then we'll do this, and it has just become impossible.'"

Twan continues to express her frustration, but then they both begin to talk about how they can remain strong through their faith in God. She claims, "And that's what they want, they want you to give up, that's what they want they want you to give up. So, once again, you go back to that rock. God, help me to do better. So, that's what I'm doing. I'm angry with the situation, but it is what it is. God's got so much more for me, and I just have to give him all the glory, and try to keep that joy. You can't let this taint your spirit. In my class at the university, I talk about being resilient, and I try to be very resilient. God, please provide for me, and I'll try to do better. And he has. That's what I tell people, is that I have made religion first. And I try to be very respectful, like when we went to Jefferson City up there to the capital and talked to the legislature, you know, I had that opportunity. But when I got up there to talk to them, I was nervous. But I'm thinking to myself, 'I'm a social worker I can do this.' I thought I *can* do this! But I'd never talked to anybody about this, like in public, you know. So when I got up there, I had a podium, I had the opportunity to speak, but *I just started crying*. I felt so stupid, you know? And Debra was sitting there beside me and she says, "Lady, are you okay?" "Are you all right?" And I'm just bawling. Now I say, 'God, you just do your part, you do what you got to do,' cause he knows that was all I could do. It's been a really long year, a really long year."

Todd asks Debra if she has finally decided to get a lawyer to help with the applications for FEMA funding. She tells us they don't have the money for a lawyer, but more than that, she confirms her belief that the community can do this themselves with the help of God. She tells us, "The lawyer that I have is the best lawyer you can get and you never have to pay him. He ain't taking chickens and he sure ain't taking no eggs! Prayer is going to have to work, 'cause I don't have anything else." With that she and Twan begin quoting Bible verses, laughing and talking over each other to complete the verses.

Twan continues to speak: "For a long time, I just couldn't talk, or I felt like I was just saying the same thing over and over again. And, you know, our job is a really hard. Social work is hard work. And we'd drive all the way to Sikeston, and back, and it was so nice when we come back to Pinhook. We would get home and we could just listen to the birds. It was just so quiet and peaceful, you know, and at night you could see the stars. I miss it. I miss everything about it. I miss my little drive when I come into my place. Sorry, I took over the storytelling, but. . . ."

At this point, Todd assured her that we need and want to hear all their stories: "This is exactly what we need to hear. And that's a part of the story we had not really heard yet. That's really good. I really appreciate you telling me that story. That seems to be why so many people are willing to fight to rebuild Pinhook somewhere because of what the town means to each of you."

Encouraged, Twan talked about why she needed her own home again. "Well, for me, I need my home. I am a single person and I need my space. It was just so nice when I needed to be alone, when I needed my own alone time, I'd just go back to my home, you know, but now we're living together with our mom. Before, if we were visiting, I could tell her, 'you're my mom, and I love you, but I just need to go and be quiet in my own home.' I'm the kind of person, I need my own space and I miss that very much. People ask us all the time, how are you all doing, living together? And I tell them we're living with Mama. And sometimes I can't do that anymore."

CHAPTER THREE

Debra "Steps Up" to Save

PINHOOK

I think, though, as African-American women, we are always
trained to value our community even at the expense of ourselves,
and so we attempt to protect the African-American community.

—ANITA HILL, *Speaking Truth to Power*

Debra Robinson-Tarver is a short, round African American woman just turned sixty. She works a long day as support staff at a mental health clinic in Sikeston, Missouri. In the winter, she arrives in the dark before 6:30 to make sure the residents have had a decent night and the social workers will have everything they need to begin another long day working with the mentally challenged. She makes coffee, kicks up the heat, turns on all the lights, boots the computers. By 7:00 she can call her daughter, who is not well; Debra worries about the debilitating headaches that keep her daughter from going to work and tries to find her help to care for her young son. He's a really good boy, generally, and stays after school with Debra's mother, Miss Aretha, who lives in the same cramped house where she and her sister, Twan, now live.

Twan, a social worker who works at the same facility as Debra, known to the family as "Lady," loves to stay in bed a few lingering minutes while Debra showers and leaves the house. Twan feels cramped by the lack of space in the house, especially in the tiny bathroom the three women must share now that each of their homes in Pinhook have been destroyed. Twan and Debra love their mother, but all three of them treasured the privacy of their own homes in Pinhook. The women feel stifled in this house, but they know they are lucky to live here through the good graces of their cousin, Larry, who owns this house and lives next door. They find it odd to live now on a cul-de-sac in "Sunset," a largely black area in Sikeston, a world apart from the peacefulness of Pinhook.

Twan arrives at work closer to 8:00 when her day begins. In the past she would tell Debra she might be a bit late so that she could post online assignments or complete a test for the Social Work Masters degree she recently completed through St. Louis University in December 2013. Now, she has a better job and does not share an office with Debra. When she first got her MA degree, she worried that she would not get the promotion she had earned, but so far it has all worked out well for her.

Since May, 2011, Debra has been checking her phone and her email, eager for news from FEMA about funding for the possible rebuilding of Pinhook. As the designated "mayor" of Pinhook—or the "manager" or the "chairman/person/woman," she answers to all—Debra is the person they know to contact. A quiet, usually demure woman, Debra has taken on the responsibility of being the lead person to work with the various government agencies in the effort to rebuild their town. Daily, she alternates between anger and hope, rage and despair, but she rarely shows these emotions. Some days she feels confident her work to rebuild the town will be successful; other days she feels invisible and fears they will never be able to resurrect their precious town. She lives in limbo, wondering. There are no emails from FEMA or SEMA or the Red Cross or Church World Service this morning. She gets up and pours herself a cup of coffee. She's going to need it.

Rising from her bed at 5:30, Debra is particularly irritated this morning because the temperatures have prematurely dropped to a new October low, and she does not have a coat. She knows that Missouri can get really cold; it could even snow. So why doesn't Debra have a coat? Because she kept all her winter clothes in a back closet at her home in Pinhook. Those coats had been the last thing on Debra's mind when she was frantically trying to make sure her mother and all the elderly residents of Pinhook were out of their homes and safely in vehicles before the floodwaters rushed in on May 2, 2011. Her coats were destroyed when the water eventually reached the roof of her house and stayed there for several weeks. This morning she hurries from the house to her car, and from her car into the cold building at work, wondering if she can manage the winter without a good coat. Probably not, but coats are expensive and her mother needs one more than she does. She always makes a joke about having enough fat to keep her warm. But her mother, Aretha, doesn't have any fat and can't walk very well anymore and is slow. She will definitely need a new coat. Debra makes a mental note to swing by Goodwill on her way home; maybe they will have one or two coats that are in pretty good shape. Being warm is more important than looking good, she thinks. But she smiles as she realizes both she and Aretha most definitely want to "look good." Debra knows the importance of both as she strikes out for town ready to do her job and work on the efforts of Pinhook at the same time. For Debra, there is no time to waste; her work to rebuild the town is vital.

Born in 1957, Debra is the oldest of Aretha and Jim Robinson's eight children. She has always lived in Pinhook. At the time of the 2011 flood, she owned her own home on one of the plots of land owned by the Robinson family. Both she and Twan have expressed how much they enjoyed owning their own homes where they could have the peace and quiet they craved when they wanted it, yet the social connections that were so important to them were just a block or two away, including the home of their parents.

Although we had met some of Debra's children at various gatherings in Sikeston, East Prairie, and at "Pinhook Day," we had not asked Debra about her own marriage and family until May 25, 2012, the day before Pinhook Day was to be held in Sikeston. We were visiting the Robinson household and eating dinner with Aretha, Debra and Twan, when we finally asked about the father of Debra's daughters. Tamyra and Tamika were 28 and 31 at the time, and one of them had a son, Gavin, who had recently turned seven. That night, Tamyra and Gavin were also at dinner, and the group, including Twan, Debra, and their mother, Aretha, had been discussing siblings across the table, so it seemed a natural time to ask about Debra's marriages. As Debra told us the stories of her marriages to Anthony Stephano Greer and Calvin Renae Tarver, Tamyra offered to show us photos of her brothers and sisters on her cell phone, which surprised us, because she explained that most of these siblings were half-brothers and sisters and most of them she had never met, yet there they were proudly displayed on their cell phones. Debra explained that both of her husbands now had several children unrelated to her, but clearly, Debra claims these other children as her own, and Tamyra claims them all as her siblings. We looked at all the photos on her phone and learned about Debra's marriages through this extended conversation.

When she was quite young, Debra tells us she was "swept off her feet" by a smooth-talking, handsome man named Anthony Greer. He set his intention on Debra, and eventually she agreed to marry him. With him, she had these two daughters, both of whom still carry the Greer name. After a good number of years of married life, Mr. Greer left Debra, and she eventually divorced him. Later, she met and married Mr. Tarver. Calvin declared his love for Debra, yet he seemed to also have an eye for other women. He had a habit of leaving her only to come back, always begging her to stay with him. She finally got tired of his lack of commitment, and eventually she also divorced Mr. Tarver. She finished her account of her marriages by saying that she had loved them both and would care for either of them if they should ever need her to do so. She seemed neither bitter nor angry about the way she had been treated by these two men, but it was clear that she has no intention of being treated poorly ever again.

Debra has a high school degree, but never went to college, primarily because she had to work full time. All of her life, after raising her own children, Debra has devoted herself to the care of her mother, other elderly residents, and to the care of the town of Pinhook. Today, she still does the planning for Pinhook Day with the help of other women and relatives from Pinhook, including her two sisters and her daughters, who have set as their collective goal the rebuilding of Pinhook. The Robinson family knows and is proud of the way Debra has stepped up to take responsibilities for the town since the flood. When Miss Aretha and her three adult children who live in the area gather in the house where Aretha, Twan and Debra now reside, the conversation often turns to their father and the brothers who no longer live in the area. Even though one of the brothers now lives in New York and one in Wisconsin, it is evident that they keep in close contact with these members of their family.

When relating the story of the 2011 flood, Debra always explains that she first heard of the breaching of the levee from her brother in New York, who called her and told her, "I tell you what—You get down there, get your shit, and get out . . . because, I am hearing it here in New York City that you need to get out—it's a mandatory evacuation." Others in the family confirm Debra's story, and also claim they first heard of the intention to breach the levee from co-workers and on the radio. An important part of this story is the fact that no one was notified personally by any governmental agency, nor were they assisted in the evacuation of the town. Debra says she kept waiting for a phone call from those involved with the breach of the levee, but it never came. To evacuate the town and get all the residents out, the Robinson family had to mobilize themselves. All that fell mostly to Debra and her brother, David. Debra also recounts that both of their distant brothers came to the area immediately following the flooding to make sure all the members of the family were out safely, arriving before the National Guard drove through to make sure every house was empty (not to assist in the evacuation, but only as a final precaution).

One particular night at the Robinson household in Sikeston we felt we were definitely staying too late, but David had stopped by to join us, and the conversation was just too good to interrupt. We were laughing and talking, making jokes, and enjoying each other's company. The jocular nature of the gatherings of Pinhook people, whether close family or not, is possible largely because they know each other so well and treat each other as family. Further, they all know the pain of what they have lost and share in the deep frustration of being ignored by those who are supposed to help them. Debra remarks that they "can't cry all the time," and "laughing sometimes helps." It was at this point in the conversation that David talked about how Debra has taken responsibility for the town. We could tell that Debra was proud to hear David remark, "Now it's Debra who's really, really stepping up."

Debra's work and David's memories illustrate her long-standing involvement in all things Pinhook, demonstrating why her move into leadership was a smooth and accepted one. They all started talking at once about how Debra organizes everything, and how much they enjoy every one of her endeavors. They make it clear that one of Debra's real strengths is the way she can mobilize other people, especially the women, to get things done. After working with her for seven years, we can attest to her ability to share her ideas without ever seeming to direct others. She knows how to quietly plant a seed, nurture it, listen to others who have a vested interest, then sit back (not too far away) and watch the ideas grow and blossom. David remembers holidays when they were children:

"Do you remember every year on the holidays and Christmas you would have T-shirts made at Boomland, and everybody would get a T-shirt from

Boomland, with their nickname on the back? We thought we were big time. And you had these sweaters made, you know, with sayings on them like "Mellow Yellow" or something on the back, and that was corny as it could be, but it was fun. Boomland made it easy to make all these shirts and sweaters and everything, even the sweatpants. And then Debra made everybody's cap, and they'd have their nicknames on them. Debra, do you remember giving us those caps."

To someone not familiar with the roadside specialties of life in the Missouri Bootheel region, "Boomland" is a large commercial gas station, convenience store, liquor store, and gift shop (offering an amazing array of "kitch" and patriotic items) in a large warehouse building often attached to a McDonalds. Boomland-type operations are a familiar sight in the rural south, and one rarely has to drive far to find one. There is likely to be one on the edge of any town in the area, and some of them offer community meeting rooms as well, serving some of the local needs that farm granges and barns did in a former time. Debra sometimes schedules Pinhook meetings at the Boomland in East Prairie.

Although Boomland may have "made it easy" for everyone to have a t-shirt, a sweater, and even sweatpants complete with their nickname on them and funny sayings on the back, it is always Debra's steady work that still makes certain all these shirts and caps are ready for her family and the community on Pinhook Day. Significantly, when asked about the celebrations, Debra's only comment was that she totally enjoyed all the activities she (and others) had planned. When Elaine asks, "Debra, what did you love about the holidays and celebrations?" Her answer is telling: "Oh, the cooking, the food, and the family being there and the fun. We always had fun, we always had games, you know like, stuff like that. So, yes, it was fun." Debra always cooked, and she loved the food. These days Debra laughs about how she needs to love her fat. She loves food and she would dearly hate to eat less, so her best bet, she says, is to embrace her fat because that means she must embrace her love of food and what food represents to her—love, family, community, sharing, and faith—all qualities she can't let go of.

Prior to the May 2011 flooding of the town, Debra had not actually served as the official "leader" of the town of Pinhook. Although she was definitely a key figure in the town and was often the one to work tirelessly on events such as the annual Pinhook Day, she had not been known in the area as the mayor or manager of the town. Debra's brother, David, indicated to us that at one time, Debra's older brother, Ronnie, who died in 1996, was tapped to be the successor to Jim Jr. as leader of the town. However, our interviews with many recent, and past, residents of Pinhook, acknowledge that when the older brother died, it unofficially fell to Debra to become the town leader. When we ask Debra about her leadership role, she seems quietly proud of her position, but remains steadily grounded in the belief that she has taken on responsibilities her father would have wanted her to assume. She often told us he would have wanted her to continue the work that he had always done for Pinhook nurturing the relationships the people had with each other and with others in the area—from the white farmers to local politicians and even to the Extension Service at the University of Missouri. After the disastrous flood of 2011, Debra has stepped up and taken on the nearly impossible task of keeping the Pinhook residents allied together, bonded as always, working as a unit in their efforts toward restitution and the rebuilding of their town. Clearly, everyone in the town has been quite happy to let Debra take on public tasks and assume the title of "mayor" at the same time. But they call her regularly, meet with her, and plan strategies with her. She tells us she does not ever make a decision on her own without calling a meeting of the former Pinhook residents to discuss it and determine what the best approach might be. Particularly following the breach of the levee, and the lack of resources to help the townspeople, it was clear that Pinhook needed a spokesperson. Without hesitation, Debra took on this role by putting herself front and center of the events, becoming educated about the controversy involving the breaching, the subsequent flooding, and the filing for the "block grants" that needed to be done immediately for disaster aid. Almost daily, she continues to speak with and email the FEMA and SEMA (Missouri State Emergency Management Agency) officials. Simultaneously, she has created a working relationship with the leaders of Church World Service, the Red Cross, local legislators, and has been the feature of several newspaper articles. Journalists and researchers alike continue to be guided toward Debra Robinson-Tarver, as we were.

✦ ✦ ✦

The experiences of African American people in this country provide a framework for understanding how and why a woman might take on the responsibility as the political leader of Pinhook following its destruction. Her father, Jim Robinson Jr., certainly modeled the role of a family and community leader to his children, neighbors, and friends. His leadership role had a particular impact on his eldest daughter, Debra. Although her father was well respected in the Bootheel region of southeast Missouri, and according to his oral history had many white friends as well as black, he also clearly understood that black people would continue to struggle to get respect and equality in southern Missouri even after they were able to buy land and farm it themselves.

Jim Jr. spent the greatest amount of his time in Pinhook farming alongside his brothers, sons and close community friends, but he also worked hard to get black people to the polls to vote for candidates he thought might work for the betterment of all people in the Bootheel. Two of his sons left Pinhook for better paying work, although their ties to Pinhook remained firmly in place. One joined the military, and another got an education and landed a job in New York City. Another son began to drive big rigs for trucking companies, living in Pinhook between his long hauls, while David, his youngest, operates a limousine and bus service in the Sikeston area. Robinson's wife, Aretha, and his daughters, Debra, Twan and LaToya stayed close to Pinhook, choosing to live there both because it was more affordable and because they loved the quiet peacefulness of the town. Over the years, the women's dedication and devotion to the town and the community served to solidify Pinhook as the home place for all who had ever lived there.

Although African American men have always resided in Pinhook, many had to find jobs away from the farms. Some moved into nearby towns in order to take jobs that would help them feed their families. Few of these men had the time, energy, or resources to also take on the responsibility as the leader of the town. Furthermore, African American men living in this region of the state, including Jim Robinson Jr., his nephew Larry, the bus driver George Williams, and others have voiced openly to us the difficulties they have had in their dealings with neighboring farmers, government officials, and nearby townspeople who would not provide them assistance when they needed it. The negative personal experiences the Pinhook men have had, which they at times attribute to underlying racial tension and deep-seated prejudice against people of color in the Bootheel region, convinced them that their involvement might cause more conflict than cooperation with their white contemporaries. For these reasons, and others, the duty of "stepping up" to defend Pinhook fell to Debra, who was both willing and able to take on the responsibilities of fighting to get restitution for the town.

Debra's act of "stepping up" should not come as a surprise. African American women have shouldered much of the responsibility for the social and cultural foundations that define the African American experience in this country. The importance of the extended family, the networks nurtured by the community, and the long-standing dedication to their faith in God and to the power of the church in their lives, have helped to establish the inter-connected strands of female strength and perseverance that continue to this day. Research on women's roles following disasters suggests that it is also typical for women of color to lead the fight for restitution and recognition following major upheavals in community life, ecological racism, and institutional discrimination.[1]

Debra Robinson-Tarver speaks at Pinhook Day, 2014. Elaine J. Lawless.

Both Jim Robinsons, father and son, took as their primary political stance the rights of African American citizens of Mississippi County to enjoy a life free from constant flooding. They went to Jefferson City, the capitol of Missouri, and argued for improvements to the levee system that would benefit the black farmers living in the spillway. Although both Robinson men felt they had gained some political authority in the area, neither of them managed to get the levee system improved. In fact, both men were often faced with the insult that even if they managed to get onto local boards of various sorts, by virtue of the color of their skin, they were consistently denied the right to be voting members. Both Debra and Twan confirm that in 2011 the practice of ignoring the African American population in discussions of politics and flooding was firmly in place. These adult women were no more likely to be consulted than had been their forefathers. Facing discrimination, ignorance, and institutional disregard, Debra took on the mantle of "mayor" with steadfast intention and pledged to keep fighting for the town.

Race relations in southern Missouri have been vexed since before the Civil War. Missouri was a border state whose allegiances were split before, during, and after the war. Stories still abound about fathers fighting sons for the gray and the blue. The fact that "Little Dixie," a multi-county region known for its southern migrants and confederate sympathies, exists (and is celebrated) in central Missouri leads credence to the argument that racial tensions can still run high in this area. Larry Robinson, one of Jim Robinson Jr.'s neph-ews, told us stories about what it was like growing up as a African American boy in Pinhook, learning to be a farmer with his father and the other black farmers. Larry made it clear to us that being an African American farmer in the Bootheel region was difficult because of the open discrimination against blacks in the near-by towns. His memories of trying to buy and repair farm machinery were rife with stories about local businessmen turning black farm-ers away, refusing to provide them with services even if the black men had the money to pay the costs. As a result, Larry told us, the black farmers became quite adept at creating their own machinery parts and providing for them-selves. He was quick to say, too, that getting angry with the whites who lived near them or who resided in town would not help their cause. Clearly, no one wanted to encounter an angry black man, and Larry was quite aware that becoming a testament to that stereotype was not in his best interest—or the interests of those who lived in Pinhook. A mild-mannered gospel musician, Larry eventually landed a good job driving a Fed-Ex truck and moved into Sikeston with his wife and daughter. Yet, he still calls Pinhook his "home." He quietly expresses his frustration and anger that FEMA, SEMA, and the Bootheel Regional Planning Commission have failed to provide any assis-tance to the residents of Pinhook for restitution and the rebuilding of their town. He is quick to point out that Joplin, on the other side of the state, received millions of dollars of aid assistance following a devastating tornado that hit the town just weeks after Pinhook was destroyed. The fact that Joplin had many white residents who were able to raise awareness as well as fund-ing to rebuild the town is very much on his mind. Larry recognizes and can articulate the racism he sees in the lack of assistance to a poor, African Ameri-can farming town such as Pinhook.[2]

Debra has told us on many occasions that her brothers are angry about the Pinhook situation. She also tells us she is careful not to encourage them to express that anger in public. She says if either Donald or David got started expressing their true feelings about how the Pinhook people are being treated, they might never quit. She is also quick to say that she does not believe their anger would forward the cause of Pinhook. Debra believes her quiet demeanor and careful attention to the paperwork will, in the end, result in funding to help them rebuild Pinhook. Her style of interaction with state and local emer-gency management agencies, FEMA, SEMA, Bootheel Regional Planning Commission, and the Army Corps of Engineers is always calm, nonassertive, thoughtful, and cooperative. It is her contention that this is the only way to reach their goals. She is quietly persistent, determined, unflinching. Others in their group might yearn to speak their minds, especially to the administrators of the agencies, but this is not the approach of Debra Robinson-Tarver. She has been a rock through more than seven years of meetings, sending duplicate upon duplicate of required paperwork to the agencies, constantly dealing with unreturned phone calls and disregard on the part of the agencies which could potentially help the town. Above all, Debra tells us that her unfailing faith in God has kept her calm and trusting and that her persistence and determination will prevail. She says God will not give "her people" more than they can bear. For her, true faith in God means remaining steadfast through the worst difficulties.

Women's Work in Times of Disaster

Debra Robinson-Tarver is not the exception. The work of disaster sociologists Emmanuel David and Elaine Enarson, editors of the 2012 collection, *The Women of Katrina: How Gender, Race, and Class Matter in an American Disaster*, draws on original research and first-hand narratives to fill in a gap they perceive in disaster scholarship: the presence and significance of gender leadership roles. In researching the aftermath of Katrina, for example, they focused on the part gender has played in women's collective struggles for post-disaster housing and assistance. Their book attests to a rich collection of testimonies about women involved in policy decisions, social inequities, and faith narratives to create a holistic picture of women's roles in disasters. According to these sociologists, the social science of disaster has emerged in recent years as a respected scholarly field that most typically focuses on the five core topics of the disaster "cycle": vulnerability, hazard mitigation, disaster preparedness, emergency response, and disaster recovery. All of these areas are of concern across a broad spectrum of cross-disciplinary studies (xi), and all five have the potential to expose glaring gaps, especially in terms of race, class and gender. These editors, and the authors of the articles in their anthology, seek to mitigate that gap by focusing on community resilience through the multiple lenses of race, class, poverty and, in particular, gender. Their research can easily be connected to our work with the women of Pinhook, Missouri.

Importantly, the researchers in this collection took time and care to attend to the concerns and agency of women involved in the disasters associated with Katrina, Rita, and other storms and their aftermath. Notably, their collective work demonstrates how "after disasters, women resist the social forces that threaten their lives and livelihoods and collectively organize for a better future for themselves and their community" (155). Articles across several different sections of this book attest to how women come together to work collectively for reconstruction:

> Grounded in a range of compelling issues, from the politics of place and the environment to struggle over collective identity, religion, and culture . . . after disaster(s), women rise to the challenge to rebuild and strengthen social ties. Their activism attests to women's agency in the face of crisis and their ability to radiate hope in the midst of destruction. (155)

In truth, sociologists do not see these patterns as new approaches for women in crisis, but rather note how women rely on what they have always done best:

> After Katrina, women began to reimagine a world transformed through care, connectedness, and concern for others. *Not unlike women's work in noncrisis times*, these efforts [are] anchored in women's families, neighborhoods, cultural practices, and memories. (155)

Thus, in identifying the importance of care, connectedness, and concern within communities, women in disaster situations often rely on narrative representations of place to anchor family and community ties. Sociologists note how places are ideas maintained by people, and women in particular, through the use of their own experiences and through their local histories—histories that provide ways of knowing and repertoires of action—repertoires that can reflect informal (and gendered) community rules and norms for planning (158). The importance of narratives of place, community, family, care and concern help define the planning for the reconstruction of family/community places. Although these "place narratives" often rely on nostalgia and a reliance on memory, still:

> listening to narratives about people's lives helps the researcher figure out what a particular place meant or means, how the actor understands the world, and how the actor perceives causality for the unfolding of life. (159)

It is important to point out how the sociologists quoted here perceive and actually utilize the narratives they have collected orally from those affected by disasters. For the researchers, "Including these first-person accounts adds a different voice and compelling context to the empirical studies that follow" (25).

✦ ✦ ✦

Notably, folklorists and oral historians have always relied on participants' oral narrative accounts, demonstrating how the actual words of the people involved provide clues to how we might better understand the communities we study. These comments relate directly to our own "reading" (which involves deep listening) of the narratives of the people of Pinhook and those of Debra Robinson-Tarver, the Pinhook leader, in particular.

Debra's role as the leader of this town illustrates how one woman located their resources in times of disaster, identified what those resources are, challenged the agencies who choose to ignore the residents, and pointed to the ways in which they can be successful in their endeavors toward restitution. Without question, Debra's efforts rely on the firm foundations of community care, connectedness, and concern—essentially the same areas of expertise women value during "noncrisis times." By examining their "place narratives" and personal accounts, we illustrate how women's efforts *are* anchored in family, community, cultural practices, and memories—and point to how these anchors provide stability for female leadership following this flooding disaster in 2011 in Missouri. Women's advocacy for restitution and compensation are more likely to be "heard" and supported by those in power when the efforts of women are framed in these non-confrontational discourses. This does not imply, of course, that these discourses are not political—surely, we do not need to be reminded that the "personal is political"—but they are politicized in less confrontational ways that may serve the community better within the racialized cultural context of Missouri's conservative Bootheel region, where power is held largely by white males who demonstrate little regard for the African American communities in their midst and often find black men intimidating and expect them to be confrontational.

Debra Robinson-Tarver's role in the aftermath of the 2011 flooding and destruction of Pinhook, Missouri, illustrates how she relies both on traditional discourses of Christian femininity and the traditional role of women as caregivers, while simultaneously establishing herself as the main conduit to the Pinhook community, strategically positioned to defuse potential racial interactions between angry (white) farmers, governmental bureaucrats, and (potentially angry) African American men. For example, on September 14, 2013, Debra called Elaine to discuss what had transpired at a meeting a week before with the Army Corps of Engineers (we refer to this meeting in the previous chapter). Although she was not expecting anything new to be revealed at this meeting, she and her two sisters, Twan and LaToya, were in attendance and were prepared to speak. The Corps representatives, however, were frank in their statement that they were not there to continue the discussions about whether or not the May 2, 2011, breach of the levee was appropriate or not;

furthermore, they informed all the locals and farmers at the meeting that they were "prepared to do it again, if necessary. And that's a fact."

The white farmers, whose large landholdings suffered when the levee was breached, were not pleased with the Corps' position, but Debra said it was evident there was nothing anyone could do. Debra and the other women from Pinhook attended this meeting because they wanted to be included in the post-flood discussions, noting that they had not been included in the discussions before the breach of the levee and the subsequent flood. She felt hopeful that their presence there—three African American women from Pinhook—might serve to bring the discussion around to the plight of the Pinhook residents who had been totally dislocated by the flood. She was confirmed in her belief. She was delighted to see several white farmers, as well as local East Prairie (white) friends of Pinhook, stand up and argue that "at the very least FEMA should come through for the people of Pinhook," naming the town perhaps for the first time in the public discourse concerning this flood's destruction. It was Debra's opinion, as she spoke with us, that having these "friends of Pinhook" speak at the meeting accomplished a great deal more than if she and her "sisters" had spoken, especially if they spoke in anger. Unfortunately, she is probably right in this as well.

Nothing in Debra's actions or her speech indicates that she took on the role of the leader of Pinhook for personal gain or in an effort to bring attention to herself. She has emphasized to us that she sees her primary job as keeping all the community of Pinhook (recent and past) connected to each other and connected to the processes of government restitution. She feels all the people who ever lived in Pinhook are members of the Pinhook extended family; thus, she works tirelessly to make certain that everything she learns about the Pinhook situation, about FEMA's intentions, about their grants for restitution, is relayed to the "body" of the community she regards as the heart and soul of Pinhook.

Before the disaster, Debra was the primary organizer for all things Pinhook. People always acknowledge her presence at community gatherings, her tireless work to provide food for everyone, her willingness to transport those who had no car or did not drive, her obvious enjoyment of events that included the full extended Pinhook "family." These stories about Debra's organizational skills, as well as her mother's, prior to the 2011 disaster set the stage for her continued efforts following the disaster. Her lifetime of displaying these skills in a totally selfless manner also helps us understand why the community was agreeable to Debra becoming their spokesperson following the 2011 flood. Importantly, Debra relies on a public discourse of modesty and female virtue that helps to frame her female leadership abilities and good intentions to care for her community.

African American women's strength and power have long been recognized in African American communities, particularly in the support and care of the family. Debra claims everyone in Pinhook as members of her family, and in doing so reifies her right to fight fiercely for the good of the entire group. Debra's role is similar to that taken by other women whose families and communities have been subjected to other environmental disasters, such as the dumping of toxic waste into the community water, lead poisoning in people's homes, and other clear instances of what we are calling political indifference (or environmental racism) to underprivileged communities. In these situations, scholars have noted the innovative, and often successful, ways in which women have forged alliances not only to fight the injustices that affect both their immediate and biological families but their community "families" as well (Bierra et al. 2007; Emmanuel and Ennarson 2012; Sterett 2012; Litt et al. 2012).

In the traditional, African American community of Pinhook, the roles of women are honored much as they are in many other African American contexts. Since slavery ripped apart families by selling fathers, sons, and daughters to other slave owners, they created ruptures between men and women and their children, African American males have had extreme difficulty locating a comfortable place within the American family structure and community. American politics and social service networks have created even more difficulties for African American males, operating as they do to disenfranchise black men and create structures that recognize black families supported in large part by strong black females, mothers and grandmothers who have learned how to survive with or without black male figures firmly attached to the family. For all the wrong reasons, black women have had to *step up*. Within this contextual understanding of 21st century African American family structures, Debra's leadership role is both expected and honored.

When her mother's home was destroyed, as well as her own and her sister's (as well as their beloved church), Debra was devastated. Yet, it was Debra who made certain they all gathered in one location for their first Christmas away from Pinhook. Her efforts to keep spirits lifted and hope instilled for a new Pinhook are reflected in this story she told us:

> I have a video—somewhere—well, maybe I don't have it anymore—of our first Christmas away from our town when we weren't home. Christmas and Easter were always the big holidays for us and we would always get together. So we made a Christmas CD, and we had a big dinner and everything together. We will always still get together with those big holidays. And we had a Christmas tree, and we gave out different ornaments to different people. One ornament was just the box—it was just a box with a ribbon on it. We made all of these, me with some

help from my sisters. This empty box stood for a "Pinhook Surprise"—meaning
that someday Pinhook would get a surprise. Each ornament had a meaning to
it. One was a drummer, it was a drum, and that one meant "we won't be beaten."
And the other one was, let me think, I think it was a bell, and it was for when we
"ring in a new Pinhook." Each one of them had a special meaning, had a special
symbol, and we told them they could keep that ornament. I hope they did. My
mom keeps saying, "now what did I do with my ornament? I don't know where
my ornament is." But she probably does. I think I packed it up somewhere when
we had to move. And when we do get to move back to Pinhook, they will all
come back and put those ornaments on the Pinhook tree.

Hearing this story, we are reminded of the assertion from earlier in this
chapter that following a disaster, women "rise to the challenge to rebuild and
strengthen social ties. Their activism attests to women's agency in the face of
crisis and their ability to radiate hope in the midst of destruction" (Emmanual
and Ennarson155). Debra's calm and collected manner serves her well in this
capacity. While she has occasionally expressed her anger and frustration to us,
she generally utilizes gentle language and a soft tone to talk about the situation of Pinhook, both in public and in the privacy of her home. In fact, con-
trasting her demeanor with her sister, Twan's, provides a good case in point.
Twan's passion and anger are never far below the surface. While we appreciate her radical claims for justice and consideration by the officials involved
in the breach of the levee that destroyed her town, her home, it is also clear
why Twan has not become the town's leader in public situations. Twan herself
acknowledges how difficult it has been for her to stay calm in the fight and
keep talking with the government officials for all the years following the 2011
flood. Her own experience trying to speak for the town left her dismayed and
broken, while they also strengthened her admiration for Debra, who continues to speak in public for the Pinhook community.

In an interview in 2014, Debra told us, "We're not out to get more than
what we had; we're just out to get what we had *back*." Her goal has been to
secure a "buy-out" from FEMA for the houses that were destroyed in the
flood, funding to help the Pinhook residents buy new land outside the spillway, and money to rebuild their homes. This seems totally logical and reasonable to Debra, yet her efforts have continued to fall short of those goals, not
because of her own inefficiency or persistence, but because the assessments
for the buy-out have taken years to accomplish. Every plot of land Debra has
identified as a possible new site for a relocated Pinhook has been rejected for
various reasons, mostly the justification that the land identified is too expensive for FEMA funding, or the zoning is not correct, or certain water or sewer

lines are not in place. To the community, it seems the roadblocks, the refusals to finish the deal, buy some land, and rebuild Pinhook, will simply continue. Debra's frustration is beginning to show. In 2015, she told us she did not know how long she could sustain her efforts. In 2016 and, now, in 2017, she tells us she is "more than a little discouraged."

Before we arrived for Pinhook Day, 2015, in Sikeston, Debra had been hinting for weeks that she would have good news to share with everyone at the annual celebration. She was excited, and it showed. However, as soon as we arrived, we could tell by her mood that the good news she hoped to share had not materialized. In fact, as we perused the various merchandise created especially for this event, the Bible verses selected for the tee-shirts, the cups, the laminated cards, the banners, were visible indications of Debra's disappointment. She was called upon, once again, to muster her faith for results that were less than satisfactory. We could read the disappointment everywhere as we read her messages. This year's chartreuse t-shirts were emboldened with the silhouette of a church flanked by pillars that read "Faith, Love, Home, Food, Faith, and Farming," the Pinhook tenets from the very beginning. The community of men, women, and children, walk toward the church holding hands beneath an image of a Bible opened to the verse that reads: "Now faith is the substance of things hoped for, the evidence of things not seen, Hebrews 11:1." Rather than wait for a joyous announcement, as soon as we had all arrived in the Legion hall for the 2015 celebration, we knew FEMA had not come through for them—again. Songs were sung, games were played, hugs and tears were shared, food was eaten, but the mood was subdued as the day drew to a close. As people gathered their belongings, their serving dishes, and their children, Debra asked for prayer, then announced the plan to meet once again in Sikeston a year later for Pinhook Day 2016. Five long years after the flood that destroyed their town, she invited the community of over three hundred African Americans to gather again to celebrate who they are—together.

CHAPTER FOUR

PINHOOK DAY
A Traditional African American Homecoming

[Our adversaries] fail to perceive the sense of affirmation generated
by the challenge of embracing struggle and surmounting obstacles.
Dr. Martin L. King, *A Testament of Hope*

Scholarship on "Homecomings" offers the argument that these celebrations are African American in origin. William Wiggins first studied African American emancipatory celebrations as physical and emotional displays of pride and dignity for black Americans who very much wanted their emancipation to be a move toward equality and recognition as true Americans. Wiggins, in his book, *O Freedom! Afro-American Emancipation Celebrations*, noted that later "Homecoming" celebrations grew out of emancipatory celebrations that began after the January 1, 1863, Emancipation Proclamation. Juneteenth celebrations sprang up, he explains, when deep-south states added their celebrations in June, since news of the emancipation did not reach them down there until months later than January. A quick internet search reveals the importance of "Homecoming" for black churches today. The African American Lectionary yields the following concerning Homecomings—a lengthy explanation of the term, complete with footnotes and a bibliography that includes the work of Langston Hughes, John Hope Franklin, Alfred A. Moses, and Clayton Carson. The major components of the African American Homecoming follows a long traditional focus, outlined by Carson, who writes about the African American struggle for freedom (2003), and is worth sharing here.

African American church Homecomings stem from the root word "home." In our community, the word "home" means more than a physical place. It is more than a plot of land, house, city, state, nation, or continent. It is also more than a family, clan, tribe, or church. It is all of that; but it is also much more. For African Americans, home is a continuum of experiences—a celebration of memories, stream of interactions, and a cacophony of feelings. It is a line of broken and unbroken relationships, and a circle of life filled with trials, tribulations and hallelujah moments. It is even more; home for us is a symphony of beliefs—a visible and invisible chain of human history that is imprinted on the DNA of each Black congregant. And, yes, home is a human library of Black hopes, dreams, disappointments, failures, successes, and achievements—personal and public. It is an ancestral map of lost tribes, muted tongues, forgotten civilizations, discarded gods, and transformed lives. It is built, brick-by-brick, by each congregant, family and community. Home, for all African Americans, is both a fixed and portable concept. However, every now and then, we have to go back to the old landmark, to that fixed place and commune together.

The Homeward Call

So, when an African American church sends its clarion call to its current and former membership and its web of friends, to join it in its Homecoming celebration, it is an invitation steeped in place and time, history and tradition, and culture and faith. That call rivals the call of the African drum that our ancestors answered centuries ago. Each congregant knows its importance and heeds its call. It was out of this landscape that the liturgical moment of Homecoming was born in the African American church.

A Celebration of Culture

Homecoming is celebrated differently in different churches by different denominations. Some congregations celebrate it for a day, while others celebrate it for a full week. Many Black churches combine their Homecoming celebration with their church anniversary. The service is always rooted in Black culture, faith, history and thanksgiving. The Homecoming service is one of the best attended services on the church calendar. It is a service to which families, friends and former church members flock from everywhere. And, usually, every age group of the church is celebrated, with particular attention given to inclusion of the church's children and young adults in the Homecoming program. The service is usually culturally rich—in that it may include various art forms, including various musical forms (e.g., Spirituals, Hymns, Gospels, Jazz, Blues, Classical, etc.), dance, films, plays, poetry, and seminars and lectures. The traditional sermon is often replaced by a message from a nationally known or a locally gifted speaker. The service often includes or ends with a congregational meal of traditional African and African American foods. [http://www.theafricanamericanlectionary.org/PopupCulturalAid.asp?LRID=44; accessed June 25, 2015]

Everything in this description applies to the annual Pinhook Day celebrated as a homecoming for Pinhook residents, more recent and past. Further scholarship on Homecomings and black celebrations attests to the importance of these events for black Americans who still have not received full citizen rights and who cling to kin and communities for their assertion of their right to respect and dignity. Both Yvonne Jones and Marilyn White have written on the importance of kinship and community. Jones, in her article, "Kinship Affiliation through Time: Black Homecomings and Family Reunions in a North Carolina County," and White, in her chapter, "We are Family! Kinship and Solidarity in the Black Community," point to the importance of kinship and the bonds of community to keep black Americans positive about themselves. The celebrations are a combination, they argue, of both the sacred and the secular, reaffirming black Christian faith and affirmation in specific communities as well as of the larger black community in the U.S.

In 1994, folklorist Doug DeNatale joined Wiggins in curating a large Smithsonian traveling exhibit on African American celebrations. The accompanying book for the exhibit, *Jubilation: African American Celebrations in the*

South offers several essays on the topic. DeNatale's introduction draws on the festival scholarship of anthropologist Victor Turner, who claimed: "During celebrations, people think and feel more deeply than in everyday life. They express the meanings and values of their societies in specific, often vivid, ways. In celebration, people mark with ceremony and ritual their triumphs, joys, sorrows, politics, and hope" (8). Turner drew upon dramaturgical models to understand the workings of celebration in human life, viewing these extraordinary moments as "distillations of the human experience with a profound inner logic and narrative movement that moves human understanding to another plane" (9). DeNatale goes on to state, "in celebrations, we see the indomitable character of the human spirit" (9), which would certainly apply to the spirit of the Pinhook people in their years of dislocation and trauma over the destruction of their town. Folklorist John Roberts, also writing in this same exhibit book, writes that celebrations are "occasions that people undertake in concert to make more of themselves than they normally do. Celebrations enrich and order their lives" (44).

Appropriate to our discussion of Debra Robinson-Tarver as the keeper of the traditions that hold the Pinhook community together, and the efforts of the Pinhook women to work for justice, DeNatale quotes from folklorist Gerald Davis, who remarked that celebrations "identify the keepers of the tradition and culture." DeNatale concludes: "In celebration, African Americans support and empower each other, incorporate and transform, challenge and modify the official and the informal social order, and Celebration as a resource for action and as a place where the individual and the society negotiate the future" (12). While affirming their past as a black farming community, Debra is certainly utilizing the homecoming celebration of Pinhook Day to remember and celebrate the past as well as "negotiate the future." She brings the Pinhook "family" together to remind them of what they have accomplished in the past and to guide them toward the possibility of a new Pinhook where they can gather in the future.

Neither Miss Aretha nor Debra seems quite sure when "Pinhook Day" as a homecoming celebration actually began, but it began perhaps in the late 1940s and early 1950s as some residents of Pinhook moved away from the town but desired to keep their connections to Pinhook secure. "Pinhookians," as they sometimes refer to themselves, have always considered all former residents and their extended family members as members of the Pinhook family. Every year from the earliest celebrations until 2011, they held a special homecoming at the Union Baptist Church, in Pinhook, for all present and former residents, family, children and grandchildren. Kinship runs deep for this community and is always inclusive. Some of the recent Pinhook residents have lived there since the early 1950s. Some only lived there for a brief time. Some children were born there and left for college never to return to live in the town; some women married outside the town and moved to their husband's communities. Some people knew Pinhook only as the place where their mothers and fathers, grandparents, aunts, and uncles have always lived. Children often spent their summers in Pinhook, even if they lived in other distant parts of Missouri, or as far away as Arkansas, Tennessee, Kentucky, Chicago, or New York. In all these cases, the close relationships with mothers, sisters, aunts, fathers, uncles, grandparents, and friends kept them tied to Pinhook. All the years of Pinhook's existence, it has been home, the place to visit as frequently as possible, even if you did not live there. Excuses to travel back to Missouri were welcomed and long-car rides were the norm; it was easy, too, to find other Pinhook family members who would provide beds for overnight stays along the way.

During the years when Pinhook was a thriving community, far more people considered Pinhook "home" than the census takers could count; Pinhook's population ebbed and flowed throughout the years and did not rely at all on how many dwelling structures one could count in the town. The Pinhook population would swell in the summers, as well as at other times throughout the year. Certainly, Pinhook Day brought everyone "home" for a weekend celebration of kin, family, food, memories, music and fun. Birthdays, weddings, and funerals also served to bring large numbers of people back home to Pinhook, some would come for a day or two, some might stay weeks, others might decide to stay even longer.

All of our collaborators on this project have different notions of the most recent population of Pinhook. George Williams, who drove the bus for the Pinhook children for forty years claimed there were more than two hundred families in Pinhook in the 1960s. His bus alone carried more than seventy-five black children from Pinhook to East Prairie when they began to attend desegregated schools. In 2012, Williams noted that there were "as many as one hundred families out there when the Corps claimed they did not know the town was there." When Twan talks about the school buses that Mr. Williams drove, she remembered the Pinhook bus carried more than seventy-five children to school. Even as the bus got overcrowded, the district did not offer to provide another bus for the Pinhook route. Seventy-five, or more, student passengers constituted a critical mass of school-aged children and pointed to a large number of young households in the Pinhook area.

Pinhook, the official town, has a place on the Missouri map. Yet, when scores of people continued to travel to Pinhook for short or long visits, for summers, or to live, their sense of "home" became much more than the place on the map. The entire community, in all its parts, constitutes what "home" means to the people of Pinhook, a conception that goes far beyond a single house or one family. In Pinhook, families intermingled and intermarried to such a degree that jokes about family lineages and kinship are often invoked, referred to as "extracurricular activities" when the kinship patterns are complicated. Someone might explain to us, "Well, she is my sister, but she is also my aunt—if you know what I mean." Such remarks are met with laughter and a chuckle as though such things are bound to happen; no one seems particularly embarrassed by it. Sometimes a favorite aunt or uncle had one family in Pinhook, left, divorced a Pinhook spouse, remarried and had another family elsewhere. Pinhookians are not exclusionary in the least. They claim those other children as family, as their brothers and sisters, even showing us their photos on their cell phones. Some of them have never met, yet they speak of them lovingly and explain in detail the familial connections. "Kin" is far-reaching and helps create strong connections between generations, primary families, and extended families. When women marry they retain their strong ties to their immediate family as well as creating new, lasting bonds with their husband's family. If both families have a connection to Pinhook, their family connections expand and their ties to Pinhook are multiplied. When their children marry, the families of the children's spouses are equally folded into the larger Pinhook extended family.

Many years ago, when Pinhook was a thriving town, Debra Robinson-Tarver enjoyed organizing Pinhook Day. She and her sisters, Twan and LaToya, joined their mother, Aretha, as well as other women in the community, in the year-long preparations for the homecoming event. Each of the adult women began to bring to the celebration what they each loved the most about the times of holidays and celebrations, particularly the homecomings. Twan loved the music and singing with the choir. Debra and LaToya enjoyed the games, the skits, the cakewalks, the laughter, the excuse to have fun and play. Aretha loved the food and helped organize the tables heavy with fish (cooked in huge vats outside by the men under orders of the women), ham, and chicken, macaroni, mashed potatoes, potato salad, corn, baked beans, slaw, and the many, many different luscious desserts that spread from one end of the room to the other.

Over the years, the women have led the Pinhook community in a celebration of food, fun, and song in Pinhook. Since 2012, after the demise of their beloved town, they have continued to organize and insure the success of Pinhook Day in local towns, including East Prairie or Sikeston. Here, in the VFW hall or the American Legion hall, hundreds of black people congregate—elders with walkers and in wheel-chairs, adult men and women, adult

Faye Mack at Pinhook Memorial Walk, Pinhook Day, 2012. Elaine J. Lawless.

children, teen-agers, young people who seem not at all bored but laughing, playing, eating and drinking, young married couples with babies, a multitude of smiling people comfortable with themselves and each other, at least for several hours on a Saturday in May.

Following the destruction of Pinhook, the women have seized upon the importance of the continuation of Pinhook Day as the mechanism necessary for the continuation of the town itself. Debra points out how this celebration serves as the place to gather with all the people who love Pinhook in order to communicate and commune with them about the year's efforts to rebuild the town. While her efforts retain the promise of a celebration full of fun and games, singing and prayer, the more recent Pinhook Day celebrations in 2012–2015 have been bittersweet occasions. The town has been destroyed, Debra reminds everyone, but the family ties have not. Just as they have come together year after year to celebrate Pinhook's history and lasting community—on Pinhook soil—they still come together to reinforce their commitments to each other and to the town they desperately hope to rebuild. To do this, the women seek the affirmation of all her Pinhook family to help her in her endeavor, to keep her strong, and to assure her that they are beside her in this journey to "save" their home.

At the Pinhook Day celebration in 2012, one year after the devastating flood, but before the church and houses had been completely destroyed by

arson and demolition, everyone first met early in the morning at the site
of the now-burned church for prayer. Attendees, including us, gathered in
a huge circle and bowed their heads in prayer thanking God for bringing
them all together and praying for God's continued help in enabling them to
rebuild their town. After the prayer and much hugging and conversation, all
the able-bodied people walked the two or three mile perimeter of the town as
a "Pinhook Fundraiser Walk," funded mostly by the sale of t-shirts and visors.

Since then, we have attended four Pinhook celebrations and have witnessed, and enjoyed, the many facets of this large gathering of black rural
Americans. The main events of communal eating, choir singing, cakewalks,
and joyous reunions occur every year. While the buildings of the town have
been damaged beyond repair, the people of Pinhook are alive and well, just
sad, angry, and confused by the continued governmental neglect and indifference. Most of them are still willing to travel further for their Pinhook Day
gatherings, even as they remember that their town lies quiet and desolate only
a few miles down the road. Each year they gather and pray for Pinhook to be
rebuilt. Before the day is done, most of the Pinhook people take a long drive
out to the town, driving slow to take in the landscape, noting the flowers that
are in bloom, exclaiming over Miss Aretha's bright red rose bushes that persist
even though no one is there to care for them. They notice cars that sit exactly
where the flood waters left them, basketball hoops standing with no net, a
few straggling shoes, a misplaced television far from its original location, a
few vinyl albums sitting on a step. Slowly, they drive away from the destroyed
houses and brown fields and head for the homes they now occupy far away
from Pinhook.

For days before Pinhook Day, women in the Pinhook family (near and far)
bake pies and cakes, brownies, cupcakes, and other desserts, using a host of
traditional and regional recipes for such delicacies as "Mississippi Mud Cake,"
"Chess Pie," "Apple Dumpling Cake," and other opulent concoctions. The
morning of Pinhook Day, they bring in their tempting desserts and fill table
after table with their donations for the cakewalk and auction. People follow
them around the table as the goodies arrive, asking if that's Miss Aretha's cake
or Thelma's dumplings. Sometimes labels are attached to the prizes acknowledging that this is, indeed, Miss Aretha's creation or some other coveted dish.
Sometimes everyone just knows which dessert has been made by whom,
and they can been seen making a mental note of where that particular pie
or cake is on the long, extended tables, ensuring they know where to find
their favorite should they win the cakewalk. Children barely tall enough to
see the desserts over the edge of the table ogle them with wide eyes as the
tables fill, drooling already over the sugary possibilities as they giggle, punch

each other, and find a numbered square on the cakewalk circle that Debra has created on the concrete floor. Pinhook Day is a day of music, laughter, intergenerational fun, barbeque, a fish fry, conversations, dancing, auctions, "ice-breakers," door prizes, photography, cakewalks, and gospel choir music that soars to the rafters.

Every Pinhook Day celebration begins with a prayer. All over the room, people join hands with whomever is nearby—including all elders, visitors, and children—and offer a prayer of thanksgiving for God's presence in their midst and in their lives for the past year. Such humble gratitude seems especially poignant because the people here have lost all their personal belongings, their homes, and their beloved church. Yet, they gather together to thank God for watching over them and helping them "make it through" until things get better. We wonder if we would be as gracious if we were in their situation. Sometimes they ask a child to offer the prayer. Somehow that strikes us as even more poignant—the children, too, know that God loves them and He "will not give them more than they can handle," something they have all heard Debra say.

After the prayer, Debra joins the choir to sing several well-known songs, mostly religious, but all contemporary, upbeat gospel tunes that declare they will "rise up" and their hearts "will be washed whiter than snow." Metaphors, we know, just metaphors. Later in the day, the choir will also offer a longer program of gospel singing that has been publicized throughout the area. This program will draw many people from the community who do not come to the regular portions of Pinhook Day, but who will travel to hear the powerfully dynamic singing of the Union Baptist Choir, a group very much alive and vibrant even though the Union Baptist church is now only a memory. The favorite song of the choir, and the Pinhook residents, is one written by Faye Mack specifically about Pinhook. Mack's song illustrates better than we can how this community feels about the town they have lost:

> When I was a little girl, living by the Mississippi,
> I called it home, my way of life, it was far, far from the city.
> I love this place, this sacred space, where I always knew
> I'd find peace and love, joy and happiness, unconditional for you—
> [the complete song lyrics can be found at the beginning of this book]

Twan joins her sister at the microphone while their younger sister, LaToya, handles the music. They are quite the team. Their mission today is to make certain everyone has a good time, everyone meets all the other members of the Pinhook family, and everyone contributes to the fundraising for their

Pinhook Day programs, 2013. Sean P. Brown.

Todd Lawrence helps hang Pinhook Memorial Quilt made by Debra Robinson-Tarver, 2013. Sean P. Brown.

"Rebuild Pinhook" fund. Every year we see tears and hear people talk about their favorite memories of Pinhook, but more than this, people come to Pinhook Day to see family members, greet the elders, meet new babies, and reconnect with old friends. Throughout the day the reality of their dislocation, the destruction of their town, the fact that they are in a rented American Legion Hall or VFW in Sikeston is never forgotten. It is, in fact, the subtext, the context, for the continuation of this event. Their longing is palpable.

On the back wall, a 36" x 56" enlargement of an aerial photograph of the floodwaters closing over the roofs of all their homes is prominently (and silently) displayed, a testament to the reality of the flood that destroyed their homes. Stacks of a booklet Debra has put together, complete with many photographs of their town following the flood, can be found on every table. People pick them up and leaf through the grim photographs as they read the many "Remembrances of Pinhook" written by their friends and neighbors, many of which we have also included in this book. The Pinhook Memorial Quilt Debra made in 2013 hangs on another wall and is generously returned each year by Faye Mack who won the quilt in a raffle several years ago. She told us she intends to gift the quilt back to Debra and the town when the church is rebuilt.

Most of the residents' photo albums were destroyed in the flood of 2011. They barely had time to get themselves and their loved ones out of the town before the floodwaters rushed into their homes, so treasures like photo albums and framed pictures were all lost. In 2013, Debra worked hard trying to locate photos of Pinhook before the flood. Few photos can be found of the actual homes, but she has located photographs of family reunions, weddings, graduation day photos, military portraits, prom photos, and a host of other historic shots that perhaps people had in their purses or had been preserved by who had already moved away. She framed them all and placed them on the tables throughout the room, asking that people try to identify the people in the photos. This is a fun and interesting exercise for everyone with ties to Pinhook. People meander from table to table looking at the photos and guessing who is in them. Debra takes notes and writes on the back of the photos, hoping to identify all the Pinhook connections. A diligent historian, Debra was convinced this project would yield new information about the photos, and she was right. Everyone loves contributing, delighted when they find a dear friend, a relative, or their own mother or grandmother in photos they have never seen or do not remember. A woman takes a framed photo over to her mother and asks, "Mama, is this your sister, Rose?" hoping to verify who she thinks is in the photo. Her mother is delighted, agreeing the young woman in the hat with a veil is her sister. Sometimes they laugh; sometimes they cry;

sometimes they argue loudly about who it is, but all in good fun, until they think they have correctly identified who is in the photo.

✦ ✦ ✦

In a perfect wedding of food and fun, music and dance, cakewalks are a common feature of community gatherings, particularly in the American south, and the game is a staple of Pinhook Day. The beauty of the cakewalk as a participatory exercise excels as an intergenerational, prize-winning contest.[1] Here, in the American Legion Hall in Sikeston, Debra and her sisters create a cakewalk with only the use of magic markers and sheets of construction paper. They assign the numbers 1–30 on the sheets of paper and tape them on the floor in a large circle. When the cakewalk is announced, LaToya blasts the room with loud, pulsating secular music and people swarm to the numbered sheets of paper, ready for the contest. Adults and children head toward a certain number; children laugh and push each other off a square only to laugh again and go find another to stand on. Everyone, young and old, is dancing to the music, as they make their way around the circle. Grandmothers gently sway to the music, children skip and hop, teen-agers do complex steps. Because everyone is having such a good time, LaToya plays the music for quite a long time, building the fun and encouraging the dancing. Then, abruptly, she stops the song. Everyone screams and scrambles to claim a numbered square on the floor. They collide with each other, bumping bodies, laughing, screaming, pushing.

When the chaos settles, Debra reaches into a bowl with numbers on scrambled cards. She announces slowly, anticipating the eagerness of the cakewalkers, "And the winner is. . . ." She has them standing with baited breath. Then, she yells out, "Number Eleven." And the chaos ensues as all the cakewalkers look at their feet and around at their neighbors' feet, asking, "Who's on eleven?" "Who got it?" This time, a small boy, perhaps four years old, is unaware that he is standing on the winning number. "Travis!" They all yell together, "You are number Eleven! You won!" Travis looks baffled, a bit terrified that everyone is yelling at him. His grin turns into a broad smile that covers his face. He squares his shoulders and heads for the dessert tables. He points without hesitation to a round tray of homemade cupcakes, perhaps as many as twenty-five on one tray. Someone reaches across to hand him the tray, entirely too large for him to hold on his own. Yet he wraps his short arms as far as possible around the tray and walks to the center of the circle. Everyone there is congratulating him as he bounces the tray with pure happiness. His mother and grandmother take his photograph with his prize. Finally, he

Pinhook Day, 2014. Elaine J. Lawless.

leaves the circle and proudly displays his trophy as he makes his way past table after table of smiling family and friends, who continue to brag on him as he carefully places the tray on his grandmother's table.

This first episode of the cakewalk has taken perhaps twenty minutes or longer. Judging from the tables full of desserts, the cakewalk will take hours to complete. It could take all day to distribute these pies and cakes. And that's the idea. The fun is extended song after song. Most of the "walks" cost the walker $1.00, but Ms. Aretha's cakes can cost the participant $2.00 per walk. Sometime the prize is announced by Debra first, to get more people to come up and choose a place on the circle. "OK. For this walk, you are competing for Miss Aretha's caramel cake and it will cost you $2.00 to join the walk. But it's well worth it! It is well worth $2.00 for Miss Aretha's cake, and it's well worth it to help Pinhook out. Come on, you all, dig deep in those pockets and come walk for this cake." As expected, on this day the cakewalk takes too long, eventually Debra begins to announce that each walk will give out two prizes. At one point, she breaks the rhythm of the cakewalk and auctions off a chocolate cake everyone has been eyeing, brought by another supreme cook in the community. That cake goes for $32.00, and all that money goes into the Rebuild Pinhook coffers.

The cakewalk will resume after lunch. And, indeed, it does take all day for the desserts to disappear from the tables in the front and find their way to the various family tables. Some are careful not to open their treasures, preferring to take them home and enjoy them alone. Others rip off the foil or cling wrap and dig right in, handing forks and spoons around to everyone at the table. Dessert, then, is special, hard-won, shared, and delicious.

The cakewalk is an inexpensive, delightful game that includes all ages. The utter delight on the face of the winner is worth watching over and over again. All they had to do was claim a space and walk, or dance, until the music stops. The suspense before the announcement of the winner is real every single time. The joy of hearing your own number called is delightful. The game is totally egalitarian, the winner random. No jealousies arise. Everyone shares in the winner's moment. And they regroup to dance the circle again and again, until only a sad little assortment of cakes and pies remain on the table. Some already look stale or are obviously "store bought," and therefore were not desired by anyone. By the time they are done with the cakewalk, Debra's coffee can is stuffed with $1.00 bills, proof of the continued contributions of everyone to the "cause."

✦ ✦ ✦

At noon, the festivities break for lunch, and people leave the circle to line up at the kitchen door for the fried catfish, pork steaks, slaw, iced tea, and potato salad. Some of the men have been manning the grill and frying kettle all morning long and continue to bring in heavy platters of meat and fish into the kitchen. Everyone eats heartily, enjoying the food and the meal with their entire community. Music continues to play from the sound system so the voices have to also turn up the volume to be heard. We hear young voices, older voices, women's voices and men's; we hear laughter and we talk to LaToya through her tears. We ask her why she cried when she saw Debra's quilt depicting Pinhook hanging on the wall. As tears roll down her face, LaToya talks about the pain of losing their town. "It's just overwhelming. . . . [I] can't go home anymore. That's all I pretty much have left of it. It's the pictures. And most of the houses are destroyed. It's just hard. It's hard" (Robinson-Tate).

Every year, Debra, her mother, her sisters, and other Pinhook women have also accumulated items to auction off to make money for the Pinhook fund. Perhaps 30 items have been quietly gracing the front of the room for hours, lovingly placed on and around a long wooden table in full view so people can view them up close whenever they pass by. New yard and garden tools sit in a pretty basket covered with cling wrap and topped with a bright red bow; another basket holds colorful kitchen utensils. A woman has been

George Williams, David Robinson, and other men cooking for Pinhook Day, 2012. Elaine J. Lawless.

"volunteered" to run the auction. She is not a "pro," so the folks at the tables do not actually seem to be listening to her as she points out the virtues of each of the items. The noise in the open, metal building is deafening as the auctioneer announces that one basket has just sold for $25—as does the one with plastic kitchen items. A plant, a bag of soil, and a garden trellis brings $30. Debra notices folks are not actually paying attention to the auction and takes the stage for a moment, feigning a Vanna White pose to gesture to the items being auctioned, coquettish, smiling, until she actually gets embarrassed when the crowd begins to laugh at her antics. After that, they seem to pay a bit more attention.

When the auction begins in earnest, someone asks how it will be run. We expect people to get numbers on a paddle like most auctions, but Debra nixes that idea, stating that she, Twan, and LaToya can "keep track." And, they do keep track—or not, as it may be. People here are honest and make certain they get their money to the table for the items they have won. Debra has done well, finding treasures others will bid on to help add to the Pinhook fund. The bidding itself is comical; sometimes the bidding becomes a game that has little to do with the items. They up the bid just for the fun of it, egging their friend to bid even more. This pattern of seeming disinterest, followed by a collective hush when the bidding gets interesting and fun, continues throughout the afternoon, allowing for conversation and "catching up" as well as making the auction a great success. They can multi-task. They know the auction is important to Debra and important for their fundraising. But today also brings beloved friends from far away and the visiting is perhaps more important. They make it all happen in an even flow of performance and collective participation.

Debra had hinted at surprises for the 2013 Pinhook Day and each one was a great success. Following the auction, she called several Pinhook folks to the front of the room—Faye Mack, "Ducky" (Reginald, one of her brothers), and her grandson, Gavin, a young member of the Pinhook family. All of them were clearly "in" on the plans for the next event.

LaToya takes the microphone from Debra and begins to tell a story: "Long ago, in the early years of Pinhook, the teenagers in the town loved their radios and they loved to listen to the music of the day, especially Chubby Checker . . . And there, in Pinhook, they got everyone dancing the . . . TWIST!" With this, the three "entertainers," ages roughly 50, 40, and 20, begin a faithful and energetic rendition of the classic dance. By now, all eyes are on the front of the room; people are laughing and singing along, accompanied by wild laughter and hoots to encourage the dancers. In minutes, others join them in the front to enjoy the dance—young and old take their place, participating in the fun. The smiles on everyone's faces began to hurt, but there was no relief, as LaToya continued: "In the '60s, the Pinhook kids bought new records and they learned the steps to dance the . . . (drum roll) slide!" And off they go, young and old dancing across the flood.

Again and again, the dances and the dancers change to fit the era and the pleasure in the room builds. Different people join in the various dances that they remember best. LaToya continues her musical story, and the dancers begin again. Soon, she announces that in the eighties, "a young black boy took the world by storm. Michael Jackson was on everybody's TV and dancing will never be the same." At this, Gavin takes the stage and does a delightful rendition of Jackson's flair, including a credible moonwalk. Folks come out of their chairs, clapping now for the boy, so proud to see him succeed as "Michael Jackson."

After the Michael Jackson revue, the dancers move with LaToya's narrative into the nineties demonstrating the different dances of each era. By now, thirty or more people are sliding along together—children, "cool" teenagers who actually look like they are having a great time, men, women, grandmothers, all take to the floor. Some are in sandals, some in spike heels, others dance barefoot on the cool floor. Without a doubt, Debra's idea for a "Dance of the Decades" has been a great success.

When we thought the day simply could not get any better, Debra called the Pinhook Choir up to prepare for the gospel singing. Every year since the beginning of Pinhook, their beloved Union Baptist Choir, dubbed the "Gospel Explosion," has had a tradition of singing at Pinhook Day. As the years went by, the choir became the Union Baptist Pinhook Reunion Choir, with an open invitation to everyone who had ever sung in the choir to join in again to sing together. This year was no different and choir members, past and more recent, gathered and began to practice a few bars of their favorite gospel songs. Within minutes, their voices rose and crescendoed in the large room astounding the ears of all those. Debra, LaToya, and Faye Mack were the leaders and the soloists; their strong voices cleared the room of all conversation. A hush fell on the crowd when LaToya began her rendition of the "The Star-Spangled Banner." It was truly mesmerizing. Such rich voices here in East Prairie, singing only for each other, for their community, and those who stand in support of their efforts to rebuild their town. It was a humbling experience.

After a few perfectly rendered songs, with solo parts worthy of a music contract, the choir members began to gently encourage an older man on the front row to join them. He laughed and resisted, saying he didn't know any of their songs. After a bit of cajoling, he took the mic at his seat and sang a few bars of the "kind of song" he said he knew. His voice was deep and sonorous; obviously, they all knew he was a very good singer. Finally, the group got him to his feet. Applause filled the room, followed by laughter and cheers. We did not know who the older gentleman was, but they all did. He stood erect, his hat sitting jauntily on his grey head, and within seconds, something happened around him. The female choir members melted back and away, leaving only men standing at several microphones. They began to sing old standards with the older man leading. The effect was astounding. Everyone listened, knowing this had turned into another magical moment. The man led them in "Swing Low, Sweet Chariot," as well as other songs everyone seemed to know from years past. This was a truly emergent moment blessed with shared love and concern as well as respect for those elders who brought such dignity to the setting.

The dynamic energy of Pinhook Day allowed for both the repetition of traditions long shared and anticipated, but the day also held the possibility for something dynamic and new to happen. The men's voices rose and joined together—young and old. As we recorded the event, we were struck by the number of African American men who were in the room, who make a point of coming to Pinhook Day every year. Stereotypes prevail in the media that the population of Pinhook had dwindled to a few "middle-aged and elderly women," now displaced. Reports that Pinhook's population had become quite small and mostly female allows for them to be more invisible, easier to be discounted. But the reality belies this gendered depiction. Men are here in numbers—young boys, teenagers, young adults holding children in their arms, middle-aged men accompanying their wives and their daughters, older men, like the featured singer and his contemporaries, all here for Pinhook Day—all part of the continued community of Pinhook, resisting easy analyses, all united with Debra in the effort to sustain the community of Pinhook and work together to rebuild their town.

Pinhook Day has been a "homecoming" celebration for this African American community for many years. It is a transformed "homecoming" for them now that the town itself is gone. But the day and the record attendance attest to the fact that the community is comprised of the people, not necessarily the land and the structures of the town. Later, after the 2014 celebration, Debra admits to us her own personal concern. How long can she, and they, continue to gather in Sikeston remembering a town that no longer exists? While it is true that the community of people is the heart and soul of Pinhook, it is also true that the people need the place, the physical site, to return to as the centered context for their community. They cannot forever exist as a free-floating group of refugees. In 2013, it had already been nearly three years since the flood that destroyed their town, and FEMA has not responded to their numerous grant requests for restitution. The celebration in 2015 was no different. The game with FEMA has become a waiting game with no real resolution in sight.

Debra quietly wonders if she can gather enough energy to keep planning future Pinhook Days, without encouragement, without money, without the land and funding necessary to rebuild their town. They need so much to sustain a community, a town, to build and grow on the historic foundations Jim Robinson Sr., Lewis Moss, and their friends created nearly a century ago. If they continue to disperse, renting houses in East Prairie, Charleston, Sikeston, Cape Girardeau, St. Louis, and Kansas City, Pinhook may become only a memory of a better time and place. For all the comparisons that can be made with other disaster sites, including the 9th Ward of New Orleans, Pinhook has its own story—and it is a different story, a unique story for a different time and place, for a group of people who chose to "make community" together and continue to farm Missouri River bottom soil.

CHAPTER FIVE

WHEN THEY BLEW THE LEVEE

But that's not all the law is. The law is also memory; the law also records a long-running conversation, a nation arguing with its conscience.
—**BARACK OBAMA,** *Dreams from My Father*

To understand the story of the Mississippi River Flood of 2011 is really to reconcile two conflicting stories—one a dominant, public narrative and the other a counter-narrative composed of individual stories that have rarely been heard outside the boundaries of Southeast Missouri. Both stories matter. The dominant narrative tells a harrowing tale of uncontrollable weather conditions and nature's cruel and uncaring force, as well as how the Army Corps of Engineers and other agencies rallied to prevent disastrous flooding all along the multiple river valleys below Cairo, Illinois, that comprise the southern half of the Mississippi River drainage basin. It is the story of a bold and audacious plan to keep the Mississippi River in its banks and what it took to execute that plan. It is the story of a success, of a heroic action, of preserving the property and lives of many. This is, without question, the dominant narrative. It is the government's narrative. It is the U.S. Army Corps of Engineers' narrative.

The other story is harrowing as well, but it is a story from the point of view of the former residents of a single small town—Pinhook, Missouri—a town that was completely destroyed as a result of the Corps' "successful" operation of the flood control "project." For the now-displaced Pinhook residents, most of whom are African American, the story of the operation of the floodway is the story of race, of people migrating great distances to establish new lives, but being forced to settle on land subject to threat—land at the mercy of the river and the whim of the U.S. Army Corps of Engineers. It is not so much the story of the unstoppable force of nature; it is the story of the shortcomings of human beings and government agencies, of the dangers of a community not being seen or listened to, and of the indifference of government bureaucracy to the lives and experiences of everyday people who lack money, power, and influence. This is the people's narrative. This is the narrative of the displaced residents of Pinhook.

This chapter relates both narratives. Part one relates the official story as told by government entities such as NOAA and the U.S. Army Corps of Engineers. We struggled deciding which story should come first in this chapter. Ultimately, we settled on relating the "official" story first, not because it is more important, but because we believe that understanding how those in power have thought about the flood is essential to comprehending the degree to which displaced residents of the community of Pinhook have been unjustly omitted from that narrative before, during, and after the levee breach. We begin, then, with the institutional account, compiled from the official publications of federal and regional government entities. While these publications together relate a narrative of triumph and success, the overt omission of Pinhook and its fate from any of these official accounts reveals an inexplicable

and indefensible abdication of responsibility to the people living inside the
Birds Point–New Madrid Floodway. What follows this official narrative is a
counter-narrative with commentary on Pinhook and the levee breach taken
from several interviews we conducted with displaced Pinhook residents over
the course of approximately three years. We present the counter-narratives,
along with our own analysis, as a challenge to the "official" stance that what
happened to Pinhook, Missouri, on May 2, 2011, was a success.

✦ ✦ ✦

Soldiers and engineers have been battling the Mississippi River and its tributaries for as long as the river has run through lands owned by the United
States. This conflict between man and nature, then, goes back at least to 1803,
when then president Thomas Jefferson purchased over eight hundred thousand square miles of land from the French. One of the most important features of that land purchase was the city of New Orleans, which sits at the
mouth of the Mississippi River. This "Louisiana Purchase," as it was called,
would eventually allow transportation and exploration throughout an area
comprising nearly half of the continental United States. Just as soon as the
United States acquired the land containing the majority of the Mississippi
River system, it was forced to begin considering how to manage and control
the river, for the land it fed could not be exploited if the river was allowed to
inundate it on an annual basis. Thus began the long struggle to keep the river
within its banks, a task well suited to human aspiration and the tendency
for our reach to exceed our grasp. According to John Barry, author of, *Rising
Tide,* one of the most famous studies of the 1927 Mississippi River Flood, "To
control the Mississippi River—not simply to find a *modus vivendi* with it, but
to control it, to dictate to it, to make it conform—is a mighty task. It requires
more than confidence; it requires hubris" (21).

The destruction of Pinhook, Missouri, took place in 2011, nearly a hundred
years later, but that disastrous destruction of a town of mostly black residents depended on decisions made about the river throughout the 150 years
since an increasing population in the states and territories of the Mississippi
Drainage Basin began to demand that the federal government take action to
curb the unpredictable and devastating natural flooding at river conventions
during the 1840s (Barry 34). The strategies and tactics that would eventually
be used in an effort to control the rising river were decided over decades
of disagreement, conflict, and debate. That Major General Edgar Jadwin's
plan incorporating floodways as a method to lower the river levels was the
foundation for the 1928 Flood Control Act was not a coincidence, but the

culmination of years of debate over how to best tame the raging flood waters
of the Mississippi and its tributaries.

The destruction of Pinhook in 2011 depended on politics, government policy, and social convention; it was animated, in part, by the realities of racism
and segregation. The people who lived in Pinhook were mostly descendants
of African Americans who had come to Missouri seeking land and opportunity. They had come seeking the chance to determine their own lives and be
able to provide for their children. For these people, the way to take control of
their existence was to acquire land of their own. Unfortunately, the only land
that was available to them was land that, in the early 1940s, no one wanted,
land located in the center of a spillway created by the flood abatement designs
of Edgar Jadwin. These aspiring black farmers did what black people often
did with what they were allowed; they took it and made it into something
good. In this case, they took what was available to them and made it into a
community—a community that was subject to the yearly backwater flooding of the Mississippi River, and more importantly, to the control of the U.S.
Army Corps of Engineers.

I.

The winter of 2010–2011 was snowy. The northern rocky mountain region and
plains, all along the basin of the Missouri River, experienced much higher
than normal snowfall due, in large part, to a strong "La Nina" weather pattern (*The Missouri/Souris River Floods of May—August 2011* 8). According to
data from the NOAA/National Climate Data Center, Wyoming, North and
South Dakota, Minnesota, Iowa, Nebraska, and Missouri all experienced precipitation between the months of January to December of 2010 that were far
above normal (*The Missouri/Souris* 10). Excessive winter snows followed by a
colder than normal spring meant that additional heavy spring precipitation
was accompanied by a late spring melt and runoff (11), bringing the Missouri
River system to its full capacity and ultimately the entire Mississippi Tribu-
tary System to flood stage.

The system designed to manage flooding on the Mississippi River is the
Mississippi River and Tributaries Project, which is managed and administered by the Mississippi River Commission (a government-citizen body)
and the Army Corps of Engineers. The Project, first conceived in 1928, and
modified several times in the intervening years, is designed to control what
is called "the Project Design Flood" (PDF) This term refers to the worst flood
that officials could imagine possible. In 1954, the National Weather Service

conceived a projection for a massive storm and flooding event by combining data from three historical storms that hit the Mississippi and Ohio drainage basins in 1937, 1938, and 1950 (Camillo 7). This projection formed the basis for the Project Design Flood—the immense storm and flooding event the MR&T was designed to control.

Controlling an event as large as the PDF required more than just levees, the tool that many early engineers had advocated. It demanded, as General Jadwin's plan laid out, other mechanisms such as floodways and reservoirs to deal with the extraordinary amount of water that would need to be drained throughout the system. The 2011 flood would put the MR&T system to the test in a way it had never been tested before. The combination of unrelenting rains and late spring snowpack runoff would push the MR&T system to its limits. For Pinhook, Missouri, located inside the Birds Point–New Madrid Floodway, this meant the very real possibility that the floodway would be operated for the first time since 1937 when U.S. Army Corps of Engineers soldiers prepared the levee for detonation under the watch of a Missouri National Guard company (Powell 44). Even then, operation of the floodway, as indicated by Jadwin's plan and the 1928 Flood Control Act, was controversial.

Early opponents of Jadwin's plan were skeptical that operation of the floodway would have a significant impact on the gage at Cairo. The official claim was always that operating the floodway would lower the Cairo gage by seven feet during the Project Design Flood, but many, including the consulting engineer for the Missouri Levee Districts claimed that "floodway operation would not bring about sufficient reduction of flood crest to afford protection again the 'project' flood" (Powell 45). Thad Snow, noted Bootheel author and activist, following the floodway's operation during the 1937 flood, questioned its effectiveness, arguing that the area from "Cape [Girardeau] to New Madrid" had been "crucified on the cross of Cairo's necessity, without ensuring Cairo's salvation'" (qtd in Powell 46). The floodway was first operated in a cloud of uncertainty, and the seventy-four years that had passed since had not provided definitive proof of its efficacy. The problem was, the practicality or effectiveness of the floodway were never the operative questions during the buildup to the 2011 flood event. The only question of any significance was: what was the reading on the Cairo gage?

There was no question that by April of 2011 the reading at the Cairo gage was high—alarmingly so. The snowpack runoff from the Missouri River Valley was being compounded by record rainfall all along the Mississippi and Ohio River Valleys. Between April 23 and 28, portions of southern Illinois, southern Indiana, and northern Kentucky received a staggering nine to ten inches of rain. Parts of the Missouri Bootheel and northern Arkansas received "more than 12 inches of rain" (*2012 Flood Season Preparedness Report* 3). According to a report by the Mississippi Valley Division of the Army Corps of Engineers, the states of Illinois, Indiana, Kentucky, and Ohio all recorded their wettest Aprils in history (3). That same report explains the ways that the 2011 flood was a uniquely historic event:

> It is the Flood of Record for many gauges between Cape Girardeau, MO and the Gulf of Mexico. The 2011 flood fight is the first time the total watershed system was required to be operated in a synchronized manner to manage the highest level of water it has ever seen, in some areas this event was near the Project Design Flood. The flood waters exacerbated weakness and created new weaknesses in the system requiring emergency response by the local levee boards coupled with technical assistance and other resources from the Corps. (4)

It is safe to say that in the 2011 flood, both local and national officials were facing an event that none of them had experienced in their lifetimes.

So as the Cairo gage continued to rise, major decision makers, most notably, Major General Michael Walsh, Commander of the Mississippi Valley District of the U.S. Army Corps of Engineers and president of the Mississippi River Commission, had to begin to consider the possibility that operation of the Birds Point–New Madrid Floodway would be required. By April 21, river forecasts predicted the Cairo gage would reach 61.1 feet by the first week of May (*Room for the River* 8). The rains had been consistently steady all month long and would certainly push the river to 60 feet and beyond at Cairo if they continued. If the Cairo gage hit 60 feet, the Army Corps would be forced to act. At that point a decision would have to be made to operate the floodway. The only question would be when it would happen. A brief lull in the rain between April 27 and 30 provided some hope that the river might level off before it reached 60 feet, but on April 30 the rain began again and the water levels continued to rise (*Room for the River* 10).

Operating the Birds Point–New Madrid Floodway would mean flooding approximately 130,000 acres of Missouri farmland with 550,000 cubic feet per second of river water (*Room for the River* 20). There were also 230 residents and private dwellings in the floodway (*RFR* 16), but the main concern seemed to be the farmland because of its economic importance. There was a danger that what some thought of as the most productive farmland in the country could be damaged by rock and sand deposits as the Mississippi flowed over it. Missouri farmers and large landowners who would stand to lose significant profit and capital if the floodway was activated appealed to the state of Missouri for help. On April 26, the Attorney General of the state of

Missouri, Chris Kloster, attempted legal intervention to keep the Army Corps of Engineers from breaching the levee and operating the floodway (*State of Missouri vs. U.S. Army Corps of Engineers*). Filed in U.S. federal court, the state of Missouri's motion for injunction was heard by U.S. District Judge Stephen N. Limbaugh. The state of Missouri's case was not based on the fact that the operation of the floodway would destroy farmland or displace residents; instead, it was argued on the only basis the state had—that the operation would "cause unlawful pollution of water under the Missouri Clean Water Act," and that the Corp's "implementation of the plan" was a violation of the Administrative Procedures Act (*State of Missouri vs. U.S. Army Corps of Engineers*).

Because the Army Corps of Engineers is an entity of the United States government, which enjoys sovereign immunity and cannot be subject to a lawsuit under Missouri statute, Kloster was limited in what he could argue to try to stop the operation from going ahead. According to Limbaugh, the power of the Corps to operate the floodway could not be contested; only the process of their decision to operate it could. He explained it this way:

> The Corps is an administrative body of the U.S. government and so they are subject to the administrative procedures act, and so that's a long drawn out series of statutes that is actually applicable to every government entity. And so not just the Corps of Engineers, but the argument there was, everybody acknowledged that, under the law the Corps of Engineers had the discretion to blow the levy if they saw fit. And so the real question was whether they were abusing their discretion in blowing a levy and whether their conduct was therefore "arbitrary and capricious." (Limbaugh)

After hearing the case, Limbaugh rendered his decision on the morning of April 29 as the Cairo gage was still rapidly approaching sixty feet. He had decided that the conduct of the Corps was not "arbitrary and capricious." His decision denied the motion brought by the state of Missouri and cleared the way for the Corp to breach the levee, to operate the floodway—an action that would destroy the town of Pinhook, Missouri.

The Corp had already begun to make preparations for the possible breaching of the levee on April 25, the day before the state of Missouri filed its motion. Barges were loaded with "materials, equipment, and personnel," including massive amounts of liquid explosive that would be used to breach the levee (*Room for the River* 13). The front side of the Birds Point–New Madrid levee runs adjacent to the Mississippi for about forty miles starting at a point just south across the river from the city of Cairo, Illinois, and extends south nearly all the way to the city of New Madrid, Missouri. The front side levee stands at 62.5 feet for most of its length, but there are three "fuseplugs" designed for breaching the levee that dip to 60 feet in height (*State of Missouri vs. U.S. Army Corps* 3). These fuseplug portions of the levee contain sections that are threaded through with buried pipe designed to be pumped full with liquid explosives in order to blow gaps or "crevasses" in the levee where river water can divert from the main channel of the Mississippi, flow into the flood-way, and eventually out of the 1,500-foot opening at its southern tip. At the moment when Judge Limbaugh issued his decision on the twenty-ninth, 150 Corps personnel were on standby poised to initiate action to breach the levee within a twenty-four hour window (*Room for the River* 16). At this point all barriers were cleared for breaching the levee. The only thing that could stop it was a continuation of a recent significant pause in the otherwise relentless rain, but when the rain began again on the thirtieth, operation of the Birds Point–New Madrid Floodway was all but assured.

The point at which state, county, and federal officials notified residents of the possibility they would operate the levee is less certain. Sheriff Keith Moore of Mississippi County declared a state of emergency and ordered a manda-tory evacuation on Wednesday, April 27 (Hevern). This evacuation plan should have included going door to door to make certain residents knew they would have to leave their homes. But on Friday, April 29th, Moore released a faxed letter asking the state of Missouri for National Guard troops to assist in making sure residents were out of the spillway by 4:00 pm that afternoon. According to the official Army Corps of Engineers account, residents were notified of decisions about the operation by "more modern means" than had been available in 1937 when "hand-written U.S. Army field notes were dropped from the sky reading, 'Levee has broken. Get out at once!'" (*Room for the River* 18). Those "more modern means" of updating residents included "news media, Facebook, and Twitter" (18). But despite the availability of more advanced methods of communication, residents reported confusion about these official notifications. Even if residents had begun to evacuate themselves and their possessions on the twenty-fifth, they would have only had five days to complete the process. And since residents (particularly Pinhook residents) may not have been aware of official notification until at least April 27 (or even April 29 when seven hundred National Guard soldiers arrived to secure the floodway and make sure that all residents had been evacuated), most residents had less than seventy-two hours to find trucks, pack their belong-ings, and move everything to temporary quarters.[1] This, of course, was a near impossible feat and explains why so much was left behind by evacuating resi-dents: vehicles, furniture, keepsakes, important documents, etc. There simply wasn't enough time to salvage the items that made up their lives. They had to leave much of it behind.

Official Corps accounts claim that all residents had been evacuated out of the floodway by April 30 (Camillo 2012: 89). By that point, Judge Limbaugh had handed down his ruling and the rain had started up again. The Corps' barges were standing by for deployment. The river was rising again.

While operation of the floodway was officially dictated by the Cairo river gage, the actual operation order would have to be given by Major General Walsh. He, along with members of the Mississippi River Commission and other government agencies had been watching the situation closely. One of the earliest indicators of the impending flood disaster had been the deteriorating condition of the levees protecting Cairo, Illinois. Cairo, which had once been an important industrial city located at the very southernmost tip of Illinois, is bounded on one side by the Mississippi River and on the other by the Ohio. The two rivers meet just south of the city at Fort Defiance State Park. There, one can overlook the two mighty rivers crashing together in swirling eddies and continuing their journey south together to New Orleans in tandem. Marking the confluence of these two rivers that form the major route to Memphis and New Orleans, Cairo has often been referred to as the Gateway to the South. It is the point where a majority of Eastern and Western river navigation meet on their journey to the Mississippi Delta and eventually the Gulf of Mexico. Once a wealthy town of thirteen thousand residents ("Cairo, Illinois Population Viewer"), Cairo was considered an important industrial, commercial, military, and navigational site throughout its history. In 1928 when the Jadwin plan was put into effect, Cairo was a prominent city of wealth and industry, as can be witnessed in the grand mansions that still occupy its northwestern corner. The historical importance of Cairo, Illinois, was now reflected in the important role the Cairo gage would play in determining the destiny of a little town inside the Birds Point–New Madrid Floodway.

The levees that protect Cairo on its eastern and western sides were in increasing jeopardy in the days and weeks leading up to Judge Limbaugh's decision. On April 28, engineers from the Memphis District encountered fast growing sand boils on the land side of the Cairo levees (Camillo 83). Boils develop when the pressure of the water in the river channel is so high that it seeks release under the levee foundation structure. Water under high pressure carrying "piped" sand and soil forces its way under the levee foundation and up to the surface on the inside of the levee wall. This "underseepage," if allowed to continue unchecked, will permit the built-up water pressure to "create voids under the levee, which can lead to an eventual collapse" (Camillo 68). The best solutions to sand boils are relief wells and seepage berms, but both of these take significant time to put in place and are not long term fixes. Sand boils are a signal of the beginning of the end of the integrity of a levee system, and by April 30, when the rains began again, Memphis District engineers, faced with some of the fastest growing sand boils they had ever seen, feared for the safety of the system. An evacuation of Cairo, Illinois, was ordered.

As the river rose, General Walsh was faced with a difficult decision. According to his subordinates and consultants, operation of the floodway was an inevitable reality. Walsh made the decision to move the barges carrying the liquid explosive to positions next to the levee on May 1st (Camillo 96). This was necessary for the explosives to be pumped into the levee walls, but it would take crews several hours to complete the preparations required for the levee breach. Walsh had, however, not yet given the order to blow the levee. As the rains continued and the Cairo gage continued to rise, Walsh met with Mississippi River Commission members and heard recommendations on the decision he had yet to make. After this consultation, the order was made to begin filling the fuseplug pipes (Camillo 101). Once this command was given there was really no going back.

On May 2, Major General Michael Walsh declared the order to "operate the project," the phrase he used during his press conference ("Operation Order"). Standing in a tent in the rain along with politicians, local and state officials, River Commission members, and Corp personnel, Walsh tried to explain his decision to the public. In the printed official order released by the MRC, Walsh wrote:

> I spent last night on the river . . . lashed to an anchor barge in the current near the top of the floodway. The rains continued to pound the deck of the Motor Vessel. The cold winds moved us around—and the current and water levels kept increasing as the rain storms continue to grow over the Ar/Miss/Ohio/TN Watershed.
>
> So, with the tool that has withstood many tests: the test of operation in 1937; decades of challenges that resulted in the 1986 operation plan; reviews and numerous unsuccessful court challenges—I have to use this tool. I have to activate this floodway to help capture a significant percentage of the flow. ("Operation Order")

At 10:02 pm CST, on the night of May 2, the U.S. Army Corps of Engineers, under the direction of Major General Michael Walsh, operated the Birds Point–New Madrid Floodway by breaching the upper levee. Television news video of the blast shows several blinding orange arcs of flame leaping into the night sky as the liquid explosives in the levee walls were detonated. Seconds later, the cacophony of the explosion's report sped across the open fields of the floodway. The levee was detonated at two points along its

Aerial image of Pinhook taken on May 3rd, 2011. The water continued to rise and kept houses submerged for approximately two weeks. AP Photo/Jeff Roberson.

frontline, allowing for up to 550,000 cubic feet per second of water to rush into the nearly 133,000 acres inside the spillway (*Room for the River* 18). The floodwater from the Mississippi filled the floodway, submerging houses and outbuildings, cars and trucks, silos and fuel tanks. Although the floodway is designed so that the diverted river water can eventually escape at its south end, this is not a quick process. To begin with, it took three days for the floodway to even fill, and water from the Mississippi River kept flowing into it until June 8th, more than a month later (Camillo 122). It took more than two weeks for water levels to diminish enough so that houses and buildings were no longer submerged. When residents were able to return to inspect their homes, they found dwellings damaged too extensively for repair. If anyone was to return to live in the floodway on the land that they owned, they would have to rebuild from scratch; furthermore, they learned later, new directives would require all structures be built on stilts, something no one wanted to do.

Reports from the Army Corps of Engineers and other government agencies declared the operation of the Birds Point–New Madrid Floodway a success. On May 5, the river gage at Cairo read 59.6 feet, four feet below what had been predicted (Camillo 122). According to the official narrative, the floodway had operated as planned and the extent of the disaster had been greatly diminished.

II.

In the months after the levee breach, journalists came to Southeast Missouri seeking to tell the story of the destruction of Pinhook. News outlets such as the *Columbia Missourian* and the *St. Louis Beacon* published stories on the aftermath of the breach and the tragedy of the dispersed community of Pinhook.[2] This is not to mention the several local newspapers, television, and radio stations that covered the flooding and the destruction of Pinhook. But at some point, most of these media outlets moved on to other stories, and the reality of what happened to the citizens of Pinhook at the hands of their own government has faded away in the public consciousness.

We contend that Pinhook and its residents were invisible before the breach occurred and that their story, following the town's destruction, has now slipped into invisibility once again after registering only a short-term recognition in the minds of those in the region. In contrast, the narrative of the government entities and the history of the levee system have been duly recorded in standard published documents that claim to tell the story of the 2011 flood. Until now, the verbal accounts, the words and voices of displaced Pinhook residents speaking their stories, their truth, could not hold their own as counter-narratives to those endorsed by the government. We seek to correct this uneven narrative history by presenting oral histories of the native Pinhook displaced residents, stories that flesh out nearly a century of hard work and community success that was demolished in one critical "operation of the project" that could have also erased their history.

The stories of the former Pinhook residents expose the lie that there is only one appropriate narrative to be told and understood about the flood of 2011 in Missouri. Their truth also exposes the gaps in the government's lack of concern for black farmers living in the Missouri Bootheel and demonstrates how ignoring these citizens through indifference and callous disregard does not erase the reality of their lives and the destruction of their town. Although their town already has been destroyed without their permission or input and, thus far, the government has not agreed to help them rebuild their town as is their due, this should not be the end of the attention to the town of Pinhook. The stories that give life to the community they had, and still have, because of their belief in each other, in a justified belief in their rights as American citizens, and their steadfast faith in God are retold here in order to redress the imbalance of a history that privileges only the narratives of the government actors who have at their disposal time, money, and a well-paid staff to spin a story that tells only one side of the story. And has the audacity to call it "Divine Providence" (Camillo).

We first began to understand the power of the oral stories of the Pinhook people as we heard them in 2012.

✦ ✦ ✦

The first day we arrived in Pinhook in 2012 was special, not just because it was our first time seeing the town together, it was also our first time meeting Debra Robinson-Tarver, the mayor of Pinhook, who would become our research collaborator and friend. We had called her out of the blue, reading her phone number in a Sikeston newspaper article on the flood's aftermath. Debra was at work when we reached her but agreed to meet us when she got off work, making the twenty-minute trek from Sikeston out to Pinhook to talk to two people she had never met before.

Debra arrived at Pinhook riding in the passenger seat of a car belonging to a journalist who also intended to write about what had happened to Pinhook. The car pulled up, both women got out and introduced themselves, then the journalist got back in her car and began to back out of the driveway. She asked Debra if she was sure it was all right for her to leave her there with us. Debra asked if we could give her a ride home to her house in Sikeston when we were done talking and we agreed without hesitation. Satisfied, the journalist shifted her car into gear and pulled off down the country road toward the setting sun. Unfazed, Debra immediately began to walk through the town, pointing out which houses belonged to which former residents, where those people were currently living, and which ones she was related to. We were still unclear about the details of what had happened or how it could have happened. At that time, it was difficult for us to get a clear picture of what Pinhook had been, and why it was now destroyed. When Elaine asked Debra whether she had any pictures of what the town looked like before the flood, Debra began to tell us a story that left both of us distressed:

E: So do you have, like, photo albums of the village before the flood?. . . .
   Does anybody? [at same time as Debra begins to speak . . .]
D: We . . . I did good to get me out [all laugh]. I don't . . . If I do, I don't know
   it, because, um, we had to get what we could. I had my mom—that house
   [points], my sister's house, my house, and then my mom's house. Well, my
   mom is older. She's more hands on. She's gotta have stuff. So we sacrificed

and got her stuff as much as we could out of hers. And then *we* just grabbed clothes and essentials. Now I don't know. We did get some stuff, but I still don't know what we got and what we didn't . . . because we had to find storage. And then, uh, we just kind of threw it in there. So—

T: And so they didn't give you any help with this at all–

D: No. [and repeats again while Todd speaks, "No"]

T: They just came and said this is what . . . its gonna be flooding . . . you have to get out—

D: No . . . and actually we didn't find that out . . . we found that out through a friend at our job. Cause we had went to work on the 27,[3] and got up and went to work and at 7:30 the lady that works behind me, she said that she saw it on the Facebook that it was to be a mandatory evacuation. So I immediately start calling, uh, Emergency Management to see, [E: "If it was true" (as if completing Deb's sentence)] you know, what's going on. I got people down here that can't walk, and they in wheelchairs, what do I . . . you know, what am I doing here? "Well, just stand down, they just getting excited, nothing's gonna happen" [mimicking the voice at Emergency Management]. At 11:30, I got a call from my brother because I got another call from the lady . . . at my work . . . and said it's there, you need to get out. You need to find out what's going on, and get down there and take care of it. So, I was on my way home, made it to Matthews—my brother from New York calls and said, "Where are you?" I said, "Well, they keep saying it's a mandatory evacuation, but I don't think nothing goin' happen 'cause ain't nobody told me nothing cause I been calling." And he say, "I tell you what—You get down there, get your shit, and get out . . . because, I am hearing it here in New York City [E: "Oh my God . . ."] that you need to get out—it's a mandatory evacuation." Well, still—we didn't hear anything until it came on TV, about 12, 12:30 . . .

E: And they didn't send out ambulances or people—trucks—anything to help you get out? [Debra shaking her head "no" through the whole question]

D: No.

E: Oh my God [emphasizes each word].

D: No—so we had to grab what trucks we had . . . See at one time my dad was a big time farmer and his brother—well, we had trucks, and tractors, and trailers [T: Mmm hmm.] and stuff, but then when he passed, we had to get rid of it, so we didn't have trailers or tractors or anything—or trucks to put anything in. So whatever trucks we were getting, we was trying to get to my mom's to get, you know, get her belongings. Cause she's . . . she's, uh, she has to walk with a wheel [gestures like using a walker], she has problems with her back . . .

And so that's, that's when we knew about it, and we came, and I started at the front, cause I had to call my sister—she live in the front—and she said,

"Ok, I heard it on the radio." She's with clients. "I heard it on the radio. I'll meet you at Momma's." I said "Ok." So then we started a chain, calling different people to see *where are you? What are you doing? And we need to get out.* You know, this, this—and that's how we just took chain of command. When I got here [points to a house]—Miss, uh, Brown had gotten contacted by her daughter. So her—the other Brown that you met—

E: Yes, Tracy—

D: Uh huh, his mom and then the other guy next door. They were all helping trying to get things together so they could get out. And then I went on down with my mother, and my sister was in, uh, Cape trying to . . . we were gonna put a new roof on the church, make it look real nice, the community center, and fix it up. Well, they were up there doing fundraising, and they got the word. My brother called and told them, and well, immediately she started panicking, and we got her here, and started getting things out. But uh, everybody got out safe. Everybody was out. Uh, the next morning, I made sure I came back and stayed until the last person got out.[4]

While "official" narratives of the flood and disaster begin in early April of 2011 when weather and river conditions were first beginning to cause concern, Debra's story of the flood begins only on April 25 when she first becomes aware of the possibility that Pinhook residents might be forced to evacuate their town. Her account consists of what is just over a twenty-four hour period—from the morning her work colleague brings the potential evacuation to her attention to the afternoon of April 26 when Pinhook residents could no longer gain entrance to the town because of flooded roads. Mississippi County Sheriff Moore did not officially declare a mandatory evacuation until Wednesday, the twenty-seventh, and it was not until Friday of that week when an official letter from Moore was faxed to Debra's workplace explaining that all residents would need to be out of the spillway. This letter, which is dated April 29 and addressed to "To Whom It May Concern," explains that all electricity to the spillway would be cut off by 5:00 pm on that day and that the sheriff was requesting the Missouri National Guard assist in "escorting any possible persons in the spillway after 5:00 pm today, Friday April 29th, 2011." Most Pinhook residents had already been out of the spillway for two days when this official notification occurred.

Debra's story is one of uncertainty, of not knowing when or if she and other Pinhook residents would be forced to leave their homes. The residents of Pinhook had lived with flooding of the Mississippi River their whole lives. Each year, backwater flooding through the open southern end of the spillway was a regular occurrence. We heard many stories during the course of our research about Pinhook farmers using tractors and trailers to ferry children across flooded stretches of road so that they could go to school. This reality of living in close proximity to the river was something the residents grew to accept. The backwater flooding rarely reached their houses; usually the biggest problem it caused was to make traveling back and forth to nearby towns such as East Prairie and Sikeston inconvenient or impossible. And while there had been bad floods over the years, 1973 in particular, the idea that the Corps would breach the levee was not a reality in the minds of Pinhook residents. The floodway had never been operated in their lifetimes. In fact, the only time the floodway was ever operated was in 1937, before most of the townspeople's relatives had even arrived and settled in the area of Pinhook.

There is also something unspoken in Debra's narrative that accompanies its uncertainly. Debra doesn't begin with any explicit statement that Pinhook residents were not warned or that they weren't assisted in their evacuation. Rather, our questions push her toward that part of the story. The two of us simply can't believe what we are hearing—or perhaps what we are not hearing. We can't accept that not one government agency provided effective notification or assistance to these residents prior to destroying their homes. It is important to consider the way Debra's narrative functions in this moment of the telling. We are drawn into her story precisely for what it cannot explain—why Debra and other Pinhook residents were left on their own in the middle of this impending disaster. Why, when the official narrative tells us that dozens of officials were scrambling here and there, making critical decisions that would affect the lives of everyone living inside the floodway, was there not effective measure taken to inform the residents of Pinhook of what was being considered? This has been one of the foundational questions of our research with the displaced citizens of Pinhook. Debra's narrative of the disaster brought it to our attention in the first minutes that we knew her, and subsequently, every interview with a Pinhook resident has been an effort to understand how this all could have happened. But where Debra's narrative was more than effective in getting us to align ourselves with the cause of Pinhook residents, it has been less so with those who actually have the power to help them. The problem is that the "they" in the narrative, the amorphous group of people who made this decision, (apparently without ever considering the town of Pinhook) are closely aligned with the same group of people now invested with the power to help them rebuild their town. When we first heard Debra's story, we fully expected their narratives to provide the basis for action from those who could provide financial resources to help them rebuild. Unfortunately, the same sort of indifference and invisibility that existed before the breach still exists after the destruction of Pinhook. Although the former residents have dutifully filed all the paperwork necessary for restitution and funding to rebuild, it seems FEMA and other agencies instituted to assist them continue to adopt an attitude of complicit indifference. Pinhook's invisibility before the flood continues after the flood over seven years later. Only their stories survive to tell what happened to them.

The government's indifference to the plight of Pinhook's displaced residents as evidenced by the lack of support from federal, state, and county agencies has not stopped them from continuing to tell their story. Speaking of their experiences in this disaster has been a way of highlighting their own existence as a town, as a community within the spillway. One of the most shocking aspects of this whole situation for us has been the degree to which the existence of an entire town was rendered invisible through silence. The word "Pinhook" seems to have never been spoken in all the discussions of the approaching flood and the sanctioned breach. Pinhook is the only organized community[5] inside the Birds Point–New Madrid Floodway, and yet we cannot find any recognition of that fact in official documents of the U.S. Army Corps of Engineers (both before and after the breach), in the lawsuit filed by the state of Missouri, or in Judge Stephen Limbaugh's written decision. In fact, when we had the chance to interview Judge Limbaugh in his office suite inside the federal courthouse named for his grandfather in May of 2013, we asked him pointedly about Pinhook. We were curious as to whether he had had any specific knowledge about Pinhook at the time that he made his decision.

> TL: So the most important question we wanted to ask you—you obviously knew there were people and houses in the floodplain, but did you know about the people in Pinhook? Did you know that town was down there?
>
> JL: Yes, yes. There was a little bit of testimony about that . . . about that area—yeah they had a couple of landowners testify and—[Here he shuffles through his papers looking for evidence but is unable to find anything.]
>
> EL: But the town itself was actually mentioned in the hearing?
>
> JL: Yeah, yeah, I'm sure it was. Yeah. Uh, but by then 60 percent of the place was already underwater anyway. By the time this came to a hearing, most of the thing, most of the area was underwater anyway—everything that was in floodplain . . . and the people of Pinhook had already been moved out—
>
> TL: Well, this not what they say—

Our timeline indicates that Judge Limbaugh is right that most of the residents of Pinhook had evacuated the floodway by the time he was hearing testimony, but his assertion that there was testimony on Pinhook is not confirmed by our research nor his own documentation. Our examination of the court papers provided to us by his office did not reveal any testimony or evidence submitted regarding the existence of Pinhook. The one thing we did find was a single illustrated one-page map of the floodway with Pinhook marked on it. Other than that, in hundreds of pages of documents, we did not find anything to support the Judge's claim. It is important to repeat what we have said and written elsewhere: we do not believe that the existence of Pinhook, the only town located inside the Birds Point–New Madrid Floodway, was ever discussed during the entire legal proceeding.

This erasure of Pinhook through collective silence has not gone unnoticed by displaced residents. They do not accept that officials did not know about their town. Consider this excerpt from an interview we did with George Williams, an important member of the Pinhook community we've mentioned before, a man who drove Pinhook children to school on the bus for over forty years. He recounted this story about speaking to the county commissioner about the impending levee breach the week before it occurred:

> The county commissioner came down one Sunday night and told me that they were going to blow it. He'd been down to talk to the governor of Missouri, and he was trying to get them not to do it—the Corps and all those groups. And, they said, they didn't know Pinhook exists. And they are all liars. They knew it existed. And they said the sheriff told us, and the representative in Jeff City, he said some guys told them they didn't know—the Corps didn't know that Pinhook exists. They are lying there. He told that to me and I said, "Lord, you know, you got to be kidding. You know there are more than a hundred families down there." And he said, "What? I thought it was only spillway in there." Well, they lied. They knew Pinhook was down there. They knew better than that. It was on the map! Now, how come they would say they didn't know it exists? It was on the map. When Pinhook was incorporated, they put it on the map. That's wrong. Why do you need to lie?

Williams's assessment of the situation conflicts with the notion that Pinhook was simply overlooked. He offers a pointed challenge to the Commisioner's claim that "they didn't know Pinhook exists." Williams's rejection of this claim is more than a criticism of the officials who made the decision to breach the levee and flood the spillway; it is an articulation of agency and presence. How is it possible that "more than a hundred families" could go unnoticed or unknown? Similar to the ways in which Debra Robinson-Tarver's narrative about her experience before the breach serves as a challenge to the official narrative that completely erases the village of Pinhook along with its residents, Williams's story offers another powerful challenge to the official narrative as well; he demands an answer to the additional critical question: how is it possible they could say that they did not know?

Although Pinhook residents are not likely to point it out directly, the answer to this question may lie in the fact that Pinhook was a small rural village composed of mostly African American farmers. One might think that a black town surrounded by an area of land occupied mostly by white farmers would be highly visible because of its contrast to the neighboring residents— first being the only incorporated town or village in the spillway, and second being composed almost entirely of black residents. We believe, however, that it is precisely the intersection of its blackness and rurality that rendered Pinhook invisible.

Our claim that Pinhook was overlooked in this situation because of a kind of racial invisibility is informed both by theories of blackness and invisibility and by the notion of rural invisibility or "urbannormativity." Recent research in the area of "critical rural studies," a sub-discipline of rural sociology, has demonstrated specific bias toward urban areas over rural ones. This bias holds doubly true when we consider the lack of visibility of black populations in rural locations as opposed to those in urban ones.

In their book *Critical Rural Theory*, Alexander Thomas, Brian Lowe, Gregory Fulkerson, and Polly Smith explain that residents of rural areas have been consistently disadvantaged by the ideology of "urbannormativity," which privileges "the urban as the normal and real" and positions the rural as "abnormal, unreal, or deviant" (5). The rural is also seen as solely agricultural or as the source of resources that cities need to survive. This perception disadvantages rural people because their value is understood mostly in terms of what products they can provide to cities. As well, rural agricultural spaces become associated in the public consciousness not with people or communities, but with the lack of people and communities. In the collective imagination, then, the rural becomes "the simple, the wild," a place of escape, a place where there is little or no organizing logic or principle, and thus a place that should always be considered subordinate to cities (Thomas et. al. 6).

Urbannormativity privileges the meaning ascribed by dominant cultural forces rather than that constructed through communal and traditional practice and renders rural spaces invisible or "unreal" even though they have enormous value to the people who make their homes there. If we allow for the ways in which the privileging of the urban in our cultural consciousness positions the rural in constant competition with and in comparison to the urban, it is not so difficult to see why it is the rural that often loses out when the destinies of the two come into conflict with one another. The city is a place, a civilization, whereas the rural is only an "undifferentiated space," or as

Thomas, Lowe, Fulkerson, and Smith put it, a "nowhere," a space "to be moved into" or space "out of which resources can be extracted" (64, 66).

When we combine this privileging of the urban over the rural with the presence of blackness we end up with a doubly disadvantaged space that is easily erased from our cultural consciousness. Over the last one hundred years there has been a significant shift in the geographical location of black people in the United States from the rural south to the urban north. And despite recent reversals of this population movement that took place during the "Great Migration," African Americans have consistently been associated with urban spaces—particularly distressed urban spaces, or "ghettos." In his book *How Racism Takes Place*, George Lipsitz discusses the ways in which society is actually structured by attitudes and assumptions about racialized spaces. Lipsitz argues for the importance of understanding how the "white spatial imaginary" in many ways determines the world we live in and how we think about it (13). For example, although African Americans are still strongly associated with urban space, the spaces where they live are not considered preferable. It is racially neutral sites that capture the imagination of citizens and government. While race-neutral sites such as "shopping malls" and "sports arenas" "loot public resources for private gain" (15), race-specific sites that are financially depressed lose resources and become even more closely associated with blackness in a negative way. Eventually, those race-specific spaces become places to fear and places to avoid according to the logic of the white spatial imaginary. Ultimately, the challenges of those spaces, challenges that have been greatly intensified by the re-allocating of resources to more "preferable" areas causes a kind of functional invisibility for communities of color that makes it difficult or impossible to access resources that could help improve the living conditions of people who live there.

This is an explanation for the kind of invisibility that occurs in race-specific areas where people expect to find black bodies. However, racial invisibility is even more extreme when we consider supposedly race-neutral areas where black bodies are not supposed to be. This may be the dynamic at play when it comes to Pinhook, a rural black village located in the middle of a Mississippi River floodway. The floodway, as a rural space, was subject to the perception that its main value could be measured in its farmland as opposed to the culture, traditions, and communal practices of black people who had established a town there. Pinhook, as a black space, was subject to the invisibility that attaches to black people who do not live in urban spaces. Our culture tends to ignore bodies that exist in spaces where we believe they should not be. Those bodies become illegitimate and unseen; they become illegible, unable to be read as significant, suffering an erasure that makes them vulnerable to acts of injustice, which are, in fact, acts of violence. As the INCITE! Women of Color Against Violence collective has written with regard to their activism efforts following the devastating disaster of Hurricane Katrina, "Invisibility can be used as a tool of oppression, because if people can't be seen, then their work can be discounted, their experience of violence and oppression can go without recourse, and their lives can be devalued" (*What Lies Beneath* xx). We see the same effect taking place with regard to Pinhook. In this case the stories that displaced residents tell about their experiences serve to make visible that which has been and could easily continue to be rendered invisible.

It is useful here to return to an interview we conducted at Pinhook Day in 2013, with LaToya Robinson-Tate, Debra's sister. In it she spoke to the emotions she was experiencing regarding the indifference shown toward displaced residents following the flood. We've quoted part of her comments in the previous chapter, but here we include her entire answer. Debra had sewn a memorial quilt to auction off during the event. On the quilt were affixed images of each of the houses in Pinhook that had been destroyed during the flood with captions underneath identifying each home's owner. When LaToya saw the quilt for the first time hanging from a wall in the VFW hall where the celebration was being held, she began to cry We asked her about her show of emotion:

> **E:** Why did the quilt make you cry?
>
> **LT:** Just because . . . it's like, you know, I can't go there and see it no more . . . but I can see it when it's . . . you know . . . it's just overwhelming . . . Can't go home anymore. That's all I pretty much have left of it. It's the pictures. And most of the houses are destroyed. It's just hard. It's hard. Like I said, I stay away from it as long as I can. Then I end up coming to Pinhook Day. Try to avoid it 'cause it's just hard to talk about, especially since, like I said, send your money to Syria . . . and everywhere else. And God bless those people in Oklahoma who need it. My goodness. I just feel like, kinda like, we were treated like, um, like the government was a pimp and just said, "Hey take this and get back on out there and do your thing." So take what you got and just keep moving. Yeah. That's why, just—it's hard.

The first part of LaToya's response to our question is about losing home as a place. This is an undeniably cruel reality of this disaster for displaced Pinhook residents. They have lost their home in that place forever. There is no going back to Pinhook in the floodway. That place will never be rebuilt or recreated. While residents have committed to reconstructing their town in another location outside of the floodway, there will always be meaning attached to the original location of their ancestral home. LaToya speaks both of how it is memory that she must rely on to keep her now destroyed home alive, but it is also memory that is the source of trauma and pain. Remembering that which can no longer be seen or experienced in that place is both something she wants to do and something that she wants to avoid because it is painful. Remembering Pinhook before, during, and after the breach is something that generates complex and conflicting emotions. Add to that the feeling of being treated with indifference and it becomes quite plain why this quilt with images of destroyed homes brought her to tears. LaToya expresses a sentiment we found quite common among displaced Pinhook residents. They feel that they lived in peace, obeyed laws, paid their taxes, observed regulations and conventions; they established a respectable community that was self-sufficient and even prosperous. But when decisions were being made about whether or not to destroy their community, they were not consulted. They were never even notified. Once the decision was made, they were not given effective warning about what was about to happen. And when it was all over, when their homes they had worked for lay ruined by water and mud, they were told neither the government nor the Army Corps of Engineers was responsible—that it was the result of a natural disaster.[5] And yet, if their homes had been destroyed because of a natural disaster, FEMA would have sped in to help them. Instead, the Corps simply explained that as an agency of the federal government they cannot be held responsible for following federal law. Just as the pimp in LaToya's analogy who will claim he is only working within the system to explain his exploitation of vulnerable women, the government, in this case, asserts its own innocence and claims no responsibility for the damage it has done. For the displaced residents of Pinhook, this is not being treated as a citizen. Indeed, this is being treated as if you do not matter or exist. Witness Twan's words, quoted earlier:

> It hurt to know that all that you did to try to build yourself up and you know get educated, and get something for yourself, and working that out in building my house there, and you had no say in it being gone. I had no say. For me that's been the hardest part for me, you know. I know the Corps did what they thought they had to do, but *put me at the table*. Engage me in conversation. Let's talk about it. But every time there was a meeting, it was with the farmers [she is referring to the area white farmers, many of whom did not actually live on their farms in the floodway.] When I read those articles now about the flood, it's all about the 180,000 or more acres. It's about those big farmers, and "a few homes," *and a few homes*.

Twan articulates a feeling of being "left out," of being overlooked, or treated with indifference. She references the fact that even after the breach occurred, news accounts focused mostly on the larger farmers who owned the majority of the acreage in the floodway. Somehow the plight of a destroyed town just didn't register compared to millions of dollars of lost crops and profit.

Worse still—while the government continues to delay remunerating the displaced citizens of Pinhook, others have cruelly accused them of being responsible for their own town's destruction. When residents began to post about their tragedy on social media websites such as Facebook, they were met with attacks and accusations. When they started to organize meetings and fundraisers to help displaced residents, they often had to answer questions about why they lived where they did from people living in surrounding towns and cities. It was as if once people finally realized that a town had actually existed in the floodway, they immediately wanted to know why it existed there. Debra talked about this in a later interview we conducted with her:

> They keep asking why were you down there? And it's like—well, it's not like I could live up here on my income. Like, I couldn't go out and buy a Cadillac if I only had bicycle money, so it's where we could live—Pinhook is where we could afford to live. And it's what we knew. We could move somewhere else, but we wouldn't have what we had in our home—Pinhook. We can say that to those who keep asking why were we there, and I answer: why do people live anywhere? Why do they live up in trailers in the woods, because they don't want to pay electric bills, for example. They live there, and that's what they chose, that's what they know and that's what they like. And that's why we were there. And I wouldn't trade it for anything! If we could go back, I mean, we would go back.

Interestingly, we see here a negative impact of speaking visibility. For the displaced Pinhook residents, the act of telling their story, in person, or through social media, can generate criticism from individuals just learning about the disaster. Why should Pinhook residents have to defend the location of their town? Debra simply compares the choices Pinhook residents made to those other American citizens have made to establish their communities where they desired. For Debra and other displaced residents of Pinhook, the choice was simple and clear about where they would live. Her explanation focuses first on the economic realities of the area. She doesn't mention that when her grandfather came to the Bootheel in the early 1940s the land in the spillway was the only land available for African American farmers to purchase. Debra only talks about the affordability. Both Debra and her sister Twan told us that it was significantly more affordable to buy land in Pinhook from neighbors or relatives than it would have been to buy land in towns like East Prairie or Sikeston. Ultimately, though, the reason they were there has to do with the people. In conversation after conversation, displaced citizens spoke about their town as a place set apart from the hustle and bustle of the larger towns in the area. They described it to us as a place where people took care of each other and cared about family before anything else. George Williams stressed this aspect of living in Pinhook as well:

> It was the people that made Pinhook what it is. Once they got that water calmed down, it was beautiful down there. You'd go by everybody's house and there'd be flowers out there, and they'd have the yard mowed. I mean, everybody just kept their property up. They'd work on their houses and if they needed help, they'd help with each other's. It was just a good place to live. Everybody knew everybody—all the kids growing up together there. Some of them grown and don't want to go back now. It just breaks your heart to go back down there now.

Aretha Robinson, Debra and Twan's mother, echoes the same sentiment about living in Pinhook:

> It is just so peaceful out there. People were loving and kind toward each other. You could get help—you could always get help. Something could happen and the community was always there for you, to help you. It was just a great place to live—peaceful and quiet. You didn't have to worry about the noise and robberies and stuff like that. We had some, of course, but very little, not like in town. And I really enjoyed living there.

Aretha Robinson's home in Pinhook, where she lived for seven years after her husband's death in 2004, was one of the largest in town. It was built by hand with stone her husband, Jim Robinson Jr., brought to the Bootheel from Tennessee. Her house became a kind of familiar landmark for us from the first time we visited the town together. Driving into Pinhook from the west on country road VV, it was one of the first houses you would encounter, and for us it was the very first house where we pulled over, got out of the car, and looked around. Venturing inside, we saw the clothes, furniture, awards, photos, and keepsakes that evidenced the lives of Aretha and Jim and their family still sitting in the house, now caked with thick layers of dried mud and dust. The windows were broken out, the walls smashed and askew, and it was plain to see that animals had been living there. Aretha finally returned to the site of her home when the ruined remains of the town were being demolished in 2015. By that time, the house had already been taken down, lovingly dismantled by her sons, as there was no hope to save the house nor of returning

Aretha Robinson home, 2013. Elaine J. Lawless.

to live on the property. Everything she'd accumulated in her life at Pinhook since 1955 was now gone. Only the memories remained.

For residents like Aretha, Twan, Debra, and George—just a few of the many who lost nearly everything they had—Pinhook was not only a place where they could afford to live, and could live without being bothered; it was a place where they had established and built a community that was theirs. They had worked the land together, worshipped together, and socialized together. When black farmers had first arrived in Pinhook, it was a place where they could exist away from the difficulties of racial strife and conflict. In 2011, it was a place where they could protect their children and grandchildren, where they could enjoy the benefits of living somewhere where people knew who they were and treated each other like family.

Buoyed by the special bonds of community, the displaced citizens continue their fight to rebuild the town destroyed by the actions celebrated in the dominant narratives constructed and disseminated by federal agencies. But their narrative, their account of their town and what it was—their stories about what happened to them that week the waters rose and that night the U.S. Army Corps of Engineers breached the Birds Point levee—serve as a counterpoint to all that. They continue to speak out, to make themselves heard, to insure that the world sees them now because it is the only way to fight against the bias that victimized them so. This continuing effort is difficult, especially

Twan Robinson at Pinhook Day, 2013. Elaine J. Lawless.

since they have been telling their story for over seven years (at the time of this book's printing) with no significant help in sight from government agencies. And yet, continuing to speak themselves into existence, to provide testimony to their experience as a community, is something they feel compelled to do. Twan described the difficulty of doing this.

> That's what they want; they want you to give up—that's what they want; they want you to give up. So, once again, you go back to that rock. God, help me to do better. So, that's what I'm doing. I'm angry with the situation, but it is what it is. God's got so much more for me and I just have to give him all the glory, and try to keep that joy. You can't let this taint your spirit. In my class, I talk about being resilient, and I try to be very resilient. God, please provide for me, and I'll try to do better. And he has. That's what I tell people, is that I have made religion first . . . and I try to be very respectful, like when we went to Jeff city up there and talked to the legislature, you know, I had that opportunity. But when I got up there to talk to them, I had that opportunity, I'm thinking I'm a social worker I can do this. And I thought I can do this! And I'd never talked to anybody about this. And so when I got up there, I had a podium, I just started crying. I felt so stupid, you know, but . . . and Debra was sitting there beside me and she says, "Are you okay?" "Are you all right?" And I'm just bawling. And I say, "God, you just do your part." But you do what you got to do.

The displaced residents of Pinhook have been doing their "part" for many years now without any success. But despite the difficulties that come with telling their story, they have continued to do so wherever and whenever they can. Their counter-narrative is essential to speak back against a dominant narrative that has subjected them to erasure, itself an act of violence. Indeed, if we, the authors, had never heard their stories, we might assume, like so many others do, that the government agencies that fought the flooding of the Missouri, Mississippi, and Ohio Rivers during the spring of 2011 had been completely triumphant in accomplishing what had to be done. We might believe that, as Major General John Peabody, current commander of the Mississippi Valley Division of the U.S. Army Corps of Engineers, argues, what was accomplished in the face of this flood was "astonishing" and "incredible," and that the narrative contained in publications like the Corps' *Room for the River* should "serve as educational tools and reference points for" future "citizens, decision makers" and "flood fighters" (1). Lives and property were saved, it is true, but the narrative contained in the glossy reports and publications of government agencies are not even close to being complete. They exclude the voices of those who suffered immeasurable loss—the loss of their homes and community. Alan Stein and Gene Preuss echo this point in their article on oral history in the aftermath of Hurricane Katrina. They assert that "oral history is a way of documenting urgent events and insights that might not be recorded" (39). More specifically, whether we call them oral histories or narratives of experience, it cannot be emphasized enough, that these stories, carried in the minds and hearts of ordinary people, can speak into existence the experience of those who have been "silenced by the dominant historiography due to race, gender, and class biases" (39).

This is why the narratives of displaced Pinhook residents—about their town, about the disaster, about the aftermath—matter so much. These stories of life in an African American town maintain the foundation of the community itself. Whether the displaced residents of Pinhook are ever able to rebuild their town—and we sincerely hope they will—the individual stories of this collective narrative will continue to guide them on their way.

CHAPTER SIX

WHY "HOME" MEANS
SO MUCH

The ache for home lives in all of us, the safe place
where we can go as we are and not be questioned.
—**MAYA ANGELOU,** *I Know Why the Caged Bird Sings*

At the "Pinhook Day" Celebration held in Sikeston, Missouri, in 2015, Robinson family members were delighted to welcome many relatives back home who now live far away, including Reginald, who lives in Wisconsin, and Donald, who makes his home in New York. We were delighted to meet many relatives—grandparents, great-grandparents, grandchildren, cousins, second cousins, uncles, aunts—and friends who had come from far and wide to share fellowship with the Pinhook community during the annual celebration. Following the festivities, at an impromptu late night meeting in the lobby of the Best Western Hotel in Miner (a section of Sikeston), where many of the Pinhook family/community were staying over the Memorial Day weekend, one of the visiting cousins explained to those who filled the hotel lobby how much it bothered him to travel so far only to meet with his family and the other former residents of Pinhook in a place other than Pinhook itself. "It doesn't feel like 'home' to me," he told them. "Why should I travel so far to come to Sikeston? 'Home' to me means actually meeting in Pinhook. Why can't we do that, even though there are no homes still standing there? Surely we could find a way to meet there, *in that place*, every year."[1] This cousin's concerns resulted in nearly an hour of discussion as the family and community members gathered in the lounge of the hotel. We were there listening to every word, openly welcomed by the Robinson family as supporters of the Pinhook efforts.

The Pinhook community took the cousin's question seriously and discussed the various possibilities. Could they raise large tents on the Pinhook property for the annual celebration? Perhaps they could erect a pole barn and keep all their necessities for the celebration in locked storage? Debra Robinson-Tarver was worried that a structure on the land would only invite more arson and that thieves would break into the locked areas because no one lived out there anymore to protect it. On the other hand, Debra's brother David was frustrated. He told the gathering he would not personally look forward to spending the weekend putting up large tents and then pulling them down. The Robinson family, he argued, already did much of the work for the celebration, and he, for one, did not want more work. He pointed out that all the food and celebration stuff would need to be taken to Pinhook. It sounded impossible to him. Debra and her sister Twan agreed the celebration had become too much work for one family and a few locals. They felt that other Pinhook former residents, even those who came from further away, needed to find ways to contribute more of their time and energy. The cousin's comments about how the place of Pinhook was actually "home" to him, even after all the structures were destroyed and erased from the landscape, relates exactly to this chapter on the importance of home and how home is directly

Intersection of state highways FF and VV with ruin of Pinhook Union Baptist Church in background, 2014. David Todd Lawrence.

connected to place for the community of Pinhook. This discussion also provides an opportunity to explore how community and place are interrelated.

That May, we had also traveled to Sikeston to document the fourth Pinhook Day celebration since the 2011 destructive flood. During a break from the festivities, we drove south from Sikeston to take more current photographs of the deserted town. Only a year after the 2014 celebration, we were astonished at how quickly the landscape of Pinhook was disappearing. We were expecting to find Miss Aretha's grand house, which the year before stood in shambles and was burned inside but still had some walls standing. We nearly drove right by the site of her house because only a flat concrete foundation remained on the property. All remnants of the house had been cleared away save for a pile of yellow stones that had been the siding on her house. We could only identify the house site by the basketball hoop still standing on the driveway and the gazebo that had been erected many years previous in honor of the civic work Jim Robinson Jr. had done for the area. The trees circling the gazebo were growing steadily, but the gazebo was collapsing and weeds prevented us from approaching it. The place was receding back into the space from whence the Pinhook men had hacked out an area that would become "home" for all the people who would eventually live in Pinhook (Tuan 6).

From the outset, Pinhook was conceived as a first "home" for a few African American farmers who traveled to Missouri. Jim Robinson Sr., Lewis

Moss, and their friends were the first African American farmers to own their own land in the area. They bought the land, cleared the land, built the town, and began farming their own crops in the 1940s. Prior to this, few African Americans had been "landed" farmers in southeastern Missouri or northern Arkansas. The historical, political, economic, and racial realities of the first part of the twentieth-century set the stage for these migrant field workers to stop traveling and create a grounded landscape, a "home" of their own, on Missouri soil. Yet, this possibility was fraught with difficulties—not the least was the fact that the only land available for them to buy was in the Birds Point–New Madrid, swampland that would need to be cleared long before any crops could be planted or houses built, land that would always be plagued with backwaters and flooding. The African American farmers who bought the land knew all of this from the outset: but what else could they do? The Flood Control Act of 1928 made it clear that the Army Corps could, if they deemed it necessary, flood the spillway.[2] Yet for nearly a century, this action had not been executed. For these farmers, losing their land and town in 2011 to a man-made flood was like losing their entire history as "landed" farmers. With the town Pinhook gone, the history of Pinhook could also disappear—a tragic loss for those who had built their dreams upon the place they had claimed as their own.

Concepts of "Home"

Sociologists, cultural geographers, environmental psychologists, anthropologists, and folklorists write about the importance of "home" and "place," defining "place" as a landscape that humans build, a "symbolic environment created by humans that confer meaning on nature and give the environment definition and form through a particular angle of vision that includes spiritual beliefs and values" (Miller and Rivera 1). Scholars have come to make a distinction between *space* and *place*—recognizing space as any undifferentiated land area that has not acquired a specific relationship with a group of humans (Tuan 6). When humans interact with space, they affect the area and confer particular meanings to it. In doing so, they create a designated place which bears a name they have given to it. Many scholars turn to Keith Basso's seminal work, *Wisdom Sits in Places*, in which he discusses the importance of "place making," which he defines as the ordinary way individuals begin to think about particular places and develop a way of understanding these important human questions: "What happened here? Who was involved? What was it like? Why should it matter?" (Basso 5). Basso's work was influenced by the work of Henri Lefebvre, who began writing about the "production of space" in the 1990s. Lefebvre, a Marxist, related a sense of place (as encountered in cultural landscapes) to the political economy, noting that societies shape a "distinctive social space that meets its intertwined requirements for economic production and social reproduction" (qtd in Miller and Rivera 12). Basso's questions relate directly to our work on Pinhook, Missouri, and the conception of "home" and "place" that was created there, beginning in 1941.

✦ ✦ ✦

The particular racialized history of African American people in southeastern Missouri had denied them the right to "stay put" in one place until 1941, when they were able to create a landscape that was their very own. Lefebvre's conceptions of the "production of space" also directly relate to the production of Pinhook, Missouri, the economic and political economy of Missouri in the early 1940s, and to how Pinhook residents aspired to create a new landscape different from those of their forbearers—as slaves, sharecroppers, migrant workers, and tenant farmers. In Pinhook they could build a grounded landscape they designed themselves. It is critical to see this effort as a political act, defying those who would rather not see African American farmers succeed. Lefebvre recognized how majority groups work to restrict the political rights and economic growth of minority groups by limiting their access to space, noting that ghettos, barrios, internment camps, Indian reservations, plantations, and migrant worker camps are all "political territories" with laws governing them to enforce the majority territories' policies and deny any rights to the inhabitants of the camps. Recent scholars are pointing to the mass incarceration of black men as a further example of a new, systematic effort to cage and control black males in this country, an effort that has been referred to as "the new Jim Crow" (Alexander 2012). In contrast, the original Pinhook residents rejected the dominant culture's efforts to ghettoize, control, and terrorize them by building instead their own environment. By establishing their own town in Pinhook, they were secure in demanding their rights as citizens of Missouri. It was not their intention to be segregated. They would have preferred to find friendly faces in the area towns and cooperative farm machinery retailers, for example, to help them with their equipment failures, but clearly they chose quiet isolation over the ghettoized African American areas in Charleston, East Prairie, Sikeston, and even St. Louis.

The notion of place-making holds particular resonance for this work on Pinhook. Sociologists Demond Shondell Miller and Jason David Rivera note how "place" comes to hold the "intersections of actions, conceptions, and the physical environment" together (13), while assisting in the "community's transference of [their] values and culture to future generations and outsiders" (14). Our interviews with the displaced residents of Pinhook, as well as the written testimonies of many who no longer actually live there but who continue to call Pinhook "home," all attest to how their creation of place was such a good example of how this implantation of meaning operates in the real world.

Most communities have so many layers of history that it is nearly impossible to peel them all off to see how the first intentions of the ancestors were carried through to later generations. With Pinhook, however, we have the possibility of seeing this creation and transference of values and culture at work within one century. The testimonies of those who lived there further support the notion that "places" have an "incorporation" ability because they act as the backdrop for human activities and interpersonal involvement: "Place-specific human activity transforms space into a place" (Miller and Rivera 13). What began as "undifferentiated space" becomes "place" as people shape it and endow it with value. Doing so provides people with the sense of belonging; those involved become allied to the "place" with attachment and love (Miller and Rivera 14).

The swampland within the spillway of the Mississippi River holds special meaning for all the people who ever lived in Pinhook. Their community history and shared stories are grounded in their collective efforts to carve out a place for themselves. Their fathers and grandfathers literally pulled the roots out of that swampland and drained the sluggish water to create a place they could call home; the most inhospitable space in southeastern Missouri, the only land they could buy, was developed by human hands to become the dearly beloved place they called Pinhook. This land means far more to these people than simply the fact that it is a small town in which they lived. Miller and Rivera remind us that people's ability to "bond" with certain places occurs through the interplay of emotions, knowledge, beliefs, behaviors, and actions in relation to a particular place. Through the production of a new landscape, this "place" comes to emphasize the quality of a community's "being in the world." This is manifested so clearly in the case of the original Pinhook families. The clearing of this land—land they now owned (regardless of the risk management factors)—the building of the town, the planting of their crops, verified for them that they could be self-sufficient citizens. Miller and Rivera might call this the "lived topography" of this part of the Missouri Bootheel.

Although they knew their town and land could be flooded, once the landed migrants accepted the mantle of citizenship, it was perfectly reasonable that this community would assume their hard work and valued participation in the "American dream" would afford them some rights and reciprocity from the government. Miller and Rivera explain that, "the role of people's attachment to a place, and ultimately a place within a physical landscape, results in their connection to the society at large" (2008:1). By no longer asking others to "take care of them," but demonstrating how they could care for themselves, build a community, plant crops, and maintain civility and proud homes, gardens and yards, they were doing what they considered their part of the unspoken bargain of citizenship.

Critical race theory would remind us how this bargain was ruptured by the destruction of the town without any discussion by the institutions that disregarded their rights to be there. The progress that had been made over nearly a century of hard work was erased within a matter of hours. Part of the former residents' frustration, now that Pinhook is gone, is the realization that, in the end, none of this seemed to matter in 2011 when the Army Corps of Engineers so easily flooded them out without even having a conversation with them about the consequences. Ironically (or not), Miller and Rivera, in their 2008 book, state the following, so appropriate for this discussion of the flooding of Pinhook in 2011: "What happened in New Orleans with Katrina has messages for all who live along the Mississippi River and its series of levees and landscape management that can, at any time, topple given natural occurrences. We all live in a 'disaster subculture,' coping with recurrent threats to our cultural and social infrastructure" (142). This may be true, but people of color are much more likely to exist within this subculture at odds with the powers that be and subject to the whims of those who continue to overlook or even ignore the rights of those on the margins of mainstream American society.

Environmental psychologists and sociologists have been at the forefront of documenting the disastrous effects Hurricanes Katrina and Rita had on the southern American coastline communities in 2005. Most of the scholarship that has emerged from Katrina and related disasters has pivoted on concepts of "home" and what happens when "home" is gone, destroyed, no longer available to those who lived there. Furthermore, folklorists and other humanists have been able to enter this discussion by offering post-disaster ethnographic research that relies on interviews with the victims of disasters to articulate both what "home" means and what the destruction of "home" also means for those people who lose their homes.

In writing about Pinhook, we are drawn to all of these conversations for the insights they can provide for our discussion of what has happened to Pinhook. In addition, scholars interested in the concept of home have helped us to identify what the ethnographic field researcher can bring to these discussions (Behar 2009; Lawless 2011; Straight 2015). Our own work interviewing the dislocated victims of the 2011 flood in southern Missouri has answered many questions for us. The words of the displaced residents of Pinhook best articulate both the concept of "home," as well as the acute devastation that ensues when a community's "home" is lost.

Sociologists are quick to note that a single neighborhood never exists separate from all the other neighborhoods that are in close proximity to it. Pinhook farmers may not have known much about the towns twenty miles away, but they knew about the white farmers who lived close by, and they knew about the towns where their children went to school. By staying in one place, they recognized their place within the region. Furthermore, to address the concerns of "double consciousness" W. E. B. DuBois so famously identified in *The Souls of Black Folk*, the African American citizens of Pinhook actually knew that the surrounding communities knew about their town and knew it as a stable African American farming community (DuBois 3). Through this identification, they might have been able to more easily manage DuBois's notion that African American people are always straddling two identities— their own and the identity that is imposed on them by white society. Establishing a secure and stable "home" may have contributed to their ability to see themselves as they had defined themselves as opposed to how white outsiders did. Escaping the system in which white landlords dictated economic and social terms was integral to this social and mental stability. Recognized neighborhoods are about people who "stayed put," as folklorist Kathy Roberts puts it in her work on Appalachian mining communities, and stable communities suggest stable residents (Roberts 407).

According to Roberts, "landowning is a distinct and powerful way that people anchor themselves and their families in place" (408). For nearly a century, Pinhook people thought of themselves as hard-working people, farmers, rural Americans, landowners, not as subaltern figures on the margins of mainstream society. Roberts rightly asserts that "Landscape is arguably one of the most publicly visible expressions of place"; yet, she argues, place studies in the field of folklore have overlooked one of the most important factors underlying the look and feel of landscapes: land-tenure (408, 409). Roberts argues, "Our understanding of attachments to place and home, and of the performative processes that bring them into being, would be enriched by insights into how people acquire and maintain the very ground on which they make their lives" (409). Consider that the Pinhook people were not only some of the first migrant workers to settle in one place, but they were the first African Americans to buy land and settle in one place in southeastern Missouri in the early 1940s. That they were successful in clearing the land, tending crops, and building a self-sufficient town that survived through several generations, makes their success even more significant. And the benefits of such success were many. Jim Robinson Sr. made a conscious decision to "not go further north" when he arrived in southern Missouri's Bootheel region where he could buy land. Robinson and his friends did not want to join the northern migration of African Americans to the northern urban areas. Instinctively and by experience, they trusted that rural residents could "enjoy the benefits of strong, stable, and geographically grounded social networks" (Roberts 429). As Roberts explains, "These benefits involve the kind of social aid many of us outsource—child and elder care; food production and exchange; transportation; home and vehicle repairs; grounds upkeep" (Roberts 429). The economic and emotional support derived from what anthropologist Anita Puckett calls "belongin' networks" are not to be underestimated (2000).

In the origin story of Pinhook, as related by members of the Robinson family in the previous chapters, several family names appear alongside the larger-than-life Jim Robinson Sr. In fact, over time, the list of families who lived in Pinhook grew to over fifty families, with many extended lines developing over the years. Many people who learn about the destruction of Pinhook today are quick to ask how many people were affected. Many are eager to note that the "good news is that no one was killed." Although these are legitimate concerns, the answers are more complex than meets the eye. County records indicate that only thirty to sixty people were actually living in Pinhook at the time of the flood. These figures are misleading, however, and do not reflect the complex living arrangements of many Pinhook residents and their extended families. For example, Miss Aretha Robinson had a house in Pinhook that was home to herself and her husband, Jim Jr., but their home was also shared with her son, Bernard "Bert" Robinson, who is a long-haul trucker. At times, her daughter, LaToya, also lived with her mother in the large Pinhook home. Grandchildren often resided at the house, as did nieces and nephews when circumstances required them to stay with her. Similarly, Debra Robinson-Tarver had a house in Pinhook where she was a "single resident." However, for long periods of time her a daughter also lived with her, as did her daughter's young son. Twan, Debra's sister, also owned her own home in Pinhook as a "single resident," yet over the years many Robinson family members and Pinhook "family" members stayed in her house as well. In truth, one could take the list of family names for the Pinhook residents and multiply each name by as many as three, four, or even ten over time. When we visit with the former Pinhook community members at "Pinhook Day" each year, they recount months, summers, and even years living in Pinhook over their lifetime and their children's lifetime. Hence, simply asking how many people lived in Pinhook when it was flooded diminishes the reality of the town as "home" to far more people than can readily be assessed.

Similarly, the media has consistently reported that Pinhook was populated by a small number of "elderly women." Again, this is a distortion of the actual people who lived there. Twan Robinson and Debra Robinson-Tarver are not elderly, and they owned homes in Pinhook until the day it was destroyed. Twan had more recently built her home there because she could build a much nicer home in Pinhook than she could other places in the area. This was an attractive benefit of living in Pinhook, the cost of living was low and land was still inexpensive. Other members of the Robinson, Moss, and other families continued to live in Pinhook, some of them middle-aged and elderly men, like George Williams and Lynell Robinson, both of whom had large families who inhabited their homes with them for many years and called Pinhook home.

Although many detractors seek to minimize what happen to Pinhook by noting how small the community was or how few people the flood displaced, the following list represents some of the surnames of the African American residents of Pinhook over the years. Debra Robinson-Tarver and her sisters worked to include all the family names for us they could recall: Adams, Smith, Ward, Simpkins, Walker, Joyner, Parker, Johnson, Thomas, Carter, Williams, Robinson, Jefro, Jones, Anderson, Moss, Bradley, Myric, Oliver, Strayhorn, Bankhed, McFadden, Spillers, Speller, Miner, Cross, Mac, Gallon, Mason, Kindle, Sutton, Franklin, Sullivan, Stokes, Verses, Rice, Craig, Garrison, and Yarbor. Many of the members of these families wrote testimonies about the loss of Pinhook and sent them to Debra when she began the laborious task of submitting paperwork for financial assistance to rebuild their town. She shared them with us. The language used by the former residents supports the scholarly discussions on the importance of home and adds many much-needed emotional aspects as well.

The Effects of Disaster on Those Who Call it "Home"

Fittingly, the disasters of Katrina and Rita in the southern states of the U.S. provided an ideal research site for scholars who had been trying to conceptualize notions of place making and place attachment. In fact, the flooding, the toxic wastes that were added to the disaster, and the ineffective governmental assistance to those in need helped to peel back some of the historical layers obscured by time and history. The racialized, classed, and gendered aspects of the disaster were laid bare as the nation watched bodies floating in waters muddied by feces and people calling for aid that did not arrive in time. Not surprisingly, the loss of "home" became the repeated refrain in the scores of books that have emerged in the years since the hurricane disasters. Miller and Rivera state that their book is interested in the cultural, economic and political landscapes more than the psychological and emotional landscapes— yet, they say the core of their book is about "loss," which demands that their book also recognizes the personal and the emotional response to loss—and it is, noting the importance of physical landscapes, psychological landscapes, emotional landscapes, social landscapes, economic landscapes, and political landscapes. Of course, we could continue the list with historical landscapes, racial landscapes, and ethnic landscapes that bear witness to the various degrees of "loss" encountered by those who once lived there.

Scholars often use the definition of disaster, and the creation of a "disas- ter landscape," first proposed by Fritz (1961) and Barton (1970), to discuss disaster as "any event concentrated in time and space in which a social or a relatively self-sufficient sub-division of society undergoes severe damage and incurs losses to its members and physical appurtenances [so] that the social structure is disrupted and the fulfillment of all or some of the essential func- tions of the society is prevented" (Barton 665). At the core of their work with disasters, scholars are concerned with the concept of loss—which for many is "so profound that some people have failed to fully recover from the environ- mental assault" (Miller and Rivera 5). A loss of culture can create an "identity crisis for the individuals" involved. Surely, this is apparent for all the former residents of this small African American town in Missouri's Bootheel. In fact, it is appropriate to quote Silverstein here, who claimed that "disasters involve an abrupt transition from the mundane, relatively safe life into an environ- ment of chaos and hell" (3). He would agree with Miller and Rivera that the key to understanding disaster is not the event itself, but the degree to which it 1) alters existing relationships between individuals and groups; 2) disrupts community norms; and 3) compels participants/victims to alter their notions of where they, as humans, fit into the cycle of life (4).

When disasters strike, scholars writing on this topic stress how an abrupt disruption of the landscape can create a multitude of reactions—from initial shock, to dismay, psychological depression, anger, disability, fear and malaise; and, the "utter contempt" for those suffering only adds to the suffering of the victims (Miller and Rivera 93). Most of the scholars on disasters similarly conclude that man-made disasters lead to a different set of responses than do "natural" disasters—although certainly some, including Chester Hartman and Gregory Squires, argue there is no such thing as a natural disaster (2006). Disasters perceived to be "natural" seem to be easier for victims to compre- hend—they are often seen as "acts of God," making it more difficult to assess blame and the incompetence of others. Certainly, Hartman and Squires point to a new "fact" of modern global realities—nature and culture are so intertwined at this point it is, indeed, difficult to say whether a disaster is "natural" or "man-made."

In the case of Pinhook, the displaced residents identify the disaster that destroyed their town as "man-made." Although there was certainly a great deal of rain in the northern U.S. that resulted in "natural" flooding of the Mississippi and Missouri Rivers in early 2011, from the Canadian border south all the way to Missouri, they mark the breach of the Birds Point levee by the Army Corp of Engineers as the "man-made" flooding of their land and the indifferent destruction of their town. Human beings made decisions about that breach, and a federal judge signed a legal decision allowing the Corps to blow the levee at Birds Point, ostensibly to "save" Cairo, Illinois, a declining post-urban space across the river from the Missouri Bootheel. Even this decision is suspect. Cairo, Illinois, is a mere shell of the booming river town it once was in 1928 when the Flood Control Act was first initiated. Both Missouri and Illinois residents know that the challenges that Cairo has endured mean that it is no longer the place it was when the plan was put into effect. This is a case where policy decisions were driven by circumstances no longer in order. Those circumstances, of course, were understood at the time in terms of privilege and presumptions that obscured any justifiable argument to save a stable African American community. Worse—the people of Pinhook did not even get the chance to make that argument—they were not "invited to the table." The first they learned of the potential breach was when they heard rumors of a mandatory evacuation. Furthermore, no governmental entity was sent to help them evacuate. They did it all on their own. These factors made this "man-made" disaster even harder for the people of Pinhook to accept. Where were their rights as citizens? How could they be so easily ignored and rendered homeless?

In their collection of essays on loss, Zinner and Williams quote Therese Rondo who identifies "group survivorship" as reflected in both acute grief and traumatic stress. In order to survive, people must develop trauma mastery and loss accommodation. Rondo is quick to assert that groups are "more than merely the sum of the members" (qtd. in Zinner xviii). She defines trauma as "any experience generating intense anxiety too powerful to be assimilated or dealt with in 'typical fashion,' overwhelming the individual and/or the group, engendering feelings of loss of control, helplessness, and other flooding affects" (qtd. in Zinner xviii). Importantly for our study of the loss of Pinhook, Rondo, Zinner, and Williams note that loss and trauma are often accompanied by "the shattering of fundamental assumptions on which life has been predicated" (xviii). Factors that lead to the most severe traumas include the lack of preparedness for the occurrence of the event, lack of controllability of the event, lack of warning, chaos accompanying evacuation, culmination of losses, duration, unresolved past traumas. All of these factors are clearly present in the case of Pinhook. Furthermore, these scholars argue, if the tragedy includes mass dislocation or relocation and property destruction, the catastrophe may challenge the very identity and structure of the community: "The essence of a stable community lies in the shared belief that a group of people 'belong.' A cohesive community affords a 'certain, safe, and wholesome environment in which individuals can lead effective, enriching, and safe lives'" (242). The importance of the restoration of this stability is the key to healing. Healing will depend on "social networks that include kinship, religious practice and beliefs, sociopolitical systems [that can help], and cultural practices."

✦　✦　✦

This discussion leads us back to the argument that African American stories in the accounts of Pinhook matter. Zinner and Williams note that "the 'cultural narrative' of the group, that is, *the life and story of the group, before the disaster* plays heavily into the drama of restoration and adjustment" (242). Unfortunately for the former residents of Pinhook, the loss of their homes, their church, and their community, the integration of their collective cultural narrative before the flood of 2011 cannot be reconciled with the dominant cultural narrative following the flood. That historical narrative was a narrative of success. Their stories dispelled the notion of African Americans who did not "belong" in the rural landscape as landed farmers. The success and the sustainability of their town defied the norms for black people in southeastern Missouri. Their story stood as a challenge to all those who might deny them their rights as citizens.

Significantly, following their loss, Zimmer and Williams ask, "How can the catastrophe be incorporated into the group's historical and cultural view?" (242). Currently, there is no way to incorporate the loss of Pinhook in the former residents' narratives. The 2016 narrative echoes the narratives of 1940 when African Americans people were denied the right to buy land on higher ground. The discrimination they've endured from the governmental agencies that were created for the sole purpose of providing aid to citizens who lose their property and their homes satisfies none of their hunger to be treated fairly as Missouri citizens. As Aretha Robinson has told us more than once, "they say this has nothing to do with race. Then why does it feel like it has everything to do with race?"

CONCLUSION: THE POWER OF
HOPE THROUGH COMMUNITY

Our struggle for racial justice, a struggle we must continue even if—as I contend here—
racism is an integral, permanent, and indestructible component of this society. The challenge
has been to tell what I view as the truth about racism without causing disabling despair.
—**DERRICK BELL,** *Faces from the Bottom of the Well*

Frustrations Abound

When we first embarked on this endeavor in Missouri's Bootheel region, our intention was to write a book about the Mississippi River flood of 2011 and the thoughtless destruction of the African American town of Pinhook, located in the Birds Point–New Madrid Floodway. We wanted to document what had happened and why. We presumed also that our work would follow the displaced Pinhook residents as they applied for funding and began the slow, but hopeful, process of rebuilding their town. We pledged to stand with them in their claim that the government had, in fact, destroyed their town, and that it should make good on the promise of funding for relocation and rebuilding Pinhook. Similarly, when we began the filming that would become our documentary film, *Taking Pinhook*, we hoped the final scenes would be filled with images of people with hammers building houses. In 2012, these outcomes seemed to be a possibility, although we all had our doubts about what might actually happen. Since those first few months of fieldwork in southern Missouri, we have come to understand much more about the racial politics in Missouri's Bootheel region and have recognized how race may have factored into the decision to flood the spillway and why destroying the town of Pinhook was not seen as problematic for government officials who made that call.

Missouri's Bootheel region, particularly the counties that were flooded (Mississippi, Pemiscot, Dunklin, New Madrid, Stoddard, and parts of other contiguous counties), has a reputation for being an underserved and under-resourced region with high levels of poverty and unemployment. Yet, we were taken aback by what Judge Stephen N. Limbaugh said to us when we asked him whether or not the existence of a town called Pinhook had been discussed during the deliberations on whether the Corps could breach the levee. Self-possessed and utterly confident, he flipped through the hundreds of pages of court documentation, while assuring us, "Yes, yes, there was a little bit of testimony about that area—yeah, they had a couple of landowners testify. . . . Yeah, Yeah, I'm sure it was. Yeah." Yet, just minutes before, he had made statements that seemed to dismiss the Bootheel as insignificant. He told us that the Bootheel was still "a feudal society." For emphasis, he reiterated, "That's how it is. It's a fact."

The Bootheel is largely a poor, rural region with little or no industry beyond agriculture and no towns larger than Sikeston, which boasted a population of 16,494 in 2013. Mississippi County, where Pinhook was located, has one of the largest populations of African Americans in the state and is also one of the poorest. Given the definition of a "feudal society," we wondered just what the judge meant with his remark. Certainly, at one time, his reference might have suggested a hierarchical social strata with (white) landowners as the "lords" and the (African American) farmworkers as "vassals" or "serfs." In 2013, when we interviewed him, his remark suggested, instead, a commonly-held negative stereotype about the Bootheel and the people who live there. For some who disparage the region as backward and of little value, there may be a generalized opinion that the rural poor in this region fit what historian Marc Lamont Hill has recently characterized as "nobodies," those who are systematically disadvantaged, particularly black and brown people who are regarded in this country as persons who can easily be ignored if they are seen as not worthy of attention or regard (Hill).

Most certainly, the judge's remark suggests that he did not know anything about the black farmers of Pinhook who owned and operated their own land in the Bootheel and had done so for over seventy years. Even though Pinhook has been clearly marked on Missouri state maps for more than fifty years, we may assume the judge had no knowledge of the actual community of Pinhook, a town complete with well-groomed yards and houses, a stately church and community center, streets marked with standard street signs, and carefully tended, productive fields. Perhaps the Army Corps of Engineers did not know anything about this town either, or they might not have been so quick to destroy what the Pinhook farmers had developed in the Bootheel. On the other hand, perhaps they would not have cared to know the facts about Pinhook and might have proceeded with the breach and the intentional flooding regardless. The result was basically the same: ignore the town and the residents who lived there; flood it, and it disappears. The implication being: those people down there are, after all, "nobodies."

As we have pointed out in the previous chapters, a wide variety of factors related to race and class were put into play even before the 1940s, continued to affect the Pinhook community up until the breach in 2011, and persist to this day. We have attempted to articulate some of the reasons the folks residing in this rural town were virtually invisible to those making decisions about the raging Mississippi River in 2011. Ignorance and incorrect assumptions about those living in the spillway worked in tandem to make it possible for the Army Corps and the legal and regional emergency agencies involved to ignore Pinhook residents and to refuse to include them in the discussions prior to the breach, to assist them in their evacuation and temporary housing, and, then, to provide the appropriate assistance for funding and restitution following the breach. Exactly what did happen to the Pinhook community immediately after the flooding, and for years following, has become a way of life for the displaced people—a life of one crushing disappointment after another.

✦ ✦ ✦

Only days after the flood, the assessment of the damage done was acknowledged as severe and worthy of federal funding for restitution. Kay Phillips, FEMA Individual Assistance Specialist, speaking after the flood, assured those who had been displaced that help was available to them.

I think the devastation here was terrible. I find that the extent of the damage to be such that folks will have to make a pretty serious decision as to whether or not they want to try to rebuild in Pinhook and be in compliance with National Flood Insurance requirements which requires elevations that they will have to verify with their local flood plain manager or make the decision to try and relocate the entire community of Pinhook as a whole and rebuild the community. After a flooding disaster, residents may get help relocating to safer ground through the Hazard Mitigation Grant Program, a FEMA-funded program administered by the State.[1]

Immediately, upon hearing this assessment, the displaced residents of Pinhook began the arduous task of filling out applications for block grants for restitution and funding to rebuild their town. Debra Robinson-Tarver, with the help of other displaced Pinhook residents, filled out mountains of paperwork, filed and refiled, revised and resubmitted hundreds of pages of grants for funding from FEMA. At first, they assumed they would be able to rebuild their homes on the original site of their town. Rather quickly, however, the Corps informed the citizens that because their town was located within the spillway, future flooding would likely destroy the town again. In addition, rebuilt structures would have to adhere to National Flood Insurance regulations, meaning they would all need to be elevated on twelve- to fifteen-foot stilts. As Aretha Robinson and George Williams both pointed out to us, building their houses on stilts was not a feasible plan for the townspeople. It seemed a ludicrous plan to them, one strategically engineered to fail. Their frustrations grew.

One year went by, then two, three, four, five, six, and now, seven years have passed.

Sometime in late 2014, we were informed by Debra Robinson-Tarver that FEMA had agreed to offer a buyout for the land owned by the Pinhook former residents. FEMA would work with them to rebuild some of their homes, she had been told, on land that was not within the spillway. While they were pleased to hear that FEMA was finally willing to talk about a buyout for their land in Pinhook, Debra described to us how devastating this proposition was for the Pinhook people. The town, as it sat centered within the fields they farmed together, was the heart of Pinhook. It sealed their community in time, place, and history. Working the fields only yards from their backyards provided a way for the community to work together and maintain their independence and sustain their way of life. Building a new Pinhook miles away from their farmland was another concession they were sad to accept. As if this was not already difficult enough, FEMA put the responsibility for locating possible town sites on the Pinhook residents themselves.

The demands were clear: find a place to rebuild and maybe we will provide the funding for a buyout. What ensued were months and years of heartbreaking negotiations. Debra and her people followed ads, contacted landowners, pleaded with those they knew to help them locate land they could buy—land that would meet all the funding criteria, which included enough acreage for the entire town, plots for each former resident who wanted to rebuild a house—land that would already have all necessary and legal water, sewer, and electricity requirements. At least twice, perhaps three times, they identified a plot of land that fit most of the FEMA requirements, but problems asserted themselves almost immediately. It was difficult for them to learn that area neighbors did not want to sell to African Americans intent upon building a town in their midst. This happened more than once. Eventually, other plots of land were identified, but FEMA found problems with each plot that was suggested—requirements were not appropriately in place, no electricity lines, inadequate water supply, inappropriate sewer, the list went on and on. More than once, we were notified that "big news" was coming, yet within weeks Debra would let us know the plans had fallen through once again.

✦ ✦ ✦

We were cautiously surprised to get a phone call from Debra Robinson-Tarver in late July 2016, informing us that some of the Pinhook community members were poised to buy plots of land on the outskirts of Charleston, Missouri, just a few miles from the original Pinhook site. She told us a plot of land had met with the approval of FEMA as an appropriate site for the relocation of their town. On land provided by a possible community development block grant, she explained, some Pinhook residents were making plans to build new homes with the help of area organizations who had already pledged their assistance, including the Mennonite Disaster Service, Church World Service,[2] and other religious and social groups.

We were eager with new questions. Which of the former residents were buying the land and building new homes? How much land had been made available? How much money was FEMA pledging for the project? As she had done so many times before, Debra was reluctant to share many details with us. Certainly, she was happy to let us know her good news—that the funding would be coming through! Yet, the more we plied her with questions, the less we seemed to learn. A few weeks later, we still did not have very many details, but that was typical of our dealings with the Pinhook community. They wanted us to share their good news, but they had learned to temper their excitement because of promises broken, plans undone, and government officials not coming through. With the blatant discrimination and disregard this community has endured for nearly a century, it is no surprise they were less than eager to spill all the still precarious details. Perhaps it was superstition; more likely it was caution bred by past experience, disappointment, and rejection.

While we sensed Debra was truly hopeful that this time this opportunity would be approved, we were hesitant to believe this long-awaited conclusion to their story was actually going to happen. To our dismay, we turned out to be correct. The city of Charleston proved an unwilling partner with the people of Pinhook, voting not to extend city services to the potential parcel of land Pinhook residents wanted to purchase. Connecting the land to necessary utilities without the city annexing the property would have been too expensive for the Pinhook residents and thus, the deal fell through. Residents found another potential plot of land near another small town in Missouri later in the year, but that deal fell through as well. After years of endless, frustrating work, the displaced residents were no better off than they were when we first met them.

The Power of Community

In our time working with the displaced residents of Pinhook, we have learned valuable lessons about institutional injustice, discrimination, disregard and ignorance. None of this has actually surprised us. The state of racial tension and unrest in our country at the present time reminds us that the injustices experienced by the displaced African American residents of Pinhook are part of a larger system and not an isolated incident. On the other hand, we have learned even more in the past several years about community solidarity, persistence, and the power of struggle by documenting the actions of our Pinhook collaborators. It is the fact of their strength and perseverance in the face of institutional opposition that has actually surprised us.

Our attempts to understand the Pinhook community's frame of mind, as perhaps different from our own (as outsiders), have guided us to develop a theory of hope for racial justice that relies not so much on institutional commitments to justice for all, but one that hinges more upon the potential power that stems from community stability, traditions, resilience, and agency. Our reading of the counter-narrative of Pinhook, recounted to us through the stories of this community's experiences, resists critical race theory (CRT) founder Derrick Bell's famous image of people of color as those residing "at the bottom of the well," an image that posits vulnerable populations as powerless victims. While Bell admits that "our actions" against racism and injustice may be "of more help to the system we despise than to the victims of that systems whom we are trying to help" (198–199), he maintains that we must all let down our "ropes" to help each other, because "Only by working together is escape [from injustice] possible" (*The Derrick Bell Reader* 311). Such an approach to justice through community solidarity and action would not preclude our helping the people of Pinhook, and certainly it does not suggest that people of color should continue to struggle on their own without aid from others, but it does suggest that hope may best be realized when a community stands in its own power and demands justice, even while working within the very institutions that operate to limit its power and keep it from succeeding. As Bell explains, African American history itself is "a story less of success than of survival through an unremitting struggle that leaves no room for giving up" (*Faces at the Bottom of the Well* 200). The survival of Pinhook is certainly a part of that story.

Our admiration for this dedicated community of African Americans confirms what those writing within critical race theory have come to recognize—that the unified struggle is what is important and that even small victories won through solidarity can change the face of racial and social justice in the United States. The kind of solidarity and agency we have seen in the efforts of the Pinhook community affirm that despair does not have to prevail. Bell reminds us that,

> The civil rights movement is, after all, much more than the totality of the judicial decisions, the antidiscrimination laws, and the changes in racial relationships reflected in those legal milestones. *The movement is a spiritual manifestation of the continuing faith of a people who have never truly gained their rights in a nation committed by its basic law to the freedom of all.* (*And Are We Not Saved* xi, emphasis added)

Bell identified the civil rights movement as a "phenomenon of rights gained, then lost, then gained again—a phenomenon that continues to surprise even though the cyclical experience of blacks in this country predates the Constitution by more than one hundred years" (*And We Are Not Saved* xi). His encouragement to fight the good fight follows from the questions that must be asked: "With the realization that the salvation of racial equality has eluded us again, questions arise from the ashes of our expectations: How have we failed—and why? What does this failure mean—for Black people and for whites? Where do we go from here? Should we redirect the quest for racial justice?" (*And We Are Not Saved* 3). Bell, with Marc Lamont Hill and other CRT scholars, admits many people are currently asking these questions without offering solutions. While we recognize it is depressing to understand that full racial equality may not be realized in our time, those in the movement assure us that "tangible progress *has been made*" (*And We Are Not Saved* 5). Nearly hidden in his discussion of the struggle for justice, Bell's most hopeful line remains more a murmur than a shout from the rooftops: "The pull of unfinished business is sufficient to strengthen and spur determination" (*And We Are Not Saved* 5). There is much unfinished business in the Missouri Bootheel.

Debra Robinson-Tarver claims she has the best lawyer anyone could possibly have and there is no way to pay him except to trust that by standing together the Pinhook community will prevail. Debra has relied on the strength of her community and her belief in God to right the wrongs that have been perpetrated against her people. And she has been consistent in her belief that truth and justice will prevail. Her generosity of spirit has prevented her from bitterness and public recriminations. Indeed, no other than Dr. Martin Luther King noted that his "adversaries expected him to harden into a grim and desperate man" (330). When that did not happen, he identified the opposition's failure as its inability "to perceive the sense of affirmation generated by the challenge of embracing struggle and surmounting obstacles" (330). Seen in this light, the struggle of the Pinhook community has been both courageous and victorious, at least to a point, and it continues to be a struggle based on hope and confidence, strength and passion, largely because they have relied on community. They have rallied in the face of terrible odds; they have faced down powerful cultural and governmental institutions without rancor; and they have relied on their faith in each other and their faith in God to get them through.

For the past seven years, we have watched the displaced people of Pinhook hold to their dignity in the face of extreme difficulties. When they are called to speak in public about their situation, they respond in measured tones, unless they crumple in tears as Twan once did at a hearing. They are slow to anger and resist becoming strident, and they reject the invitation to be perceived as helpless victims. We sincerely hope our book honors their accomplishments and dedication to their community and their shared traditions, strengths, and faith. Even Marc Hill ends his rather depressing history of how African Americans have been, and continue to be, devalued in American life on a note of hope: "The People have asserted that they are, in fact, Somebody. In doing so, they offer hope that another world is indeed possible, that empires eventually fall, and that freedom is closer than we think" (184).

✦ ✦ ✦

This case study of one African American town's plight in the face of what we are calling persistent discrimination, indifference, disregard, and environmental racism may not help prevent a repeat scenario anytime in the future, but we are committed to documenting injustices where they occur, to naming the offenders and the offences, and to take a stand that openly rejects all actions that suggest that some communities of American citizens are "less-than" others and therefore not eligible for the government's very best efforts at protection and assistance for their bodily safety, their happiness, and their preferred way of life. By exposing what happened to Pinhook, Missouri, and by highlighting the difficulties displaced residents continue to have in their efforts to rebuild their town, our intention is to keep governmental institutions responsible to all citizens, regardless of race, creed, class, or nationality. If people know the on-the-ground story of what happened to Pinhook, that story can be evaluated alongside the published stories propagated by the institutions with the most power. The voices of the displaced Pinhook residents in this book resonate with the truth that people of color matter, their lives matter, their experiences, and their stories, matter. Ethnographers such as ourselves are obligated to expose injustices and call for their restitution by publishing the counter-narratives of the people with whom we collaborate. We have been honored to hear the counter-narratives of the Pinhook community and share them alongside the public ones endorsed and distributed by the agencies involved. Our intention is to elevate the people's stories to the same narrative plane as that occupied by those in power.

Coda

On June 18 of 2017, Debra texted Todd. "There should be something in the semo paper about Pinhook today," her brief message read. We had heard from Debra about a community development grant possibly coming through in the few weeks preceding the 18th. Debra had let us know that the possibility for displaced Pinhook residents to be able to relocate and rebuild their town together was growing smaller and smaller. There was still a chance, however, that individual families would finally get money to help them rebuild their houses outside the Birds Point-New Madrid Floodway.

The article in the *Southeast Missourian* Debra told Todd about announced that the state of Missouri had agreed to pay for the rebuilding of homes through a Community Development Grant. An agreement had been reached at a meeting in Charleston. Displaced Pinhook residents could purchase land and rebuild or they could purchase existing houses and renovate them. After seven long years, the people of Pinhook were finally getting something, even if it wasn't what they had been asking for. We, of course, saw this as just another way the government has treated Pinhook residents unjustly. The article in the *Missourian* even suggests that the reason Pinhook could not be relocated is because the residents themselves could not agree on a location. Statements by Missouri Department of Economic Development[3] spokesperson Amy Susan quoted in the article sound as if no one is responsible, as if things just didn't work out. The agreement residents would have had to come to to relocate the town "was never reached" (Bliss). This explanation flies in the face of everything we have been told by Debra in our ongoing communications with her.

Once again, it seems, the residents of Pinhook, a community of people we have come to admire and respect so much, have gotten a raw deal. They will get their money, but they will get it seven years too late. Some may be able to rebuild their houses, but they may not be able to do it together. Worse, the government will claim credit for providing this assistance to Pinhook even while it has never admitted its culpability in the town's destruction. As we have argued from the beginning of this book, what happened to the people of Pinhook was an entirely preventable disaster, one that was done by the hands of powerful entities unwilling to see the pain they would cause or right the wrong once they'd done it.

The people of Pinhook have shown us, however, that they will survive the injustice that has been done to them. They are an amazing community of people. And though we may never witness the triumphant reconstruction of Pinhook done nail by nail and plank by plank, maybe we have already seen something even more inspiring: how a community called Pinhook endured and survived when they blew the levee.

ACKNOWLEDGMENTS

We want to thank the entire Pinhook community for inviting us into your lives after losing your beloved town in 2011. Especially, we thank Debra Robinson-Tarver, Twan Robinson, David Robinson, LaToya Robinson-Tate, Aretha Robinson, Larry Robinson, and George Williams who have served as our primary collaborators, friends, and comrades during the past six years. We thank you for your time, your generosity, all the conversations and laughs we shared together, and the good food you fed us along the way. We thank Faye Mack for sharing her memories of Pinhook with us and for allowing us to use the lyrics to her song for the pages of this book. We thank Laura Hatcher of Southeast Missouri State University for several sessions discussing "takings law" and for sharing what she has learned over the years about the legal battles of other communities who have lost their homes because of flooding and other disasters. We thank Jeff Corrigan of the Missouri State Historical Society on the University of Missouri-Columbia campus for his invaluable help in locating documents pertaining to Pinhook, for inviting us to speak at the Historical Society along with Debra, and for his interest and willingness to assist in this project, including finding Will Sarvis's interview of Jim Robinson Jr. in the Historical Society archives.

For our film, *Taking Pinhook*, we were very fortunate to work with filmmaker and artist Emilie Sabath, who came on board a bit late with the project but saved it from being just another amateur production. Emilie's professionalism and faith in the Pinhook project helped us believe in the power of this story on film. Emilie got up at the crack of dawn to photograph the expanse of the mighty Mississippi, was willing to hang out of car windows when needed, and suffered through an insanely hot day when we took her and her camera to Cairo, Illinois. We also thank videographer Sean Brown of Columbia

Twan Robinson, Todd Lawrence, Debra Robinson-Tarver, LaToya Robinson-Tate, Elaine Lawless, Aretha Robinson, and Emilie Sabath, 2014. Darcy Holtgrave.

Access Television, who traveled with us to Pinhook Day in 2013 to get footage for the film. The way he could put people at ease with his cameras was inspiring. We also thank Dr. Clyde Ruffin, former chair of theatre at the University of Missouri, for narrating our film. The power of Clyde's voice continues to help viewers feel the power and importance of this story.

We'd also like to thank our friends, families, and loved ones. Each of us has a special connection to Missouri through family, history, and heritage. Writing about the state we both love has been both a challenge and a privilege. Our families have supported us all these years as we embarked on this emotionally taxing journey alongside the brave people of Pinhook. Friends and family members who have never met our Pinhook friends asked us constantly how things were going for Pinhook. Their powerful response to the story of the people of Pinhook and the injustice done to them has only confirmed that we needed to make sure that the story of Pinhook gets heard.

Finally, we cannot overstate how much the people of Pinhook have meant to us over the years of this project. If there is any small way that our work together with all of you has made any positive difference in your lives, that is all we could ever ask for. You will never know how much your kindness, generosity, and strength of spirit has meant to us. We have been blessed to meet each and every one of you.

NOTES

Prologue

1. These are the exact words of the newscaster on KFVS 12 in Cape Girardeau, Missouri, as the station reported live on the breach of the Birds Point levee.

2. This semi-fictionalized account of the days leading up to the breaching of the Birds Point levee and the destruction of Pinhook, Missouri, was inspired by oral narratives shared with us by displaced Pinhook residents. The events, dates, and times are to our knowledge accurate. We imagined here what residents must have been going through prior to the breach; we now know the true devastation of what occurred.

Introduction

1. Major General Michael Walsh, commander of the U.S. Army Corps of Engineers, gave the order to operate the Birds Point-New Madrid floodway under the authority of the Flood Control Acts of 1928. This order, whose procedures have been amended and adjusted over the years by subsequent acts (particularly 1965), tied the operation of the floodway to the reading on the Cairo river gage. Accordingly, the actions of the Corps in breaching the levee were legal. The state of Missouri filed an injunction to stop the breach in federal court. The decision by federal judge Stephen N. Limbaugh allowing the breach to go forward was based partially upon his determination of whether the Corps was acting in an "arbitrary and capricious" manner. He ruled that they were not, and thus, the actions of the Corps were perfectly legal. FEMA, then, has had no responsibility to provide remuneration to the residents of the floodway. Legally speaking, they "chose" to live in the floodway. All along, according to government accounts, the government had purchased easements on the property within the floodway, which gave it permission to flood that land whenever they felt it was necessary. The legitimacy of those easements has been challenged in court as part of a class action lawsuit filed the day after the breach by J. Michael Ponder on behalf of 140 floodway farmers. The displaced Pinhook residents were not invited to be a part of this lawsuit.

2. The authorized narrative published by the Army Corps of Engineers is available in a publication written by Charles A. Camillo, entitled *Divine Providence: The 2011 Flood in the Mississippi River and Tributaries Project*, available online at http://cdm16021.contentdm.oclc .org/cdm/ref/collection/p16021coll4/id/181 (last accessed March 4, 2017).

3. Laws affecting African American land ownership varied from state to state before, during, and after slavery. While there may have been no state laws prohibiting the ownership of land in southeastern Missouri by African American citizens at that time, informal and unofficial practices could make it difficult, if not impossible, for African Americans to purchase land. As scholars such as George Lipsitz and Richard Rothstein have shown, local, state, or federal laws did not have to explicitly deny African Americans the right to freely purchase land. Covenants, denial of insurance, discriminatory lending practices, and individual bias could make it so that African Americans were effectively restricted from buying land. So while in certain parts of the state free African Americans owned property and even operated businesses prior to the Civil War, this does not mean that African American migrants coming to Mississippi County in the early 1940s would have been able to purchase land wherever they desired. It is likely that their choices for land purchase were extremely limited. See George Lipsitz, *How Racism Takes Place*, 2011; and Richard Rothstein, *The Color of Law: A Forgotten History of How Our Government Segregated America*, 2017.

4. We have long suspected that the sale of land inside the Birds Point-New Madrid Floodway to former sharecroppers was in some way connected to the 1939 Sharecroppers Strike in southeast Missouri, but have been unable to prove a direct connection. The story of the strike, or "uprising," as it is sometimes called, sheds light on the environment the families who established Pinhook in 1941 were moving into. In January of 1939, over a thousand sharecroppers and tenant farmers, who had been evicted by wealthy landowners, occupied the roadsides at the intersection of highways 60 and 61 in southeast Missouri, just south of Sikeston. Their demonstration attracted a great deal of attention, including, ultimately, that of President Roosevelt and the First Lady Eleanor. The protesters were eventually removed from the highway to various locations including a camp inside the Birds Point–New Madrid Floodway near what is now Ten-Mile Pond Conservation Area. This highly visible demonstration resulted in the implementation of several state and federal policy changes intended to improve wages and living conditions for sharecroppers and tenant farmers. Subsidized housing or the opportunity to purchase homes and land also resulted from this demonstration. See Lewis Cantor, *A Prologue to the Protest Movement: The Missouri Sharecropper Roadside Demonstration of 1939*, 1969; and Jarod Roll, "'Out Yonder on the Road': Working Class Self-Representation and the 1939 Roadside Demonstration in Southeast Missouri," 2010.

5. Between that first visit Elaine made to Pinhook in November 2011 and our first visit there together in April, 2012, Lynell Robinson's wife, Mary Nell Robinson, passed away. He is still living, but his house, along with all the other houses and structures in Pinhook, has been demolished.

6. In 1991, Elaine proposed an ethnographic method that "begins with the one-on-one interview and grows into a series of dialogic sessions with the flow of interactions taking on multiple forms and overlapping functions" such that the "conclusions (if there are

any) emerge from the discourse between and among participants, ethnographer included" (36–37). Instead of conducting interviews and then leaving to analyze and write our ethnographies, the reciprocal ethnographer returns to work with research collaborators time and again, sharing the data and writing, and engaging in meaningful conversations about the research in general. We would argue that while we were not able to engage in "dialogic sessions" with Pinhook residents regarding what we had written, we did engage in countless conversations with them where we asked a lot of questions, offered our analyses, and engaged with them about what had happened to their town. Throughout our nearly six years of fieldwork, their ideas shaped our understanding of their situation. We have come to see our work with them as collaborative, though we recognize our power as authors to shape and construct this work as a narrative of their experience. We have striven whenever possible to bring their voices to the fore and to let their point of view inform our understanding of what has happened to them. At the same time, we have endeavored not to hide our presence in this study or to deny our position as researchers and authors of this book.

7. Pinhook is incorporated as a village in the state of Missouri. In Missouri incorporated communities are classified as villages when they have a population of less than five hundred people. For more information see chapter 72, section 72.080.1, of the Missouri Revised Statutes, published by the Missouri legislature.

Chapter 1

1. See Arvarh E. Strickland, "The Strange Affair of the Boll Weevil: The Pest as Liberator" in *Agricultural History* 68.2 (1994): 157–168. Here Strickland discusses the role of the boll weevil before and during the great migration which brought millions of African American workers to the north from the south during the first half of the twentieth century.

2. This interview is used with the permission of the State Historical Society of Missouri. It is available in its entirely in their *Politics in Missouri Oral History Project* Digital Collection: http://digital.shsmo.org/cdm/singleitem/collection/ohc/id/596/rec/1.

3. Robinson is referring to Edward Hull Crump Jr., the famed head of the "Political Machine" in Memphis, Tennessee, which ruled the region from roughly 1900–1954.

4. As Missouri is a land "nondisclosure" state, the actual sale price of any plot of land cannot be disclosed to interested parties.

5. See note three from the Introduction.

6. Jim Robinson Jr. spent much of his life appealing to the federal government to improve the flood control mechanism at the Birds Point-New Madrid Floodway. His principle concerns were that the front side levee height be raised, and that the quarter-mile gap at the south end of the floodway be closed. This gap, which was designed to allow water to drain out of the floodway if it was ever "operated," also allowed significant amounts of water from the Mississippi to flow into the floodway from the south. The residents referred to this as "backwater flooding." According to Pinhook residents, it happened nearly every year and caused them significant problems.

Chapter 2

1. The following list represents the surnames of the African American residents of Pinhook over the years. This list of surnames was provided to us by Debra Robinson-Tarver. We believe it to be complete, but we do not know for sure. The fact that the list is not in alphabetical order and does not list the Robinson family at the top of the list suggests the egalitarian perception of the Pinhook families as equal in importance: Adams, Smith, Ward, Simpkins, Walker, Parker, Johnson, Thomas, Carter, Williams, Robinson, Jefro, Jones, Anderson, Moss, Bradley, Myric, Oliver, Speller, Miner, Cross, Gallon, Mason, Kindle, Sutton, Franklin, Sullivan, Stokes, Verses, Rice, Craig, Garrison, Yarbor.

2. This statement by Aretha Robinson is one of a very few statements we heard asserting race as a factor in the breaching of the levee. Most residents, foremost among them Debra, avoided making this claim, at least openly or publicly. Yet it must be said that the question was not entirely absent from discourse surrounding the breach or far from the minds of the people we talked with. This claim was often offered in coded language, phrased as a question that asked us, the researchers, to decide what was the most likely explanation. We have, of course, come to the same conclusion that Aretha Robinson expresses here.

Chapter 3

1. Research on the aftermath of Hurricane Katrina has yielded much theorizing on the role of women in advocating for community preservation and development and grassroots organizing in the face of environmental injustice, governmental indifference, and institutional racism. We have been greatly influenced by writing on gender and class post Katrina. In particular, we are indebted to Alisa Bierra, Mayaba Lieberthal, and INCITE! Women of Color Against Violence (In *What Lies Beneath: Katrina, Race, and the State of the Nation* Ed. South End Press Collective); and Emmanuel David and Elaine Enarson, *The Women of Katrina: How Gender, Race, and Class Matter in an American Disaster.*

2. Joplin, Missouri, was hit by an EF-5 tornado on May 22, 2011, just 20 days after the levee breach of the Birds Point levee. The massive tornado killed 161 people and injured over a thousand others, causing more than $3 billion in damages. According to the National Institute of Standards and Technology, this is the single deadliest and costliest tornado on record in U.S. history. Following so closely on the heels of the flooding in southeastern Missouri, the disaster in Joplin understandably took center stage with state and federal disaster agencies, not to mention with media outlets. While we do not intend to suggest that the attention and aid Joplin received is unfair, it is worth noting that Joplin has received multiple millions of dollars in aid from various government agencies—county, state, and federal—to rebuild and redevelop the city. In the years since Pinhook was destroyed, displaced residents have received a community block grant in 2014 that paid to demolish their houses (they received no rental assistance or any kind of aid in the interim), and have been promised aid to assist them in rebuilding their houses if the residents themselves are able to identify and secure land on which to rebuild their town. Some time ago we heard from Debra that after many failed efforts to purchase land parcels for the entire town to rebuild, they had been told that

to move forward, they would have to purchase land individually. This meant that the dream of relocating and rebuilding Pinhook as an entire town would likely not come true. Though in a recent phone call, Debra told us that she had just submitted paperwork that would enable residents to buy seven contiguous plots of land within the city limits of Sikeston, Missouri. It wouldn't be a new Pinhook, but at least some of the displaced residents might be able to live next to one another once again.

Chapter 4

1. Not to be confused with the traditional dance called the "cakewalk," which began on slave plantations and was popular up through the first part of the twentieth century. This dance, in which pairs of dancers would parade down an aisle lined by other dancers has roots on the slave plantation and later in minstrel shows. Like the cakewalk of carnival fame, the dance gets its name from the prize that was awarded to the winning couple—a fancily decorated cake.

Chapter 5

1. As it turned out, the way Debra explained it to us in later conversations, many residents did not find out about the *possibility* of an evacuation until the morning of Monday April 25th, just one week before the levee breach. Debra and her family were not able to begin moving out their belongings until the morning of the next day. Unfortunately, access to their houses was restricted sometime after 11:00 am that morning when road access into the town became impossible because of flooding. According to Debra, all Pinhook residents were out of their homes by that afternoon; however, they had only barely been able to move a few of their possessions. They took only the most essential items.

2. Newspapers publishing stories about the destruction of Pinhook included *USA Today,* the *Columbia Missourian,* the *Columbia Tribune,* the *Southeast Missourian,* the *Sikeston Standard-Democrat,* the *New York Times, Time Magazine* and others. This attention was limited mainly to the time period immediately before and after the levee breach. Some media outlets did stories on the ongoing struggles of displaced Pinhook residents, but those stories became more infrequent in the second and third years after the breach. More stories were written in August of 2015 when what was left of the town was demolished, but there has been very little attention paid to the story since then.

3. In a phone conversation on February 25, 2016, Debra corrected this date. She explained that she had made a mistake and that the real date was April 25th. This would have been a Monday immediately following Easter Sunday of that year.

4. The correction to the earlier date would mean that this day is April 26th, a Tuesday. This means that residents had less than four hours to remove their belongings from their houses.

5. Major General Michael Walsh, commander of the U.S. Army Corps of Engineers, gave the order to operate the Birds Point-New Madrid Floodway under the authority of the

Flood Control Act of 1928. This order, whose procedures have been amended and adjusted over the years by subsequent acts, tied the operation of the floodway to the reading on the Cairo river gage. Accordingly, the actions of the Corps in breaching the levee were legal. The decision by Judge Limbaugh allowing the breach to go forward was based upon his determination that the Corps was not acting in an "arbitrary and capricious" manner. He ruled that they were not, and thus, the actions of the Corps were perfectly legal. FEMA, then, has no responsibility to provide remuneration the residents of the floodway.

Chapter 6

1. Pinhook Day 2017 was held at Pinhook on property that was formerly owned by Pinhook residents before the 2015 FEMA buyout. The buyout only paid for the demolition of all the remaining homes in Pinhook, those that had not been destroyed by arson after being submerged during the 2011 flood. The buyout did not cover the cost of building new houses. The agreement allowed that the remaining land would still belong to the town of Pinhook. Nothing can be built on that land, however; it can only be used for park or green space. After Pinhook Day 2014, more and more displaced Pinhook residents and relatives expressed interest in holding at least part of the Pinhook Day celebration on the newly cleared Pinhook property. In May of 2017 residents took campers and tents out to Pinhook and held their annual fish fry and meal on the grounds of the former town. It was held on property where George Williams' house used to stand. The theme was "Pinhook Reclaimed: 2017."

2. According to Charles Camillo in *Divine Providence*, the government purchased flowage easements from landowners in the Birds Point-New Madrid Floodway beginning in 1928. He asserts that by 1936, "the district had obtained 77% of flowage rights, surpassing the 50% necessary to degrade the fuseplug levy," and by 1942, "The federal government completed acquisition of flowage rights on the necessary acres within the floodway—a figure that did not include acreage in the backwater area. The cost of flowage easements totaled $2,385,546 at an average price of $22.34 an acre" (42). He also claims that landowners were paid between $1 and $100. Oral history accounts frequently cite the amount of $50 per family plot. The 2011 class action lawsuit filed by floodway farmers (not including Pinhook farmers) argues that, among other issues with flowage easements purchased from farmers by the government, easements "were acquired for value far below the value of the property taken by defendants, so as to be inequitable" (*Big Oak Farms et al. vs. U.S.A.*). Certainly, many Pinhook residents would agree with this claim. If 77 percent of the easements were purchased before Pinhook residents even arrived in the area, then they did not benefit financially from the easement purchases, and indeed they may not have even known about the purchase of easements at all.

Conclusion

1. This quote was taken from a FEMA video of a question and answer session that happened in Charleston, Missouri, on June 7, 2011, just over a month after the levee breach. The

video was posted on the FEMA.gov website for some time, but currently we can no longer locate the video or the excerpted transcribed comments which also appeared on the FEMA.gov website. A still photo of Kay Phillips and Pinhook resident Rosetta Bradley still exists on the site and on the National Archives website. It can be accessed at: https://www.fema.gov/ar/media-library/assets/images/59430.

2. We were always told by Debra that Church World Service, an international assistance organization, had committed to help with the rebuilding of residents' houses from almost the very beginning. In fact, we met with and interviewed Barry Shade, a CWS representative, who was present at Pinhook Day the first time we attended in 2012. Church World Service was one of a number of agencies that had committed to help Pinhook with supplies or labor over the years. Their offers of assistance depended, though, on Debra and her fellow Pinhook residents securing land and being granted funding.

3. When we talked to Debra over the years about her efforts to secure financial assistance for the displaced residents of Pinhook to relocate and rebuild their town, she almost always referred to FEMA as the agency involved. The Community Development grant that will pay for Pinhook residents to individually rebuild their houses or buy new ones is being administered by the Missouri Department of Economic Development and the Bootheel Regional Planning Commission. Both are state agencies that sometimes work in partnership with FEMA. We have used FEMA in the book to refer generically to any agency responsible to the displaced residents of Pinhook largely because that is the way they themselves represented those agencies—county, state, or federal.

BIBLIOGRAPHY

2012 Flood Season Preparedness Report. Greenwood, MS: U.S. Army Corps of Engineers (Mississippi Valley Division).

Adichie, Chimimanda Ngozi. "The Danger of a Single Story." *TED: Ideas Worth Spreading.* 6 March 2016. Web. 25 February 2016.

Alexander, Michelle. *The New Jim Crow: Mass Incarceration in the Age of Colorblindness.* New York: The New Press, 2012.

Ancelet, Barry Jean, Marcia Gaudet, and Carl Lindahl. *Second Line Rescue: Improvised Responses to Katrina and Rita.* Jackson: University Press of Mississippi, 2013.

Basso, Keith. *Wisdom Sits in Places: Landscape and Language Among the Western Apache.* Albuquerque: University of New Mexico Press, 1996.

Barry, John M. *Rising Tide: The Great Mississippi Flood of 1927 and How It Changed America.* NY: Simon and Schuster, 1997.

Barton, Allen. *Communities in Disaster: A Sociological Analysis of Collective Stress Situations.* New York: Anchor Press, 1970.

Baskin, John. *New Burlington: The Life and Death of an American Village.* New York: Norton and Co, 2000.

Behar, Ruth. "Folklore and the Search for Home." *Journal of American Folklore* 122 (2009): 251–266.

———. *The Vulnerable Observer: Anthropology that Breaks your Heart.* Boston: Beacon Press, 1996.

Bell, Derrick. *And We Are Not Saved: The Elusive Quest for Racial Justice.* New York: Basic Books, 1987.

———. *Faces From the Bottom of the Well: The Permanence of Racism.* New York: Basic Books, 1992.

———. *The Derrick Bell Reader.* Edited by Richard Delgado and Jean Stefancic. New York City: NYU Press, 2005. Print

Bierria, Alisa, Mayaba Liebenthal, and INCITE! Women of Color Against Violence. "To Render Ourselves Visible: Women of Color Organizing and Hurricane Katrina." *What*

Lies Beneath: Katrina, Race, and the State of the Nation. South End Press Collective. Cambridge, MA: South End Press, 2007.

Bliss, Mark. "Pinhook Reclaimed: State Grants Set to Help Former Village Residents Relocate." *Southeast Missourian*, 18 June 2017. Web. 18 June 2017.

Brunsma, David L., David Overfelt, and J. Steven Picou, eds. *The Sociology of Katrina: Perspectives on a Modern Catastrophe.* New York: Rowman & Littlefield Publishers Inc, 2007.

"Cairo, Illinois Population." *Census Viewer.* Web. 5 October, 2014.

Campbell, Rex R., and Thomas E. Baker. *Negroes in Missouri—1970.* Missouri Commission on Human Rights, University of Missouri, 1972.

Cantor, Louis. "A Prologue to the Protest Movement: The Missouri Sharecropper Roadside Demonstration of 1939." *Journal of American History* 55.4 (1969): 804–822.

Camillo, Charles. *Divine Providence: The 2011 Flood in the Mississippi River and Tributaries Project.* Army Corps of Engineers, Omaha District. U.S. Department of Defense. 2012. www.digitalcommons.unl.edu/usarmyceomaha.

Clifford, James, and George E. Marcus. *Writing Culture: The Poetics and Politics of Writing Culture.* Los Angeles: University of California Press, 2010.

Coates, Ta-Nehisi, *The Beautiful Struggle: A Memoir.* NY: Spiegal and Grau, 2008.

———. *Between the World and Me.* New York: Spiegal and Grau, 2015.

Cook, Fannie. *Bootheel Doctor.* Dodd, Mead Publishers, 1941.

Conrad, David Eugene. *The Forgotten Farmers: The Story of Sharecroppers in the New Deal.* Urbana: University of Illinois Press, 1965.

Crenshaw, Kimberle, Neil Golanda, Gary Peller, and Kendall Thomas. *Critical Race Theory: The Key Writings that Formed the Movement.* New York: The New Press, 1996.

David, Emmanuel and Elaine Enarson, eds. *The Women of Katrina: How Gender, Race, and Class Matter in an American Disaster.* Nashville: Vanderbilt University Press, 2012.

Delgado, Richard, and Jean Stefancic. *Critical Race Theory: An Introduction, Second Edition.* NY: New York University Press, 2012.

Dyson, Michael Eric. *Come Hell or High Water: Hurricane Katrina and the Color of Disaster.* New York: Basic Books: 2006.

DuBois, W. E. B. *The Souls of Black Folk.* New York: Oxford University Press, 2007 (1903).

Felman, Shoshana, and Dori Laub. *Testimony: Crisis of Witnessing in Literature, Psychoanalysis and History.* New York: Routledge, 1992.

"Flood-Besieged Town Seeks Buyout." *Columbia Daily Tribune*, 25 April 2013. 15 March 2015. http://www.columbiatribune.com/20630a68-add2-11e2-9b78-10604b9f6eda.html.

Fried, G., "Grieving for a Lost Home." *The Urban Condition.* Edited by L. J. Duhl. New York: Basic Books, 1966. 151–171.

Fritz, Charles E. "Disaster." *Contemporary Social Problems.* Edited by Robert K. Merton and Robert A. Nisbet. New York: Harcourt, 1961. 651–694.

Graef, Tyler. "Former Pinhook Residents Watch as Bulldozers Level What's Left of the Town the 2011 Flood Destroyed." *Southeast Missourian*, 7 August 2015.

Greene, Lorenzo J., Gary R. Kremer, and Anthony F. Holland. *Missouri's Black Heritage.* St. Louis: Forum Press, 1980.

Gregg, Garry S. *Self-Representation: Life Narrative Studies in Identity and Ideology.* New York: Greenwood Press, 1991.

Grubbs, Donald. *Cry from the Cotton: The Southern Tenant Farmers' Union and the New Deal*. Chapel Hill: University of North Carolina Press, 1971.

Hartman, Chester, and Gregory D. Squires, eds. *There is No Such Thing as a Natural Disaster*. New York: Routledge, 2006.

Hatcher, Laura. *Disasters, Property and Politics*. Blog. 12 January 2016. Web. 11 February 2016.

Hevern, Erin. "Mississippi Country Sheriff Orders Mandatory Evacuation of Spillway." *Southeast Missourian*, 27 April 2011. Web. 23 February 2016.

Hill, Marc Lamont. *Nobody: Casualties of America's War on the Vulnerable, From Ferguson to Flint and Beyond*. New York: Atria Books, 2016.

Interagency Recovery Task Force. *Operation Watershed—Recovery: Responding to the Historic Mississippi River Flood of 2011*. Washington DC: U.S. Army Corps of Engineers, 2011.

Inland Waterway Navigation: Value to the Nation. Washington: U.S. Army Corps of Engineers, 2009.

Janoff-Bulman, R. *Shattered Assumptions: Toward a New Psychology of Trauma*. New York: The Free Press, 1992.

Jasper, Pat, and Carl Lindahl. "The Houston Survivor Project: An Introduction." *Callaloo* 29.4 (2006): 1504–1505.

Johnson, Jay. *A Deeper Sense of Place*. Lincoln: University of Nebraska Press, 2013.

Jones, Yvonne V. "Kinship Affiliation through Time: Black Homecomings and Family Reunions in a North Carolina County." *Ethnohistory* 27.1 (1980): 49–66.

Jensen, Robert. *The Heart of Whiteness: Confronting Race, Racism and White Privilege*. San Francisco: City Lights Publishing, 2005.

Keen, Judy. "Pain is Still Fresh from Blasted Levee." *USA Today*, 11 October 2011. Web. 12 October 2011.

King, Martin Luther. *A Testament of Hope: The Essential Writings and Speeches of Martin Luther King, Jr*. Edited by James Washington. New York City: Harper Collins Publishers, 1986.

Kremer, Gary R. *Race and Meaning: The African American Experience in Missouri*. Columbia: University of Missouri Press, 2014.

Kummu, Matti, Hans de Moel, Phillip J. Ward, and Olli Varis. "How Close Do We Live To Water? A Global Analysis of Population Distance to Freshwater Bodies." *PLoS One* 6.6 (2011): 1–13. 23 February 2016.

Lawless, Elaine. "'Reciprocal' Ethnography: No One Said It Was Easy." *Journal of Folklore Research* 37, no. 2/3 (May–December 2000): 197–205.

———. "Folklore as a Map of the World: Rejecting 'Home' as a Failure of the Imagination." *Journal of American Folklore* 124.493 (2011): 127–146.

———. "Women's Life Stories and Reciprocal Ethnography as Feminist and Emergent." *Journal of Folklore Research*. 28.1 (1991): 35–60.

Lee, Spike. "If God Is Willing and da Creek Don't Rise." *HBO*, 23 August 2010. Television.

Lefebre, Henri. *The Production of Space*. Hoboken: Wiley-Blackwell Press, 1992.

Limbaugh, Stephen N. Personal Interview. 23 May 2013.

Lindahl, Carl. "Survivor to Survivor: Katrina Stories from Houston." *Callaloo* 24.4 (2006): 1506–1538, 2006.

Lipsitz, George. *How Racism Takes Place*. Philadelphia: Temple University Press, 2011.

Litt, Jacquelyn, Althea Skinner, and Kelly Robinson, "The Katrina Difference: African American Women's Networks and Poverty in New Orleans after Katrina." *The Women of Katrina*. Edited by Emmanuel David and Elaine Enarson. Nashville: Vanderbilt University Press. 2012. 130–154.

Liu, Amy, Roland V. Anglin, Richard M. Mizelle, Jr., and Allison Plyer, eds. *Resilience and Opportunity: Lessons from the US Gulf Coast after Katrina and Rita*. Washington DC: Brookings Institution Press, 2011.

Miller, Demond Shondell, and Jason David Rivera. *Hurricane Katrina and the Redefinition of Landscape*. Lanham, MD: Lexington Books, 2008.

Missouri: The WPA Guide to the "Show Me" State. 1941.

The Missouri/Souris River Floods of May—August 2011: Service Assessment. Washington DC: U.S. Department of Commerce. 2012. Web, 23 February 2016.

Moody-Turner, Shirley. *Black Folklore and the Politics of Racial Representation*. Jackson: University Press of Mississippi, 2013.

Nussbaum, Martha. *Cultivating Humanity: A Classical Defense of Reform in Liberal Education*. Harvard: Cambridge University Press, 1997. Print.

O'Connor, Candace, Lynn Rubright, and Steven John Ross. *Oh Freedom After While: The Missouri Sharecropper Protest of 1939*. California Newsreel, 1989.

Pipher, Mary. *Writing to Change the World*. New York: Riverhead Books, 2007. Print.

Powell, Betty F. *The History of Mississippi County: Beginning Through 1972*. Independence, MS: BNL Library Service, 1975. Print.

Puckett, Anita. *Seldom Ask, Never Tell: Labor and Discourse in Appalachia*. Oxford: Oxford University Press, 2000.

Reed, Adolph. Interview by *The North Star*. March 22, 2013. http://shout.lbo-talk.org/lbo/RadioArchive/2013/13_03_07.mp3 50004100 audio/mpeg (last accessed March 4, 2017).

Reilly, Morse, "Advancing Social Equity in Post-Katrina Mississippi," *Resilience and Opportunity: Lessons from the U.S. Gulf Coast after Katrina and Rita*. Edited by Amy Liu, Roland V. Anglin, Richard M. Mizelle, and Allison Plyer. Washington, D.C.: Brookings Institute Press, 2011. 131–147.

Roberts, Katherine. "The Art of Staying Put: Managing Land and Minerals in Rural America." *Journal of American Folklore* 126 (2012): 407–433.

Robinson, Aretha. Personal Interview. 23 April 2012.

———. Personal Interview. 27 May 2012.

Robinson, Aretha, and Larry Robinson. Personal Interview. 1 August 2012.

Robinson, Aretha, David Robinson, Debra Robinson-Tarver, and Twan Robinson. Personal Interview. 1 August 2012.

Robinson, Aretha, Debra Robinson-Tarver, and Twan Robinson. Personal Interview. 23 April 2012.

———. Personal Interview. 4 June 2013.

Robinson, Bernard. Personal Interview. 26 May 2012.

Robinson, Jim, Jr. "An Interview with Jim Robinson, Jr. at His Home in Pinhook." Interviewed by Will Sarvis. October 28, 1998. Print. [C3928, Politics in Missouri Oral History Project, Jim Robinson, Jr., a.c. 239, 240, The State Historical Society of Missouri.]

Robinson, Larry. Personal Interview. 4 June 2013.

Robinson, Twan. Personal Interview. 23 April 2012.

Robinson-Tarver, Debra. Personal Interview. 7 September 2012.

———. Personal Interview. 23 April 2012.

———. Personal Interview. 2 August 2012.

Robinson-Tarver, Debra, and Oneatha Boldridge. Personal Interview. 2 December 2012.

Robinson-Tate, Latoya. Personal Interview. 26 May 2012.

Roll, Jarod. "'Out Yonder on the Road': Working Class Self-Representation and the 1939 Roadside Demonstration in Southeast Missouri." *Southern Spaces*, 16 March 2010. (https://southernspaces.org/2010/out-yonder-road-working-class-self-representation -and-1939-roadside-demonstration-southeast)

———. *Spirit of Rebellion: Labor and Religion in the New Cotton South*. Urbana: University of Illinois Press, 2010.

Room for the River: Summary Report of the 2011 Mississippi River Flood and Successful Operation of the Mississippi River and Tributaries System. U.S. Army Corps of Engineers and Mississippi River Commission. 2012. Web. 23 February 2016.

Ryden, Kent C., and Wayne Franklin. *Mapping the Invisible Landscape: Folklore, Writing and the Sense of Place*. Iowa City: University of Iowa Press, 1993.

Sehgal, Parul. "Fighting 'Erasure.'" *New York Times*, 2 February 2016.

Silverstein, Martin Elliot. *Disaster: Your Right to Survive*. Lincoln, NE: Potomac Books, 1992.

Snow, Thad. *From Missouri*. Houghton Mifflin Publishers, 1954.

The South End Press Collective, *What Lies Beneath: Katrina, Race, and the State of the Nation*. Cambridge, 2007.

Stack, C. *All Our Kin: Strategies for Survival in a Black Community*. New York: Harper and Row (1973) 1987.

State of Missouri vs. U.S. Army Corps of Engineers. No. 1:11CV00067 SNLJ. United States District Court Eastern District of Missouri Southeastern Division. 26 April 2011. Web.

Stein, Alan H., and Gene B. Preuss. "Oral History, Folklore, and Katrina." In *There Is No Such Thing as a Natural Disaster: Race, Class, and Hurricane Katrina*. Edited by Chester Hartman and Gregory D. Squires. New York: Routledge, 2006. 37–58.

Snow, Thad. *From Missouri*. Cambridge: Cambridge University Press, 1954.

Stepenoff, Bonnie. *Thad Snow: A Life of Social Reform in the Missouri Bootheel*. Columbia: University of Missouri Press, 2003.

Sterett, Susan, "State Policy and Disaster Assistance: Listening to Women." In *The Women of Katrina: How Gender, Race, and Class Matter in an American Disaster*. Edited by Emmanuel David and Elaine Enarson. Nashville: Vanderbilt University, 2012. 118–129.

Stevenson, Bryan. *Just Mercy: A Story of Justice and Redemption*. New York: Spiegel and Grau, 2015.

Straight, Belinda, ed. *Women on the Verge of Home*. Albany: State University of New York Press, 2015.

Thomas, Alexander R., Brian Lowe, Greg Fulkerson, and Polly Smith, eds. *Critical Rural Theory: Structure, Space, Culture*. Lexington, KY: Lexington Books, 2012.

Tillmann-Healy, Lisa M. "Friendship as Method." *Sage*, vol. 9, issue 5, 2003, 729–749.

"Tiny Missouri Town is Finally Getting Buyout Money." *Columbia Tribune*, 28 June 2015.

Tuan, Yi-Fu. *Space and Place: The Perspective of Experience*. Reprinted edition. Minneapolis: University of Minnesota Press, 2001.

Turner, Victor, ed. *Celebration: Studies in Festivity and Ritual*. Washington DC: Smithsonian Press, 1982.

Walsh, Michael. "Operation Order." Mississippi River Commission. 2 May 2011.

Watriss, Wendy. "Celebration Freedom: Juneteenth." *Southern Exposure* 5 (1977): 80–87.

White, Marilyn M. "We are Family!: Kinship and Solidarity in the Black Community." In *Expressively Black: The Cultural Basis of Ethnic Identity*. Edited by Geneva Gay and Willie L. Baber. New York: Praeger Publishers, 1987.

Wiggins, William. *O Freedom!: Afro-American Emancipation Celebrations*. Knoxville: University of Tennessee Press, 1987.

Wiggins, William, and Doug DeNatale, eds. *Jubilation!: African American Celebrations in the Southeast—A Traveling Exhibition Catalog with essays*. Charleston: University of South Carolina Press, 1994.

Williams, George. Personal Interview. 24 April 2012.

Wortham, Robert A, ed. *W.E.B DuBois and the Sociological Imagination: A Reader, 1897–1914*. Waco: Baylor University Press, 2009.

Young, Kevin. *The Grey Album: On the Blackness of Blackness*. Minneapolis: Greywolf Press, 2013.

Zinner, Ellen S. and Mary Beth Williams. *When a Community Weeps: Case Studies in Group Survivorship*. Ann Arbor: Edwards Bros: 1998.

INDEX

CPSIA information can be obtained
at www.ICGtesting.com
Printed in the USA
LVHW090856180120
644101LV00001B/144